T0347084

WHY WE HATE

WHY WE HATE

Understanding the Roots of Human Conflict

Michael Ruse

OXFORD
UNIVERSITY PRESS

OXFORD
UNIVERSITY PRESS

Oxford University Press is a department of the University of Oxford. It furthers
the University's objective of excellence in research, scholarship, and education
by publishing worldwide. Oxford is a registered trade mark of Oxford University
Press in the UK and certain other countries.

Published in the United States of America by Oxford University Press
198 Madison Avenue, New York, NY 10016, United States of America.

Library of Congress Control Number: 2022900031

ISBN 978–0–19–762128–8

DOI: 10.1093/oso/9780197621288.001.0001

1 3 5 7 9 8 6 4 2

Printed by Lakeside Book Company, United States of America

To the memory of the members of the Warwickshire Monthly Meeting of the Religious Society of Friends (Quakers), who, in the years after the Second World War, gave so much to the children in the group and whose loving influence has guided and enriched my whole life.

CONTENTS

Illustrations ix
Preface xi
Acknowledgments xv

Introduction 1

1. The Biology of War 22

2. The Biology of Prejudice 60

3. The Culture of War 118

4. The Culture of Prejudice 161

5. Moving Forward 208

Epilogue 260

REFERENCES 263
INDEX 281

ILLUSTRATIONS

I.1. The history of life on Earth. 2

I.2. The tree of life. From Ernst Haeckel, *Generelle Morphologie der Organismen* (1866). 7

I.3. Structure of the argument of the *Origin*. 8

1.1. The Bayeux Tapestry. 24

1.2. A US recruiting poster from the First World War. 30

1.3. The population density of humans over the past 200,000 years. 36

1.4. Average number of wives of unokais compared to non-unokais. 42

1.5. Average number of children of unokais compared to non-unokais. 42

1.6. A wall painting of a supposedly killer human. 49

2.1. The history of European hunter-gatherers. 70

2.2. The spread of Beaker pottery to the British Isles. 71

2.3. World War I graves. 79

2.4. Neanderthal. 84

2.5. Neanderthal ancestry in today's humans. 86

2.6. Denisovan ancestry in today's humans. 87

2.7. Well-known Shakespearean actor Brian Bedford playing Lady Bracknell. 88

2.8.   Greek homosexual activity. 91
2.9.   Duration of secular communes as against religious
       communes. 98
2.10. Franklin Roosevelt in wheelchair. 100
2.11. *In Bedlam* (Hogarth, The Rake's Progress). 103
2.12. Jews as vermin. 110
2.13. Poster for *Jud Süss.* 111
4.1.   The change over thirty years, 1985–2015, between those
       with degrees and those with no such qualifications. 171
4.2.   Poster for the sale of slaves. 177
4.3.   Memorial window to Oscar Wilde in Westminster
       Abbey. 184
4.4.   Richard III skeleton. 193
4.5.   Hitler and children. 202
5.1.   Brexit: Educated vs. uneducated. 226
5.2.   Brexit: Rich vs. poor. 227
5.3.   Brexit: Happy with lot vs. unhappy with lot. 227
5.4.   A 1918 recruitment poster aimed at African
       Americans. 237
5.5.   Robert E. Lee High School. 240

PREFACE

I was raised a Quaker in the years after the Second World War. Quakers don't have the usual trimmings of religion—preachers, churches ("steeple houses" as we called them of old), or creeds and dogmas and that sort of thing. However, to conclude that Quakers have no strong beliefs is to make a major mistake. They could give St. Paul a run for his money. Above all, for me, being a Quaker meant being part of a community with my fellow human beings. We were never very good at literal readings of the Bible, but my goodness we took the Sermon on the Mount seriously. "Ye have heard that it hath been said, An eye for an eye, and a tooth for a tooth: But I say unto you, That ye resist not evil: but whosoever shall smite thee on thy right cheek, turn to him the other also" (Matthew 5:38–39). And: "Ye have heard that it hath been said, Thou shalt love thy neighbor, and hate thine enemy. But I say unto you, Love your enemies, bless them that curse you, do good to them that hate you, and pray for them which despitefully use you, and persecute you" (43–44).

That is our role in life and how we serve our Lord. Loving other human beings. Quakers talk of the "inner light," that of God in every person, and that resonates to this day. Always inspiring me, haunting me in a way, is the great elegy of the metaphysical poet

John Donne that hung on the wall of nigh every meeting house, where Quakers met to worship in silence.

> No man is an island,
> Entire of itself,
> Every man is a piece of the continent,
> A part of the main.
> If a clod be washed away by the sea,
> Europe is the less.
> As well as if a promontory were.
> As well as if a manor of thy friend's
> Or of thine own were:
> Any man's death diminishes me,
> Because I am involved in mankind,
> And therefore never send to know for whom the
>   bell tolls;
> It tolls for thee.

(Meditation 17, from *Devotions
Upon Emergent Occasions*, 1624)

Here was the paradox that has never left me, unchanged by my loss of faith when I was twenty years old. If we are such social beings, how can we be so hateful to each other? In my early years, memories of the Second World War hung over us all: Poland, the Fall of France, the Blitz, Barbarossa, Pearl Harbor, Stalingrad, and on down to the end, the Battle of the Bulge and the bombing of Dresden. Across the world, Hiroshima and Nagasaki. Yet this only confirmed what we already knew. The Second World War was the more recent, but it was the First World War—the Great

War—that permeated every aspect of our culture. My teachers in primary school were single women, who had lost fiancés and husbands on the battlefields of Flanders. Parks had lonely men wandering aimlessly—"shell shocked," as we were told in pitying terms. Go into the front parlor, the room unused except for Sundays and special occasions, like funerals. There stood a picture of Uncle Bert, eighteen years old, proud in his new uniform. Dead at twenty at Passchendaele. Then I went to Canada when I was twenty-two and soon found that it was the Great War that defined that country—as it did other parts of the Commonwealth, notably Australia and New Zealand. The triumphs—when the Canadians at Easter 1917 took Vimy Ridge, that had withstood so many earlier attempts—and the tragedies—when on July 1, 1916, the first day of the Battle of the Somme, some eight hundred members of the Newfoundland Regiment went over the top, and the next morning at roll call there were but sixty-eight who responded. Every day, walking to and from my university, I passed the birthplace of John McCrae, author of the most-quoted poem of the war: "In Flanders Fields."

Add to all of this the dreadful ways in which we behave to each other in our daily lives. Above all, in the years after the war, as we became increasingly aware of the horrors of the Holocaust, we saw the depths to which we humans could fall. It is but part of a general story of prejudice, and there is not one of us who can look back on history without guilt and regret. No one living in the American South, as do I, can avoid daily reminders of the appalling treatment of white people toward black people. Over two centuries of slavery followed by a century of Jim Crow. Contempt, belittlement, lack of respect—toward strangers, toward people of different classes, toward members of other races, toward those with minority sexual orientations, toward adherents of different religions, toward the disabled, toward Jews, and of men toward women. Was it not naïveté, bordering on the callous, to go on talking about the social nature—the inherent goodness—of human beings? It is this, our conflicted nature—so social, so hateful—that has driven me to write this book. I have found that, in the past two decades, there have been incredibly important discoveries and reinterpretations of our understanding of human evolution. Discoveries and reinterpretations highly pertinent to my quest. Finally, there seem to be some answers. I am amazed at and grateful for what I learned. It is this new understanding that I want to share, less concerned about whether you agree or disagree with me than that you appreciate the importance of the problem and the need to continue the inquiry. It is a moral obligation laid on us all. If you doubt me, think Ukraine.

ACKNOWLEDGMENTS

Working on such a project as this, I realize my fortune at being embedded in a community of scholars who share with me the conviction that, in some important sense, tackling the issues of this book must be a joint effort. Above all, I want to thank the anthropologists and archaeologists whose focus is on war and its origins. Most importantly, Douglas Fry, of the University of North Carolina at Greensboro, has been as helpful as he has been inspiring. Others, who have responded in a friendly and encouraging way to endless questions from a complete stranger, include Brian Ferguson, of Rutgers University; Jonathan Haas and Matthew Piscitelli, both of the Field Museum in Chicago; and Brian Hayden of Simon Fraser University, in British Columbia. Closer to my home fields of study, as always I am in debt to John Kelsay, my colleague here at Florida State University and an expert on just war theory in Islam; and also to Robert J. Richards of the University of Chicago and to Joe Cain at University College, London, both of whom have been very important in helping me to put evolutionary thinking into a broader context. And I am especially grateful to my graduate students who went with me on a trip to the battlefields of northern France, where, in the Great War, so many of all nations died because their leaders failed them.

These young people, those living today and those dead yesterday, convinced me that I had to write this book.

More immediately, at the professional level, Peter Ohlin at Oxford University Press has been all that one could desire as one's editor. He is thoughtful, encouraging, and—important when dealing with someone such as I—able to show when I am going off track and need to rethink what I am saying and writing. At the personal level, as always my wife, Lizzie, has given me love and understanding—able to show when I am going off track and need to rethink what I am saying and writing! My beloved cairn terriers, Scruffy McGruff and Duncan Donut, are ever ready to tell me I need to take a break and go for a walk in the park. In this book, I focus on the evolution of humans. We are a very small part of the whole story.

WHY WE HATE

Origins

The prehistory of humans starts with the Big Bang about 13.8 billion years ago (Morison 2014). (See Figure I.1.) Our solar system, about halfway through its life span, is about 4.5 billion years old. The planet Earth was formed from detritus circling the sun. Life appeared about 3.8 billion years ago, in other words about as soon as it could, after the oceans cooled enough to support its existence and continuation (Bada and Lazcana 2009). For about half of the subsequent time, life was primitive, one-celled organisms—prokaryotes. Then came multicelled organisms—eukaryotes.

Although it did not come out of the blue, the big event—at least as far as we humans are concerned—was the Cambrian explosion, about 550 million years ago. That was when the major life groups appeared—including chordates, a subset of which were the vertebrates, animals with backbones. Things were now racing ahead—fish, amphibians, reptiles (including the dinosaurs), and then mammals and birds. Mammals first appeared about 225 million

Why We Hate. Michael Ruse, Oxford University Press. © Oxford University Press 2022.
DOI: 10.1093/oso/9780197621288.003.0001

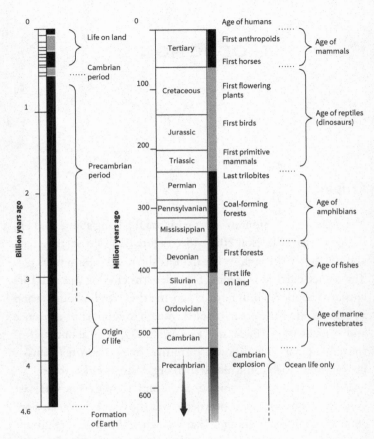

FIGURE 1.1 The history of life on Earth.

years ago, rat-like, nocturnal creatures, careful to keep out of the way of the dominant life group, the dinosaurs. The dinos went extinct around 65 million years ago, thanks to the planet's disruption by the impact of a meteor or similar body from space—birds, their direct descendants, survived—and the way was opened for mammals to thrive and diversify, and so came the primates about 50 million years ago. Going down in time, finally we get the great apes, and the important action—at least, with respect to humans—takes place in the last ten million years. Amazingly, we now know our human line—hominins—split from other apes, gorillas, and chimpanzees, around seven million years ago, or less. Even more amazing is that we are more closely related to the chimpanzees than they are to gorillas.

The break with the other great apes came with our move out from the jungle and onto the plains. This led to bipedalism. There is speculation about the reason for this. Being able to stand upright and look for predators is one plausible suggestion. As is the point that, being bipedal, we are not that fast, comparatively, but we can keep going for much longer than an ape that uses its front legs for motion. Whether as cause or effect, it is thought that these early hominins moved to a hunter-gatherer type of existence. Being bipedal could be of value in hunting down prey, which outrun us but collapse finally from exhaustion. As we moved to walking on two legs, so also our brain started to grow, marking an increase in intelligence. The famous missing link, Lucy, a member of *Australopithecus afarensis*, is about 3 million years old. She walked upright, if not as well as we modern humans. Compensating, she was probably better at climbing trees. Her brain was about 400 cubic centimeters, about the size of a chimpanzee's, compared to our brains of about 1300 cc. It is important to note that, while her brain was the size of a chimpanzee brain, she was well on the way to having a human brain (Johanson and Wong 2009). Our species, *Homo sapiens*, appeared half a million years ago or a bit later. Apart from our line, there were two other subspecies, the Neanderthals (in the West) and the Denisovans (in the East). Both are extinct. Apparently in our history we went through bottlenecks. The whole human population comes from about fourteen thousand individuals, and out-of-Africa humans from less than three thousand individuals (Lieberman 2013). This will be a part of our story.

Charles Darwin

What caused all of this? Evolution through natural selection. In his *On the Origin of Species* (1859), the English naturalist Charles Darwin made the case simply and strongly. Organisms have a reproductive tendency to multiply geometrically—1, 2, 4, 8—whereas food and space supplies at best multiply arithmetically—1, 2, 3, 4. Hence, there will be what the clergyman-economist Thomas Robert Malthus (1826) called a "struggle for existence." Darwin took this up unchanged: "as more individuals are produced than can possibly survive, there must in every case be a struggle for existence, either one individual with another of the same species, or with the individuals of distinct species, or with the physical conditions of life" (Darwin 1859, 63). Truly, it is reproduction rather than bare existence that counts. Taking this insight, and combining it with the belief—reinforced by a decade-long study of barnacles—that in natural populations new variation is constantly appearing, Darwin argued for an equivalent to the selective breeding that farmers and fanciers apply so successfully in creating new forms—shaggier sheep, beefier cattle, more melodious songbirds.

> Can it . . . be thought improbable, seeing that variations useful to man have undoubtedly occurred, that other variations useful in some way to each being in the great and complex battle of life, should sometimes occur in the course of thousands of generations? If such do occur, can we doubt (remembering that many more individuals are born than can possibly survive) that individuals having any advantage, however slight, over others, would have the best chance of surviving and of procreating their kind? On the other hand, we may feel sure that any variation in the least degree injurious would be rigidly destroyed. This preservation of favourable variations and the rejection of injurious variations, I call Natural Selection. (80–81)

Change. Change, but of a certain kind. Organisms look as though they were designed. They show purpose. Their formation is guided by what, following Aristotle in his *Metaphysics* (Barnes 1984, 1013^{b}25), are called "final causes." In today's language, they are "teleological." The eye is like a telescope. It looks that way, not because of the direct intervention of the Great Optician in the sky, but because of natural selection. Those organisms that work—that have design-like features, features that serve the purpose of seeing, whose final cause is sight—will survive and reproduce, and those that don't, won't. Such features that help their possessors, Darwin called "adaptations." We see them "most plainly in the wood-pecker and missletoe; and only a little less plainly in the humblest parasite which clings to the hairs of a quadruped or feathers of a bird; in the structure of the beetle which dives through the water; in the plumed seed which is wafted by the gentlest breeze; in short, we see beautiful adaptations everywhere and in every part of the organic world" (60–61).

Thus, the key argument of the *Origin*. With his mechanism on the table, as it were, Darwin could move quickly to the fact of evo-lution. Through the years, natural selection brought on what was known as the "tree of life"—we start at the base, at the bole, with the simplest organisms, and then grow as the branches spread, leading to plants and animals of all kinds. "As buds give rise by growth to fresh buds, and these, if vigorous, branch out and over-top on all sides many a feebler branch, so by generation I believe it has been with the great Tree of Life, which fills with its dead and broken branches the crust of the earth, and covers the surface with its ever branching and beautiful ramifications" (130). (See Figure I.2.) Then, for the rest of the *Origin*, Darwin set about the hard work—showing that natural selection was the causal force behind what his mentor, the historian and philosopher of science William Whewell (1840) called a "consilience of inductions." Darwin looked at a range of subdisciplines in the life sciences—behavior, the fossil record ("paleontology"), geographical distribu-tion ("biogeography"), systematics, morphology, and embryology, showing how he could explain many hitherto unsolved problems. (See Figure I.3.) Finally, the most famous passage in the history of science:

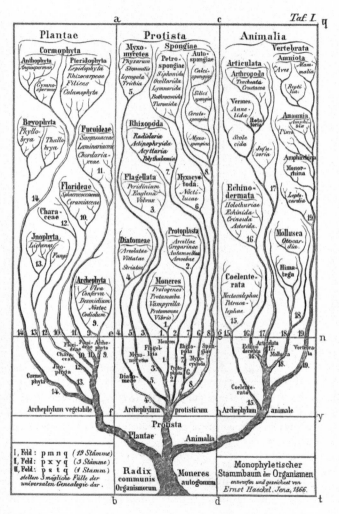

FIGURE I.2 The tree of life. From Ernst Haeckel, *Generelle Morphologie der Organismen* (1866).

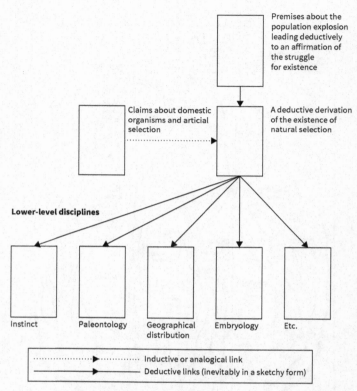

Premises about the
population explosion
leading deductively
to an affirmation of
the struggle
for existence

Claims about domestic
organisms and articial
selection

A deductive derivation
of the existence of
natural selection

Lower-level disciplines

Instinct   Paleontology   Geographical   Embryology   Etc.
distribution

┈┈┈┈▶┈┈┈┈ Inductive or analogical link
─────────▶ Deductive links (inevitably in a sketchy form)

FIGURE 1.3 Structure of the argument of the *Origin*. Darwin was (consciously) following Newton's *Principia* in putting the causal laws first and then using them to explain empirical phenomena: the heliocentric universe; the organic world.

There is grandeur in this view of life, with its several powers, having been originally breathed into a few forms or into one; and that, whilst this planet has gone cycling on according to

the fixed law of gravity, from so simple a beginning endless
forms most beautiful and most wonderful have been, and are
being, evolved. (490)

Expectedly, in the 150 years since Darwin wrote, there has been
a massive increase in our knowledge of the workings of evolution.
Most particularly, in the area of heredity (Bowler 1984, 1989).
Darwin was convinced that new variation keeps coming into natural populations. These are the building blocks on which natural
selection works. But Darwin had little idea about the nature of
these variations or their causes. The only thing about which he was
adamant was that, however caused, the variations are "random"
in the sense of not appearing according to the needs of the possessor. The adaptive nature of organic characteristics comes from
the external force of natural selection rather than some force from
within guiding organic development. Confirming this insight has
been one of the great triumphs of science, as first Mendelian and
later molecular theories of heredity, genetics, have been developed
and extended, underpinning Darwin's intuitions. Natural selection, adaptation, evolution.

Cui bono?

Before we get to the extension of Darwin's theorizing to humans,
let's pause for a moment, and ask an important question about
Darwin's understanding of natural selection. Who benefits? Who
loses? Did he think that selection was always for the benefit (or
loss) of the individual or did he think that selection could be,

perhaps often is, for the benefit (or loss) of the group? If two animals (or plants) compete and one wins and is the parent of members of the next generation, and one loses and has no offspring, then this is between two individuals—hence *individual selection*. If two groups of animals (or plants) compete and one group wins and has offspring and the other loses and has no offspring, then obviously in a sense this is between two groups—hence *group selection*. Not so fast. The fact that groups are involved does not at once imply that evolutionists would speak of "group selection" as opposed to "individual selection." Their interest is in who or what caused the success and who benefits. If one group has members that overall do better than the members of the other group, then it is the members who are benefiting—the individuals—and so this is individual selection. We obviously think in terms of actual organisms; but, now we know that it is the units of heredity (genes) underlying everything, individual selection can be thought of in terms of genes as well as organisms. Individual selection means some genes doing better for themselves than others in the struggle to leave copies of themselves in the next generation. In Richard Dawkins's (1976) memorable metaphor, they are "selfish genes" who won. If, however, when the groups compete, the winner is determined by the group rather than individuals, meaning that individuals give or sacrifice themselves to the group, without necessarily expecting or getting any return—some individuals in the group win while others get nothing, even though they have contributed to the success of the winners—this now is "group selection." The individual organisms were not "selfish." They were "altruistic." You give in a disinterested fashion for the benefit of group members even though you yourself get nothing (West, Griffin, and Gardner 2007, 2008).

Darwin was from first to last a completely determined individual selectionist. Why did he feel so strongly this way? In part, at least, for the very reason that today's evolutionists reject group selection. He did not think it could work. Alfred Russel Wallace, who was the co-discoverer of the theory of natural selection, was, from boyhood, a socialist rather than a capitalist. He was always enthusiastic for group selection. He and Darwin fell out over the sterility of the mule. Wallace thought it advantageous to the parent species—horses and donkeys—that their inefficient hybrid offspring be sterile. Darwin simply could not see how, having committed oneself to producing a hybrid, it would now be of advantage to either parent that the offspring, the mule, be sterile. It must simply be a function of different inheritances not meshing and working well together.

> Let me first say that no man could have more earnestly wished for the success of N. selection in regard to sterility, than I did; & when I considered a general statement, (as in your last note) I always felt sure it could be worked out, but always failed in detail. The cause being as I believe, that natural selection cannot effect what is not good for the individual, including in this term a social community. (Darwin 1985–, 16, 374; letter to Wallace April 6, 1868)

As his socialism influenced Wallace, social factors were also at work on Darwin. He was a great revolutionary, but he was not a rebel. He was the author of one of the greatest advances in the history of science. He was also a member of his society—as it happens, a very secure member of the British, upper-middle classes. His grandfather (and his wife's, Darwin having married a first cousin) was Josiah Wedgwood, founder of the pottery works bearing his name and one of the most successful entrepreneurs of the Industrial Revolution. The Darwin-Wedgwood family was both respectable and Silicon Valley–level rich. Naturally, Charles Darwin imbibed the norms of his family and his class, and above all this meant free enterprise. The figure behind the throne, as it were, was the eighteenth-century Scottish economist Adam Smith (1776), who—with the aim of improving the whole—preached the virtues of self-interest. "It is not from the benevolence of the butcher, the brewer, or the baker that we expect our dinner, but from their regard to their own self-interest. We address ourselves not to their humanity but to their self-love, and never talk to them of our own necessities, but of their advantages."

This line of reasoning is virtually a priori true for someone like Darwin. Whatever the effects on the group, it starts with the individual. Unsurprisingly, Smith's thinking about the virtues of a division of labor—everyone should focus on one job rather than trying to be Jack of All Trades—appears in very significant ways in the *Origin*. First, there was the "physiological" division of labor. "No naturalist doubts the advantage of what has been called the 'physiological division of labour'; hence we may believe that it would be advantageous to a plant to produce stamens alone in one flower or on one whole plant, and pistils alone in another flower or on another plant" (Darwin 1859, 93). Then there is what we might call an "ecological" division of labor: "in the general economy of any land, the more widely and perfectly the animals and plants are diversified for different habits of life, so will a greater number of individuals be capable of there supporting themselves. A set of animals, with their organisation but little diversified, could hardly compete with a set more perfectly diversified in structure" (116). A group picture but brought on by everyone being a butcher, a brewer, or a baker.

Humankind

Now, what about that ever-interesting organism *H. sapiens*? A decade after the *Origin*, Darwin took up this topic, and in 1871 he produced *The Descent of Man*. Much of this work is unexceptional. We are functioning organisms just like other organisms, with our special adaptations—hands, eyes, teeth, noses. Darwin draws attention to similarities—homologies—between humans and apes, using them as evidence of common ancestry. No one is claiming that we are descended from apes or monkeys extant today, but apes and monkeys were our ancestors. Darwin thought that a secondary mechanism, sexual selection, where the competition is more for mates than for resources, might have been significant in human evolution; but, overall, the treatment is orthodox. No special spirit forces to explain our existence and nature. What was particularly innovative was Darwin's treatment of human sociality. We may be produced by a struggle for existence, and obviously, sometimes, it is a very bloody struggle for existence. Ask an antelope in the jaws of a lion. However, Darwin was adamant that this is not the human way, at least it is not the fundamental human way. We humans succeed by cooperating. Half a loaf is better than none at all. We are not that fast or strong. Probably we have evolved that way, in tandem with our abilities to get along together, for mutual benefit. A pertinent metaphor is that of the computer (Newson and Richerson 2021). At first, the emphasis was on brute power—the brain the hardware, the culture the software. But then it became clear that the real power of the computer lies less in the simple ability to do sums and more in facilitating sociality—the internet and email. That is the story of humans. Our brains grew, our hardware got way more power-ful and efficient. But the real breakthrough was how this aided communication, sociality—our linguistic abilities, our emotions, our religious susceptibilities, and everything else that helps us to work together.

Darwin's great supporter Thomas Henry Huxley (1893) argued that natural selection always promotes abilities to fight and attack and that morality means going against our evolved nature. Darwin will have none of this. Tribes of people who get along and help each other do better than tribes who don't.

> It must not be forgotten that although a high standard of morality gives but a slight or no advantage to each individual man and his children over the other men of the same tribe, yet that an advancement in the standard of morality and an increase in the number of well-endowed men will certainly give an immense advantage to one tribe over another. There can be no doubt that a tribe including many members who, from possessing in a high degree the spirit of patriotism, fidelity, obedience, courage, and sympathy, were always ready to give aid to each other and to sacrifice themselves for the

common good, would be victorious over most other tribes; and this would be natural selection. (Darwin 1871, 1, 166)

"Victorious over most other tribes"? Surely this is an appeal to group selection? Not at all! Shortly before this passage, Darwin implies that (what today is known as) "reciprocal altruism" is a major causal factor. You scratch my back and I will scratch yours: "as the reasoning powers and foresight of the members [of a tribe] became improved, each man would soon learn from experience that if he aided his fellow-men, he would commonly receive aid in return" (1, 163). This is not the disinterested altruism of group selection. The individual alone is benefiting: individual selection. But it seems also in the passage above that Darwin is appealing to the interests of the group: "sacrifice themselves for the common good." Again, there is individual-based understanding at work here. It is the good of the individual that is all-important, where individual might apply to the family—or what Darwin, in the letter to Wallace, called a "social community." If members of your family reproduce, then you, sharing elements of heredity, reproduce by proxy as it were. "Thus, a well-flavoured vegetable is cooked, and the individual is destroyed; but the horticulturist sows seeds of the same stock, and confidently expects to get nearly the same variety; breeders of cattle wish the flesh and fat to be well marbled together; the animal has been slaughtered, but the breeder goes with confidence to the same family" (Darwin 1859, 237–38). Today this is known as "kin selection." In other words, a form of individual selection.

So, what about Darwin and morality? The key notion is that of a "tribe." Does he think it an intrarelated group, which he must if he is to be consistent with his individual-selectionist stance? He does. He endorses an article by Herbert Spencer on tribes, where it is clearly argued that tribes think themselves united by a common ancestor, whether this be strictly true or not. "If 'the Wolf,' proving famous in fight, becomes a terror to neighbour- ing tribes, and a dominant man in his own, his sons, proud of their parentage, will not let fall the fact that they descended from 'the Wolf'; nor will this fact be forgotten by the rest of the tribe who hold 'the Wolf' in awe, and see reason to dread his sons." Indeed, the rest of the tribe will want to get on board. "In proportion to the power and celebrity of 'the Wolf' will this pride and this fear conspire to maintain among his grandchil- dren and great-grandchildren, as well as among those over whom they dominate, the remembrance of the fact that their ancestor was 'the Wolf'" (Spencer 1870, 535). Darwin agrees: "names or nicknames given from some animal or other object to the early progenitors or founders of a tribe, are supposed after a long inter- val to represent the real progenitor of the tribe" (Darwin 1871, 66, ft. 53). Morality for Darwin comes from a proto-form of kin selection—our thoughts and actions are driven by our belief in part of a related community, whether or not this is actually true. Anticipating, today's evolutionists agree: "we are evolutionarily primed to define 'kin' as those with whom we are familiar due to living and rearing arrangements. So genetically unrelated indi- viduals can come to be understood as kin—and subsequently treated as such—if introduced into our network of frequent and intimate associations (for example, family) in an appropriate way" (Johnson 1986, 133).

Hatred

Accept with Darwin that the key to evolutionary success is being adapted and *the* crucial adaptation for human success has been our sociability (Ruse 2019). This is likely a cause-and-effect feedback relationship. We are not that strong or fast or fierce, but we are very good at getting on with our fellows. And the causes are not just psychological, but physiological too. It is hard enough as it is teaching an undergraduate logic class. Imagine if three students in the class were in heat. Being sociable and friendly is what makes us tick. And yet, while one hates to spoil this hymn of self-congratulation, it is so obviously—so painfully obviously—only part of the story. As the last century alone shows too well, humans are vicious haters. Our thoughts and behaviors toward our fellow human beings make one cringe. Or, if they don't, they should. The Great War, the First World War (1914–1918), depending on how you count the numbers, produced twenty to forty million dead. The Second World War (1939–1945), sixty to eighty million dead. The Russian Civil War (1917–1922), five to ten million dead. The Chinese Civil War (1927–1949), about ten million dead. It is hard to draw a line between soldier and civilian. Fifty million of the deaths in the Second World War were civilian. Then there are the pogroms and the like within countries. During the Great War and for some years after, over three million Armenian Christians were murdered by the Turks. There were the Kulaks, the wealthy peasant farmers, whom Stalin regarded as enemies of the Soviet state. In the 1930s, at least a million were liquidated, perhaps more. And this is not to mention the resulting famine caused by their elimination. The Germans and the Jews—at least six million deaths—will forever be a stain on humankind (Friedlander 1997, 2008). Europeans are not alone in this. In Rwanda, in 1994, up to a million Tutsis were murdered and up to half a million Tutsi women were raped, often as a preliminary to grotesque mutilations of their genitalia.

We Anglophones should beware of being smug. Not all hatred involves massive wars. In Amritsar in the Punjab, India, on April 13, 1919, Acting Brigadier-General Reginald Dyer ordered his troops to fire on unarmed Indian civilians (Gilmour 2018). At least 379 people were killed and 1,200 other people were injured. In Tulsa, Oklahoma, on May 31 and June 1, 1921, mobs of white residents attacked black residents and businesses of the (very successful and middle-class) Greenwood District (Ellsworth 1992; Brophy 2003). Between one hundred and three hundred black people were killed. No convictions. If you think this hardly compares to the sufferings elsewhere, remember that these are but tips of the iceberg of ongoing vile treatment by those in power against those less fortunate. Tulsa is a metaphor for the whole dreadful story of America and its exploitation of black people. July 4 is America's most significant national holiday, celebrating the signing of the Declaration of Independence on that day in 1776. From then, until the beginning of the Civil War in 1860, America's slave population grew from seven hundred thousand to over four million. This, at a time when other countries, not to mention the northern states of the Union, were realizing the grotesque immorality of enslaving other human beings. African Americans were not the only people who suffered. By end of the nineteenth century, thanks to harassment and eviction from their native lands, consequent starvation and the like, the numbers of indigenous people were down to a quarter of a million from at least five million when Christopher Columbus first crossed the ocean. You don't have to murder someone to make their lives miserable to the point of elimination. Ask the British in the 1840s about the Irish Famine. From 1845 to 1849, a million Irish died and another million emigrated. True it was not the British who invented or imported the potato blight. Business had to go on. "In the year A.D. 1846, there were exported from Ireland, 3,266,193 quarters of wheat, barley and oats, besides flour, beans, peas, and rye; 186,483 cattle, 6,363 calves, 259,257 sheep, 180,827 swine" (Jones 1849, 10). At least enough food to feed half of the Irish population.

The Problem

In the face of the rosy picture painted above about our social nature, how do we speak to this dreadful side to our nature? Do we just blame a few perverted members of our species? Or are we all tainted with the Sin of Adam, as Calvinists assure us? If we turn to biology for insight about our social nature, turn to biology also for insight into our satanic nature. The answer comes as readily. As Charles Darwin told us, life is a struggle and winner takes all. In the world of selfish genes, the winner wins and the loser loses, it is as simple as that. Thomas Henry Huxley spoke truly after all. Might is right. General Friedrich von Bernhardi, a sometime member of the German General Staff, put the case starkly in his *Germany and the Next War*, published just before the First World War. "War is a biological necessity of the first importance, a regulative element in the life of mankind which cannot be dispensed with, since without it an unhealthy development will follow, which excludes every advancement of the race, and therefore all real civilization. 'War is the father of all things'" (von Bernhardi 1912, 18). Happy to use the authority of Darwin: "The struggle for existence is, in the life of Nature, the basis of all healthy development" (18).

This all seems so mixed up. It is natural to be nice, so that is okay. It is just as natural to be nasty, but that is not okay. How do we reconcile this? In this book, I am going to focus on two aspects of hatred—war and prejudice. These, involving hatred at the group level and hatred at the individual level, are clearly major parts of the story. The already-quoted numbers of deaths in the two worldwide conflicts confirms the place of war in my tale. The attitudes, from the beginnings of European life in the New World, toward people not of that ancestry, confirm the place of prejudice in my tale. Are war and prejudice always entirely separate? Probably not. David Hume points out that in war we tend to think of the enemy as inferior, not the best quality people: "whoever harms or displeases us never fails to excite our anger or hatred. When our own nation is at war with any other, we detest them under the character of cruel, perfidious, unjust and violent" (Hume 1739–40, 225). One suspects this overlap points to shared causes; but, leave this for a moment. Here my concern is that both involve hating one's fellow humans. Is all hatred covered by war and prejudice? Again, probably not. I am not sure that genocide— mass killings of groups by other groups: Turks of Armenians (1915–1923), Soviets over Kulaks (1932–1933), Germans over

Jews (1939–1945)—quite fits these categories. Else my topic gets away from me, I have squeezed it in.

My first two chapters will look at what scientists have to say about war and prejudice, their natures and their causes. I am an evolutionist, so I believe that the answers to the present are to be found in the past. Simply put, we shall learn that we humans were hunter-gatherers and that natural selection made us highly suited to our lifestyle. Experts at avoiding conflict and with little reason to look down on others. Then came agriculture and all changed. Our formerly efficient adaptations were too often not adequate for our new circumstances and lifestyles. Conflicts, group and individual, arose. In the next two chapters, I shall look at what those who focus on culture, the humanities—especially philosophy, literature, religious studies (not excluding theology), and history—have had to say about war and prejudice, their natures and their causes. These chapters complement rather than contradict the earlier chapters. I shall show how we have wrestled with understanding how things have so changed, and the full implications for where we find ourselves now. In my final chapter, I shall ask whether we can reconcile the tensions in our position. Can we move forward, bringing the knowledge of our biological past combined with the awareness of our cultural present to speak positively and creatively to the challenges that lie before us? Can we moderate or eliminate war and prejudice? The wonderful thing about our human nature is that, although it buckles under the course of history, it does not let that history be the sole determinant. It has the spirit and abilities to fight back and reset our path through time in a far better manner. I am ever an optimist. Is my optimism justified?

THE BIOLOGY OF WAR

Kinds of War

Let us start with a somewhat informal taxonomy of war or, rather, wars. The categories are intended as a guide and, as we shall see, often depend on different perspectives, rather than something strictly objective. First, when one thinks of war, there is *Offensive* War. One side goes after another. A paradigmatic example occurred in England in 1066, the Battle of Hastings, when the Duke of Normandy—"William the Conqueror"—wanting the crown for himself, invaded and defeated the reigning Anglo-Saxon king, Harold Godwinson. The former king, Edward the Confessor, died childless early in 1066, setting up a struggle for the succession. The Norwegian king, Harald III, joined by Harold's brother Tostig, invaded in the North. Their army was defeated by Harold at the Battle of Stamford Bridge (in the East Riding of the northern county of Yorkshire) in late September, and both Harald and Tostig were killed. The only remaining rival claimant was William—he maintained that Edward had promised

Why We Hate. Michael Ruse, Oxford University Press. © Oxford University Press 2022.
DOI: 10.1093/oso/9780197621288.003.0002

him the crown—who landed in the South of England, also in late September, and thus forced Harold to march his exhausted army south to confront the invader. They clashed on a hill just outside Hastings, a seaside town in what is now East Sussex. The battle on October 14 lasted all day. At first, Harold's forces were doing well, holding their own. Then William's forces feigned defeat, pretended to retreat, fleeing down the hill. Harold's forces followed, found themselves in an ambush, and that was it. Harold himself was killed toward the end of the battle, pierced through the eye by the most famous arrow in English history. The victorious duke then marched north. He was crowned William I (1066–1087) in London on Christmas Day 1066. After that, it was simply a matter of dividing England up between William's nobles, and the Norman Conquest was over. A perfect example of an Offensive War. (See Figure 1.1.)

A paradigmatic example of a *Defensive* War is that waged by the Russians in 1812, when faced by the invasion of Napoleon's troops. This began on June 24, when Napoleon's *Grande Armée* crossed the Neman River aiming to engage and defeat the Russian Army. The reason behind the invasion was less to do with Russia as such, being more an attempt to stop Russia from trading with the British, Napoleon's chief foe, that he hoped thereby to force to sue for peace. As those who have read Tolstoy's *War and Peace* know full well, at first the French forces were stunningly successful, overpowering the Russians at the Battle of Smolensk in August. But the Russians retreated, destroying all in their wake, thus preventing the French from replenishing themselves as they advanced. A second French victory was the Battle of Borodino in early September, followed by more Russian retreat. In mid-September,

FIGURE I.I The Bayeux Tapestry. A seventy-meter-long embroidered tapestry, probably made in England in the late eleventh century, showing the events of the Battle of Hastings.

Napoleon entered an empty Moscow, aflame from Russian arsonists. The Russian tsar, Alexander I, still free, refused to surrender, and, in late October, short of supplies and fearing the oncoming Russian winter, Napoleon left Moscow and began a retreat to Poland. Decimated by the ferocious weather, lack of supplies, and constant harassing by the Russian forces led by Mikhail Kutuzov, it was the beginning of the end for Napoleon. Russia was defended and the French humiliated. History was on its way to the Battle of Waterloo, June 18, 1815.

Then there is *Civil* War. Look briefly at the English Civil War, in the middle of the seventeenth century, between Cavaliers (supporters of Charles I) and Roundheads (supporters of Oliver Cromwell). It all started the century before with Henry the Eighth (reigned 1509–1547), he of six wives fame, declaring England a Protestant country when the pope would not give him permission to divorce his first wife, Catherine of Aragon, and marry Anne Boleyn (Brigden 2000). After Henry, first briefly came his son, Edward VI (1547–1553), Protestant; then, after a nine-day reign by Lady Jane Grey, Protestant, came Henry's older daughter, Mary (1553–1558), daughter of Catherine of Aragon, Catholic; and following her, for a long time, his younger daughter, Elizabeth (1558–1603), daughter of Anne Boleyn, Protestant. She, famously dying a virgin, was followed by (from Scotland), James I (1603–1620), Protestant, and then his son Charles I (1620–1649), also (somewhat wonkily) Protestant (Kishlanski 1997). The trouble began with Mary, who was fiercely Catholic, burning her citizens at the stake for their heretical Protestant beliefs. Many escaped to the continent and joined the Calvinists in Geneva. When they returned, they ("Puritans") were very much more Protestant than those who remained, who were much given to the trappings of Catholicism (buildings and ceremonies) blended into a mild Calvinist theology. These differences continued into the seventeenth century and were a major issue under Charles I, whom many considered dangerously close to Catholicism. His French wife was Catholic, for a start, and he had a suspicious liking for high Anglican rituals. Charles II, the son of Charles I, was secretly probably Catholic, and his brother James II was overtly Catholic, which led to his being overthrown and replaced by his Protestant daughter, Mary, and her Protestant Dutch husband, William.

These religious tensions, increasing through the 1630s, were matched by a struggle between Charles I and his parliament. Although the king had the authority and power to convene and dismiss parliament, it was parliament that passed the tax laws and provided the money. Things came to a crisis in the 1640s, with a series of intermittent wars between the king's supporters, the Royalists (Cavaliers wearing fancy clothes well captured by Anthony van Dyck) and the Parliamentarians (Roundheads, wearing sober clothing with inverted-bowl-shaped helmets). Eventually, the Parliamentarians prevailed, Charles I was captured, found guilty of treason, and beheaded (January 30, 1649). Through the 1650s, the Interregnum, England was ruled by the leader of the Parliamentarians, Oliver Cromwell, the "Lord Protector." In 1660 Charles II was restored to the throne, although from then on the British Parliament had far greater control than that of the absolute monarchs of the continent. At the beginning of the First World War, Kaiser Wilhelm in Germany, Emperor Franz Josef in Austro-Hungary, and the tsar in Russia all had power that the British monarchs had relinquished over two centuries earlier.

Next, there is *Revolutionary* War, as in America, between 1770 and 1783, when the American colonies broke loose from British suzerainty and declared themselves independent, a fact that the British finally accepted (Middleton 2011). Since the colonies were part of the British Empire (as it was later called) at the time of the beginning of the war, one might then call it a Civil War. By the time it was finished, it was revolutionary. The background to what happened was most obviously a function that, almost from the first, in the seventeenth century, the American colonies had been left to fend for and govern themselves. Thus, great umbrage was taken when, in the 1770s, to cover debts incurred in earlier wars—for example, the "Seven Years' War" between England and

France—the British government decided to spread the costs to the colonies. Conflicts broke out and, in August 1776, the colonies made their Declaration of Independence. Fighting continued, somewhat exacerbated by France seizing the opportunity to get at the British by signing formal alliances with the new American government. Eventually, after the British (led by General Cornwallis) were defeated (by Americans led by George Washington and French led by the Comte de Rochambeau) in the Battle of Yorktown (in Virginia) ending October 19, 1781, negotiations were begun. On September 3, 1783, the Treaty of Paris was signed between Great Britain and the United States, granting or acknowledging (depending on one's perspective) American independence.

Going on, one might want to distinguish *Nuclear* War, as at Hiroshima and Nagasaki in Japan in 1945, although in a sense one might say it was all part of what started as a Defensive War, as the United States girded its loins after Pearl Harbor and fought back against the Japanese (Gordin 2007). The list grows. Most obviously there is *Guerilla* War, as in Kenya between 1952 and 1960, when rebels attacked the British Army as well as citizens loyal to the British Colony: "The insurgents' lack of heavy weaponry and the heavily entrenched police and Home Guard positions meant that Mau Mau attacks were restricted to nighttime and where loyalist positions were weak. When attacks did commence, they were fast and brutal, as insurgents were easily able to identify loyalists because they were often local to those communities themselves" (Anderson 2005, 252). In other words, not full-scale battles, but attacks on weak positions. The British won the battle and (horrifically) executed over a thousand rebels. The Kenyans won their independence.

One could continue. What about *Private* War, where one individual (or perhaps a small group) takes on a whole nation over some perceived grievance? John Brown, in the nineteenth century, over slavery; Osama bin Laden, in the twentieth century, over perceived attacks by the United States on Muslims in the Middle East. The list now is adequate for our needs. War comes in different forms or situations. All-important are the similarities, most obviously that people set out or feel forced to kill other people.

Killer Apes?

Wars are about humans killing other humans. The overriding Darwinian premise/conclusion is that what distinguishes humans is that we are so obviously and clearly a social species. A moral species. But none of this precludes or makes impossible intraspecific conflict. Just as well. After the Battle of Stamford Bridge, only 24 boats out of the original 300 were needed to carry away the Norwegian survivors. Against a total population of rather more than 3 million, probably at Hastings each side had about 10,000 men. It is thought that 4,000 of the English were killed and about 2,000 of the Normans. A tiny number compared to what was to come, but still not figures that a recruiting sergeant would parade. Moving forward down the centuries, numbers are far higher. A mere 27,000 of Napoleon's troops survived the journey home. Left in Russia were some 370,000 dead and 100,000 prisoners. In the English Civil War, about 34,000 Parliamentarians and about 50,000 Royalists died. Add to this at least 100,000 civilian men and women who died from war-related diseases. In other words, in total almost 200,000 out of a population of around 5 million. Hiroshima and Nagasaki are even more horrific. Pre-bomb Hiroshima had a total population of 255,000. There were 66,000 dead and 69,000 injured—over half the population. Pre-bomb Nagasaki had a total population of 195,000. There were 39,000 dead and 25,000 injured—around a third of the population. What price sociality now? The Harvard psychologist Joshua Greene writes: "We have cooperative brains, it seems, because cooperation provides material benefits, biological resources that enable our genes to make more copies of themselves. Out of evolutionary dirt grows the flower of human goodness" (Greene 2013, 65). The flower of human goodness? Rank weeds more like.

Many have thought that we need to add an extra ingredient to the stew. There is a very popular line of thought—perhaps unsurprisingly, popular in the years after the Second World War—that has an answer to explain our violent nature. Appearances apart, for all the surface skin of sociality, we humans are the unrestrained ape, evil to the core. (See Figure 1.2.) The apes with weapons, killing other apes at the beginning of the movie *2001*, epitomize this kind of approach. It represented a much-rehearsed theme. Paleoanthropologist Raymond Dart was its modern originator. Rightly celebrated as the person who in 1924 identified Taung Baby, *Australopithecus africanus*—a human ancestor (hominin)—by the 1950s Dart was venturing into speculation. To use an appropriate metaphor, he made no bones about his views. We were flesh-eaters. And we were not that fussy about whom we ate. Whether by choice or need we ate each other. That explains a lot: "The loathsome cruelty of mankind to man forms one of his inescapable characteristics and differentiative features; and it

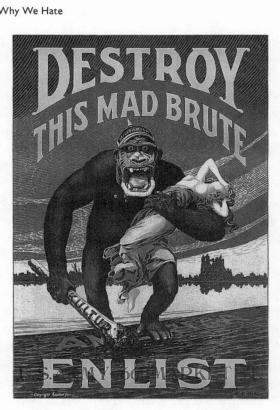

FIGURE 1.2 A US recruiting poster from the First World War.

is explicable only in terms of his carnivorous, and cannibalistic origin" (Dart 1953, 208). Warming to his theme:

> The blood-bespattered, slaughter-gutted archives of human history from the earliest Egyptian and Sumerian records to

the most recent atrocities of the Second World War accord
with early universal cannibalism, with animal and human
sacrificial practices of their substitutes in formalized religions and with the world-wide scalping, head-hunting,
body-mutilating and necrophiliac practices of mankind in
proclaiming this common bloodlust differentiator, this predaceous habit, this mark of Cain that separates man dietetically from his anthropoidal relatives and allies him rather
with the deadliest of Carnivora. (208–09)

Dart was taken up by Robert Ardrey, an American film-script
writer who, having run afoul of the McCarthy anticommunist
hearings, moved to Africa, where he became a best-selling writer
about human origins, pushing a view of humankind—*African
Genesis*—that he admitted openly (and proudly) he got from
the often-neglected and -derided Dart. Ardrey was serious and
respected, but he was not on the way to a Nobel Prize, unlike
the father of ethology, Konrad Lorenz. In his best-selling *On
Aggression*, he too embraced the killer-ape theme with enthusiasm. All animals have built-in mechanisms to save them from
harming members of their own species. "This is certainly the case
in the dog, in which I have repeatedly seen that when the loser in a
fight suddenly adopted the submissive attitude, and presented his
unprotected neck, the winner performed the movement of shak-
ing to death, in the air, close to the neck of the morally vanquished
dog, but with closed mouth, that is, without biting" (Lorenz
1966, 133). Humans alas are the exception. "In human evolution, no inhibitory mechanisms preventing sudden manslaughter
were necessary, because quick killing was impossible anyhow; the

potential victim had plenty of opportunity to elicit the pity of the aggressor by submissive gestures and appeasing attitudes" (241). Natural selection let us down. We did not develop inhibitions against killing each other. Then came the invention of artificial weapons. We were helpless: "man's position was very nearly that of a dove which, by some unnatural trick of nature, has suddenly acquired the beak of a raven."

Moving rapidly through the next fifty years, the killer-ape thesis continues to ride high. The prominent evolutionary psychologists John Tooby and Leda Cosmides wallow in it. They assure us that: "War is found throughout prehistory." Unsurprisingly: "Whenever in the archaeological record there is sufficient evidence to make a judgment, there traces of war are to be found. It is found across all forms of social organization—in bands, chiefdoms, and states. It was a regular part of hunter-gathering life whenever population densities were not vanishingly low, and often even in harsh marginal habitats" (Tooby and Cosmides 2010, 191). The University of Southern California anthropologist Christopher Boehm tells us: "Thus, for at least from 45,000 BP to 15,000 BP, or a bit later, it seems likely that in all human societies a combination of chronic male competition over females and recurrent intensive resource competition were stimulating some level of lethal conflict between bands" (Boehm 2013, 326). Philosophers join in the chorus. "Violence has followed our species every step of the way in its long journey through time. From the scalped bodies of ancient warriors to the suicide bombers in today's newspaper headlines, history is drenched in human blood" (Livingstone Smith 2007, 8). Elaborating: "Human beings wage war because it is in our nature to do so, and saying that war is just a matter of choice without taking account of how our choices grow in the rich soil of human nature is a recipe for confusion." Our writer is in good company. "War itself, however, is in need of no special stimulating cause, but seems engrafted in human nature, and is even regarded as something noble in itself to which man is inspired by the love of glory apart from motives of self-interest" (Kant 1795, 151). More recently, there is best-selling, academic superstar Steven Pinker. We humans are a violent folk—"most of us—including you, dear reader—are wired for violence, even if in all likelihood we will never have an occasion to use it" (Pinker 2011, 483). It is true that "when men confront each other in face-to-face conflict, they often exercise restraint. But this reticence is not a sign that humans are gentle and compassionate." Pure and simple. We are nice only out of prudence.

Which raises the question: Is there no more to be said? "Job's comforters" is the term that comes first to mind as these Cassandras end their discussions. First, Ardrey gives his take on human nature. "It is a jerry-built structure, and a more unattractive edifice could scarcely be imagined. Its greyness is appalling. Its walls are cracked and eggshell thin. Its foundations are shallow, its antiquity slight. No bands boom, no flags fly, no glamorous symbols invoke our nostalgic hearts." Then, he offers a way forward. "Yet however humiliating the path may be, man beset by anarchy, banditry, chaos and extinction must at last resort turn to that chamber of horrors, human enlightenment. For he has nowhere else to turn" (352–53). We have all the makings of a novel by Thomas Hardy.

Darwinian Explanations

If we mean by "Darwinian" in the spirit of Charles Darwin himself, then none of this is very Darwinian. We could be killer apes, but we need some adaptive reason why. Killer apes are predisposed to violence, but Darwinian humans are social, getting into war only when there are good reasons. We are not going to go after our fellow humans spontaneously. For insight, let us turn to the "chamber of horrors." Specifically, turn to an approach that pays attention to what our theory tells us about human nature: Darwinian thinking. The anthropologist Douglas P. Fry (2013a) points out that the slogan that should be chanted endlessly is: "Does this behavior (or thinking) promote Darwinian processes? Does it lead to increased survival and reproduction?" We might be brutes. Prove it. Don't assume it. Why do we do—why would we do—what we do? War is dangerous. Unless it pays off, no one is going to do it. The assumption is peace, until shown otherwise. Peace does not always win. This last century shows that, tragically. But it is the null hypothesis, as it were. So why war? How do you set about answering a question such as this? Three lines of evidence seem promising. First, archaeology: what do we learn from the remains of hominins and their artifacts? Second, people: what do we learn from groups of people who seem to have been least affected by modern civilization? Three, primates: what do our closest relatives tell us?

Archaeology

What do we learn from archaeology? The evidence shows, clearly, that war is a relatively recent invention. For most of hominin existence since the break from the apes, there was no war. As anthropologist Brian Ferguson says, "We are not hard-wired for war. We learn it" (Ferguson 2013a, 126).

> True, in some cases, war could be present but not leave any traces. However, comparison of many, many cases, from all different regions, shows some clear patterns. In the earliest remains, other than occasional cannibalism, there is no evidence of war, and barely evidence of interpersonal violence. In Europe's Mesolithic [15,000–5,000], war is scattered and episodic, and in the comparable Epipaleolithic [20,000–8,000] in the Near East it is absent. (Ferguson 2013b, 191)

For most of our existence, until the last 15,000 years or later, as I outlined in the introduction, members of *Homo sapiens* were hunter-gatherers. We lived in nomadic bands, about fifty people give or take, hunting and gathering, going after game and picking berries and roots and the like. Cooperation was needed, and this would have led to the forces propelling our evolution. We left our relatives in the jungle and moved out onto the plains. With this came bipedalism and for the same or related reasons our brains—and consequent reasoning powers—started their climb upward. We were in groups, able to move around, using (and using up) available resources, and then moving on as need be.

Look at Figure 1.3, showing relative population density on Planet Earth in the past 200,000 years (Haas and Piscitelli 2013, 177). I suspect that your immediate reaction is the same as mine. "Why are you bothering to show me this? It is just a bunch of identical empty spaces." A more careful look shows that it is

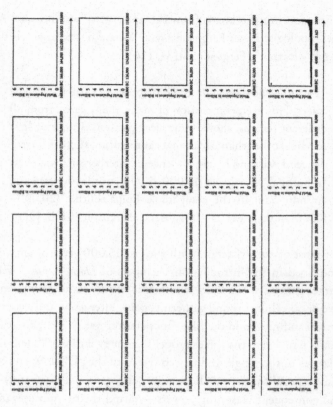

FIGURE 1.3 The population density of humans over the past 200,000 years. (Courtesy Jonathan Haas.)

not entirely a bunch of empty spaces. The picture, down in the bottom right-hand corner, shows a graph which starts slowly, and then suddenly shoots up out of sight. Something happened. Leave that, for now, and focus on the time before it happened.

There was room for everyone, masses and masses of it. We were in groups, able to move around, using (and using up) available resources, and then moving on as need be. The hunter-gatherers did not just stay on open African plains. Sometimes we were living relatively cheek by jowl with other groups, but there was still plenty of room for everyone. Why fight? Why put your lives at stake? While you might get some of their women, they might take more of your women. Perhaps some of the young braves saw more career prospects in another group. No doubt these things did happen sometimes, enough so that, over time, the genes of the species got spread around. That is hardly of concern to hunter-gatherers. In any case, it could as like have been a peaceful exchange. There is plenty of room for everyone. Move on and out of their way.

This is the crucial Darwinian point. There was no need of war. So, no war and no innate propensity to make war. Those who moved on were those who survived and reproduced. So, what changed all of this? In one word: *agriculture*. One must acknowledge other contributing factors, most particularly those which make it possible for humans to wage war. As the anthropologist Frank Marlowe points out, small groups are not fitted for systematic fighting. "If warfare were very prevalent, we should expect foragers to prefer, when at all possible, to live in larger local groups to defend themselves more effectively" (Marlowe 2010, 264). Douglas Fry and colleagues elaborate that: "changes associated with the development of social complexity—such as settling down, development of social inequalities, population increase, rise of ambitious leaders, accumulation of food and other items to plunder—greatly increase the likelihood of warfare" (Fry, Keith, and Söderberg 2020, 303). But something triggered everything and that was agriculture. "The first clear evidence of warfare arrives with the development of agriculture" (Fry 2013b, 112); quoting Raymond Kelly (2000, 2) in justification: "following the 'global conditions of warlessness that had persisted for several million years.'" Starting in force around ten thousand years ago, biologically agriculture was a smash hit. Serendipitously, from one corner came animals and plants ripe for domestication. Cattle, sheep, pigs, chickens, rice, wheat, potatoes. Not to mention dogs for guarding and helping generally. From the other corner came the ability to fashion helpful tools and artifacts. Pottery possibly goes back another ten thousand years (Craig et al. 2013). It now starts to play a major supportive role. Sophisticated grinding stones appear, opening up massive new energy sources. And where does this all lead? No surprise: "farmers pump out babies much faster than hunter-gatherers" (Lieberman 2013, 188).

Today, I suspect most of us who are parents tend to think of children as a drain on resources—clothing, schooling, housing, video games, and more. Then, it was the reverse. "After a few years of care, a farmer's children can work in the fields and in the home, helping to take care of crops, herd animals, mind younger children, and process food. In fact, a large part of the success of farming is that farmers breed their own labor force more effectively than hunter-gatherers which pumps energy back into the system, driving up fertility rates."

And so started that population explosion that we see in that last picture, bottom right.

Only during the Holocene did humans undergo exponential population growth. Just prior to the Holocene (19,000 to

13,000 BP), the Late Pleistocene populations of Australia, Asia, Europe, and Africa combined have been estimated at about 500,000 people, or .3 persons per 100 sq. km (Haas & Piscitelli 2013). By way of comparison, for an extant sample of Holocene foragers from Africa, Asia, Australia, North America, and South America . . . , the average population density is 34.12 persons per 100 sq. km, which amounts to 113 times the estimated population density for the world-wide forager population near the end of the Pleistocene. (Fry, Keith, and Söderberg 2020, 311)

The trickle-down consequences were immediate and deadly. No longer was there space just to move away from potential competitors. Increasingly, you had to live side by side, and increasingly the pressure to grab neighbors' land grew. Moreover, if the neighbors were successful farmers, increasingly there was reason to go and grab it, even in the face of potential danger. It was not as if the neighbors could simply get up and go. That is the whole point of agriculture. You are no longer nomadic. You are stuck on your land. War started. "In most formulations, some basic parameters appear: higher populations, more sedentism, foraging concentrated on spatially limited and highly productive sites, food storage, definition of more distinctive social groups, and sociopolitical hierarchy. These all apply, with local variations, to the European Mesolithic" (Ferguson 2013b, 199). Or something similar. "On Kodiak Island [Alaska] the archaeological record goes back at least 7500 years. For the first 5000 years, evidence of war is non-existent" (Fry, Keith, and Sönderberg 2020, 313). Then we get "the first use of small defendable land-forms such as placing camps on steep slopes and promontories at about 1100 BP. A few centuries later, large defensible villages appear in the archaeological record." And so "inequality arose along with the development of whale hunting and eventually expands to embrace large-scale, endemic warfare mobilized by large boats and long-distance raids." We are not hard-wired for war. We sure do learn it.

Societies Today

The second line of evidence is societies today. Again, there is evidence that war is not innate and inevitable. The Hadza are a hunter-gatherer society, about 1,200 individuals, living in East Africa (Tanzania). As with so many other such societies, civilization keeps impinging and altering the traditional ways of life. Alcohol has had a devastating effect. But we know enough to make some general observations. "Traditional Hadza may be classified as an egalitarian, tolerant, and autonomous people. They tend to avoid conflicts by avoidance and tolerance, as members of most nomadic societies do. . . . In conflict situations, the Hadza, like other nomadic foragers, prefer to retire . . . , and most men and women have never killed anyone. Blood revenge is not practiced" (Butovskaya 2013, 292). Societies like this—and it is not atypical—do add to the general thesis.

"Not atypical"? Is this true? Many would think there is massive counterevidence to this, most notably Napoleon Chagnon's extensive and detailed studies and findings of the Yanomamö—about 15,000 individuals in 200 communities—in southern Venezuela and the adjacent northern Brazil.

Studies of the Yanomamö Indians of Amazonas during the past 23 years show that 44 percent of males estimated to be 25 or older have participated in the killing of someone, that approximately 30 percent of adult male deaths are due to violence, and that nearly 70 percent of all adults over an estimated 40 years of age have lost a close genetic relative due to violence. Demographic data indicate that men who have killed have more wives and offspring than men who have not killed. (Chagnon 1988, 985)

Revenge for past wrongs is almost always the explicit motive. About 10 to 20 members of a group go out on a mission, often requiring several days journeying, and the victims—usually one or two—are felled by arrows. Most attackers have killed only one, but, like fighter pilots, some are aces with over ten kills. Those who have killed are known as "Unokais." These tend to be the leaders, and since the Yanomamö are polygamous, with leaders having six or more wives, expectedly the Unokais tend to have more wives than the non-Unokais. (Figure 1.4, based on Chagnon 1988, table 3, 989.) This cashes out in the number of offspring of Unokais versus non-Unokais. (Figure 1.5, based on table 2, 989.) Put into context, the conclusion follows. Becoming a unokai pays off. It is "one of a number of male characteristics valued by the Yanomamö and an integral component in a more general complex of goals for which ambitious men strive. All the characteristics just mentioned make some males more attractive as mates in arranged marriages and dispose some of them to take the risks involved in appropriating additional females by force. Both paths lead to higher reproductive success" (990).

	Unokais			Non-unokais		
Ages	n	Number of wives	Average number of wives	n	Number of wives	Average number of wives
20–24	5	4	0.80	78	10	0.13
25–30	14	13	0.93	58	31	0.53
31–40	43	49	1.14	61	59	0.97
>41	75	157	2.09	46	54	1.17
Total	137	223	1.63	243	154	0.63

FIGURE I.4 Average number of wives of unokais compared to non-unokais. (From Chagnon 1988.)

	Unokais			Non-unokais		
Ages	n	Number of off-spring	Average number of offspring	n	Number of off-spring	Average number of offspring
20–24	5	5	1.00	78	14	0.18
25–30	14	22	1.57	58	50	0.86
31–40	43	122	2.83	61	123	2.02
>41	75	524	6.99	46	193	4.19
Total	137	673	4.91	243	380	1.59

FIGURE I.5 Average number of children of unokais compared to non-unokais. (From Chagnon 1988.)

Expectedly, Chagnon has had (many) critics. From our perspective, two are particularly salient. First, Chagnon is not talking about small hunter-gatherer groups on very large African plains. "Contrary to the widespread view at the time of Chagnon's early fieldwork, pre-Columbian native societies of northern Amazonia were not characterized by the small size and simple organization of ethnographically known shifting horticulturalists." To the contrary: "Ethnohistory and archaeology reveal large riverine settlements, bordering on urban scale, linked together with connections of trade, marriage, war, alliance, and ritual. These systems reached into smaller scale societies in highland interiors. Without any doubt, these were social worlds full of tumult, change, and conflict" (Ferguson 2015, 382). Second, there was a lot of action after that. For example: "Slave raiding by or for Europeans reached the Negro, Branco, and Orinoco rivers that encompass Yanomami highlands from the 1620s onward, more or less rapidly devastating lowland societies." Continuing: "In the 1730s, captive-taking reached a peak, with some 20,000 going to the Portuguese from 1740 to 1750. These wars for captives totally transformed the indigenous world of northern Amazonia" (382).

The Yanomamö are not relevant to our discussion, and, even if they were, claims that the most ferocious are those that have the most offspring are suspect. On the one hand, age seems to be at least as strong a causal factor. The longer you live, or not, the more offspring you are likely to have, or not. On the other hand, being that ferocious might well be counterproductive. You get killed when you are young and your reproductive chances are brought to an abrupt conclusion. The Yanomamö "do not represent humankind in a state of nature, but were mightily 'touched' by the imperial world for centuries. The society Chagnon studied was drastically restructured by western contact, both within and between local groups" (403). In any case: "There is no evidence that participating in killings leads to any increase in reproductive success and, much more likely, reduces it" (403).

Primates

What then of primate analogies? Here, surely, the war-is-not-innate thesis comes crashing down. Since the long-term studies of chimpanzees in Africa by Jane Goodall (1986), we know that chimpanzees are indeed killer apes. Bands of chimpanzees go out and kill other chimpanzees (mainly males but also females). "As the number of chimpanzee study sites has increased across Africa, and with accumulating information from long-term study sites, it has become clear that intraspecific aggression constitutes a pervasive risk for chimpanzees" (Wilson 2013, 370). Some killing occurs within groups. However, "the majority of killings (67 percent) involved intergroup attacks. . . . Intergroup killing thus appears to be a widespread trait of chimpanzees, rather than the result of circumstances peculiar to one or a few study sites" (Wilson 2013, 370).

That seems definitive. Humans as killer apes is a hypothesis back in play (Pinker 2011). Not so fast! First, remember, we are equally related to the pygmy chimpanzees, the bonobos. Their rule to life seems to be: Make love not war! "Male bonobos do not form the tight bands that are associated with the male cooperative killing behavior of chimpanzees. Instead, bonobo aggression is mild. Disputes and social tensions among bonobos are often diffused through sexual behavior" (White, Waller, and Boose 2013,

392). Apparently, bonobos and chimpanzees separated about a million or so years ago (give or take a million!) with the growing size of the Congo River keeping chimpanzees to the north and bonobos to the south. A number of suggested-but-not-definitive hypotheses have been proposed for the different tracks they took with respect to violence. One, most obvious, is that the bonobo habitat is richer in low-lying plant foodstuffs ("terrestrial herbaceous vegetation"). One study found that whereas 37 percent of bonobo diet was of such stuffs, only 7 percent of chimpanzee diet was of comparable stuffs. There is less need of competition by the bonobos for access to this source. A second hypothesis is that whereas tree fruits are eaten by both species, they are more abundant and consistently available in the bonobo habitats. Likewise, less need of competition for access to this food source. Third, the food patches are thought to be larger in the bonobo habitats than in the chimpanzee habitats. The bonobo males are not thrown upon each other, striving for mates and so forth, in the way of chimpanzees. As importantly, bonobo females can more easily form bonds, working together, making it less easy for a male just to come in and have his way. Or a bunch of males to come in and have their way. Social grace is more important than group force.

A second note of caution about treating chimpanzee behavior as definitive for humans is that, as we have seen, since the break humans have taken a very different reproductive strategy, getting out of the more restricted jungle onto the plains, with much more room and less inclination or need to fight for food and space. Daniel Lieberman writes: "The biggest benefits of bigger brains was probably for behaviors we cannot detect in the archaeological record." Among these is an ability to cooperate. We are really good at working together, sharing food, raising others' children—yes, said this author in agreement, nodding vigorously after fifty-five years of teaching—and much more. "Cooperative behaviors, however, require complex skills such as the ability to communicate effectively, to control selfish and aggressive impulses, to understand the desires and intentions of others, and to keep track of complex social interactions in group." Apes simply are not up to this. "Apes sometimes cooperate, such as when hunting, but they cannot do so very effectively in many contexts. For example, chimp females share food only with their infants, and males almost never share food" (Lieberman 2013, 110).

Complexity?

This is the case for war as something relatively recent—ten thousand years or so—and triggered by the move to agriculture. For most of our existence, certainly going back before we were fully modern humans, we were hunter-gatherers with little inclination to get into big fights with others. This doesn't mean that human evolution had long ceased. There were always going to be ongoing challenges, for food and shelter so forth. From about 200K years ago, we clearly did develop in such a way that increasingly we were able to do many advanced things, helping us to hunt and gather sufficiently well that we throve. We learned to speak to each other and all that that implies, we learned to make sophisticated tools, we started to process our food like smoking meat for preservation—as a bonus, surely all a part of group harmony and identification, we got into cave painting about ourselves and our hunting successes and we seem sometimes to have developed bonding techniques including something, as we shall see, remarkably like religion. Now it is plausible that simple societies stayed away from conflict; but, as our societies got more complex, isn't it even more plausible to suppose that they might have started to covet the things of other groups—their women, their better territories, their possessions—or fear that others might covet what we have? And so comes planning and warlike conflict.

These are controverted questions. There seems to be general agreement that, reasonably, one must have a somewhat complex society to wage war. "War both invites and requires organisation" (Grayling 2017, 121). That is a necessary condition. We have noted the comment by Frank Marlowe (2010) that small groups simply are not going to be able to wage war in any significant fashion. Is complexity/organisation sufficient? Some argue that it is. Marc Kissel and Nam C. Kim argue for what they call "emergent war." They point out that the "cognitive and behavioral capabilities associated with 'behavioral modernity' [language, toolmaking, and the like] would have afforded our ancestors the ability to produce cultural ideas and attitudes about violence, and to cooperate in ways to use or avoid it" (Kissel and Kim 2019, 143). They stress how important the development of linguistic abilities would be in waging war successfully. Overall: "We contend that: (a) warfare stems from sophisticated abilities of sociality, higher cognition, symbolic thought and communication; and (b) these abilities emerge gradually throughout the Pleistocene, giving ancestral groups the capacity to engage in intergroup aggression and violence."

True. The question is: Did they ever use that capacity? Presumably, they had the capacity to produce operas like Mozart, but one doubts they ever did. Basically, the proof is in the pudding.

Do we find any evidence of war—bodies of people who died in conflict, for instance? There are certainly lots of Pleistocene bodies and many do show signs of a violent end. That does not mean war. If my brother and I go after the chap who pinched his wife and if we kill him, that is not war. If we gang up on an obstreperous group member and kill him, that is not war. If we bump off a resource-draining grandma, that is not war. When you start to put the question in the light of these sorts of things, the evidence of war before around 10K years ago starts to look vanishingly small. The sociologist Robert Bellah writes perceptively:

> Although there is no peaceable past to hark back on—hunter-gatherers often have homicide rates higher than our inner cities—war does seem to be correlated with economic intensification and to emerge in relatively recent prehistoric times. Much depends on what we mean by war: homicide, revenge, even occasional raiding are not rare among hunter-gatherers. But organized warfare oriented to territorial conquest does seem to appear only when resources are locally concentrated and other options are less appealing. (Bellah 2011, 195)

No war before 10K years ago? Famously, there is the case of Jebel Sahaba in the Nile Valley where 61 dead bodies were found, almost half by violence (Kelly 2005; Haas and Piscitelli 2013). However, the evidence-of-war interpretation has been challenged and, in any case, its date of about 11½ thousand years ago brings it just within our bounds. The same is true of a smaller group of remains found in Kenya. Their date is about 10 thousand years ago, and in this case also the war interpretation has been challenged (Lahr et al. 2016a, b; Stojanowski et al. 2016). War could have happened, but there is no solid evidence. Contingent evidence, like cave art, is not that helpful either. Even though some of the most-cited figures might show killing, that they are human is another matter. One of the most famous has a tail! (See Figure 1.6.) In short, while we have increasing understanding of our hunter-gatherer ancestors, their warlike nature is unproven. Until the coming of agriculture, that is—including aquaculture for coastal regions.

FIGURE 1.6 A wall painting of a supposedly killer human. (From the Pech Merle cave in South West France, about 20,000 years ago.)

Reasons

Can we relate the taxonomy of war, given at the beginning of the chapter, with the causal discussion through the middle of the chapter? Do the types of wars that were cataloged mesh with the "agriculture changed it all" hypothesis? Certainly, however advanced the hunter-gather societies truly were, one can hardly expect an exact mirroring, or much of one at all. It is bad enough separating types in the present. Was the Crimean War, fought in the mid-nineteenth century, between Russia and the allied Britain and France, offensive or defensive? More immediately, the tsar was seen as threatening his Roman Catholic subjects in favor of the Orthodox; in the longer term, it was the unwillingness of the allies, Britain in particular, to let Russia move in and grab territory from the declining Ottoman Empire (Turkey). Both sides, with reason, would have allowed that they were on the offensive. Both sides, with reason, would have said they were defending the status quo.

This said, we can say some things about the agriculture hypothesis and modern-day war. Suppose wars usually or always came about spontaneously, because people were getting bored and decided that they would rather kill other people than simply watch television or play soccer. It would not then really seem that what we have been talking about in these last causal sections has much relevance. Why didn't hunter-gatherer societies sometimes decide that they would like to go out and decimate other such societies, for the fun of it. No real reason. Just to avoid ennui or some such thing. Well, if that does happen, it would be nice to have some examples from the present to make it plausible. William the Conqueror setting sail for England does not fit the needed pattern. William was not in it for the "fun of it." He wanted the crown of England, which he got. It turns out that Napoleon made a terrible mistake invading Russia. Mistake or not, he did not make his move for the "fun of it." He wanted to put pressure on his arch-rival, Britain. Of course, in the spirit of Kissel and Kim, you might argue that, in the distant past, people went to war for other reasons. If so, you must tell us what reasons, and why today's evidence is irrelevant. It might be; but, tell us why.

Not all wars have the same underlying reasons. The English Civil War was in major respects about who was going to have power—the king or parliament. But a determining underlying reason was that causing much conflict—the Thirty Years' War— on the continent. Was England to be Protestant or Catholic? Protestantism prevailed, although the final stake was not driven through the heart of Catholic aspirations until toward the end of the century, when James II was deposed. We shall take up some of these issues in more depth in chapter 3, but even here we can see that there is no need to invoke killer-ape hypotheses. Most, if not all, of the tension was about who was going to rule the roost. Unlike the hunter-gatherer times, when one could simply walk away from strangers who did not share one's ideas and values, the English were stuck with each other. Eventually this led to conflict. As always, the truth is in the details. The causes of the English Civil War are not the causes of the American Civil War; but, in these as in related cases, the answers lie not in simplistic assumptions about human nature but in seeing why the human nature that might have served us through most of the history of

H. sapiens might come under strain and break down in the new world. A new world started by agriculture, and now grown to a very different society with altogether new challenges.

Innate Killers?

A sense of unease might still hover. Go back to the killer-ape hypothesis. Have we brushed it aside too quickly? Even if it is not the obvious product of human evolution as we now understand it, have we missed something? The surprising answer is that there is such a missing piece of evidence. The irony is that it points away from the killer-ape scenario. Accounts of actual warfare strongly suggest that the urge and ability to kill our fellow humans is very far from being confirmed. For most of us such an urge is nonexistent! "During World War II U.S. Army Brigadier General S. L. A. Marshall asked these average soldiers [whom he was interviewing] what it was they did in battle" (Grossman 2009, 3). His findings were staggering: "of every hundred men along the line of fire during the period of an encounter, an average of only 15 to 20 'would take any part with their weapons.' This was consistently true 'whether the action was spread over a day, or two days or three.'" Marshall was at pains to stress that the nonfiring soldiers were not wimps or cowards. Often the very opposite. Asking those who had recently been in close combat with either European or Japanese foes: "The results were consistently the same: only 15 to 20 percent of the American riflemen in combat during World War II would fire at the enemy." However: "Those who would not fire did not run or hide (in many cases they were willing to risk great danger to rescue colleagues, get ammunition, or run messages), but they simply would not fire their weapons at the enemy, even when they were faced with repeated waves of banzai charges" (3–4). Measured by terms of psychological stress, medics are in very good shape. So, perhaps somewhat surprisingly, are officers. You might think that they, above others, would be stressed out. Not so. "Indeed, it is a generally accepted tenet of modern warfare that if an officer is shooting at the enemy, he is not doing his job." This isn't because he is a coward. In the First World War, 27% of officers serving on the Western Front were killed, as opposed to 12% of the men. It is rather that he doesn't have the psychological strain of killing another human being. "Over the men, officers in that war had a 50% less chance of being psychologically disabled" (63).

So how do armies kill so many of their opponents? The answer does not lie in special killing squads of crazies—James Bond types. Where the answer does lie is obvious. It is done at a distance. Think this way. If, in the Second World War, you had asked a nice young Brit—a nice young Yank, for that matter—to take up a gun and go into town and kill five hundred people taken at random—men, women, and children (in war, probably more of the latter than the former)—they would look at you as a moral monster. Put him in a Lancaster bomber, as navigator say, and he has no qualms about dropping bombs on the city below him. It is the same elsewhere. Why don't "sailors suffer from the same psychiatric ailments that their brothers on land do? Modern sailors suffer and burn and die just as horribly as their land-bound equivalents. Death and destruction fall all about them. Yet they do not crack. Why?" Same answer as before: "most of them don't have to kill anyone directly, and no one is trying, specifically, personally, to kill them" (58).

That is the point. Hunter-gatherers did not kill neighboring groups—no need, and they might get hurt themselves. In fact, there was a real adaptive advantage not to want to kill others. They, in turn, might want to kill you. But no one gave them the option of hopping into a bomber and going in search of other groups. So, they didn't set up emotions about those sorts of situations. And note, incidentally, that this is all individual selection. I don't want people killing me or my family. You may have noticed, Konrad Lorenz appeals to group selection, a big favorite in the 1950s when he was writing. He assumed that we don't kill the loser for the good of the group. That makes one suspicious right there. Humans don't do things for the good of the group save there are going to be some returns—reciprocation, help for relatives, and so forth. The killer-ape hypothesis is built on rotten theoretical foundations and goes against the empirical evidence.

Hobbes vs. Rousseau

A cynic's question. Are we simply invoking that old chestnut, the "noble savage"? The myth that all was sweetness and light until civilization came to mess it all up? What else would you expect from someone (like me) who had a Quaker childhood, the effects of which (by his own admission) are still powerful? Although he never actually uses the term "noble savage," it is usually laid at the foot of the French Enlightenment figure Jean-Jacques Rousseau, who supposedly saw us all originally in a happy state of nature, somewhat akin to that proposed earlier in this chapter (Lovejoy 1923). In this, he was in opposition to the thinking of the seventeenth-century, English political philosopher Thomas Hobbes, who is generally credited with having a more realistic take on things. Hobbes wrote at the time of the English Civil War, and he saw conflict as our natural state. "Whatsoever therefore is consequent to a time of war, where every man is enemy to every man, the same consequent to the time wherein men live without other security than what their own strength and their own invention shall furnish them withal" (Hobbes 1651). No industry, no culture, no navigation of ships and hence no trading, no significant building, no geography or geology, no arts, letters, society—"and which is worst of all, continual fear, and danger of violent death; and the life of man, solitary, poor, nasty, brutish, and short."

It is certainly true that Rousseau had a different take on things. In the case of "savage man, being destitute of every species of intelligence, . . . his desires never go beyond his physical wants. The only goods he recognises in the universe are food, a female, and sleep: the only evils he fears are pain and hunger" (Rousseau 1755, 14). This all adds up to a pretty peaceful state of affairs.

> With passions so little active, and so good a curb, men, being rather wild than wicked, and more intent to guard themselves against the mischief that might be done them, than to do mischief to others, were by no means subject to very perilous dissensions. They maintained no kind of intercourse with one another, and were consequently strangers to vanity, deference, esteem and contempt; they had not the least idea of meum and tuum, and no true conception of justice;

they looked upon every violence to which they were subjected, rather as an injury that might easily be repaired than
as a crime that ought to be punished; and they never thought
of taking revenge, unless perhaps mechanically and on the
spot, as a dog will sometimes bite the stone which is thrown
at him. (20)

Hobbes and Rousseau. In a way, they are the yin and yang of
things. Both are right, and it is taken together that the true picture starts to emerge. No one is denying that war can lead to a
Hobbesian state of things. Certainly not we, who have taken the
English Civil War as one of our examples. Certainly not Rousseau,
whose complete picture is that the original state of humankind
gives rise to progress and the development of intelligence and culture and technology, including agriculture. Which opens up the
possibility—the certainty—of war. Property, civilization, new
passions, gave rise to "perpetual conflicts, which never ended but
in battles and bloodshed. The new–born state of society thus gave
rise to a horrible state of war; men thus harassed and depraved
were no longer capable of retracing their steps or renouncing the
fatal acquisitions they had made, but, labouring by the abuse of
the faculties which do them honour, merely to their own confusion, brought themselves to the brink of ruin" (29).

It really doesn't seem to be a question of going with Rousseau
because he makes you feel good, or because he justifies the Sermon
on the Mount. He offers an empirical hypothesis—nonviolence
and then, given property (in which agriculture had a significant
causal role), conflict. This does, in major respects, anticipate the
position taken in this chapter, the null hypothesis, as it were, and

war therefore is an intruder brought on by circumstances. In his way, Rousseau is as ultra-Darwinian as you can get. There is no question of rejecting Hobbes. It is just a question of what fits where. A conclusion, incidentally, that is in harmony with modern anthropological thinking on these topics. Alan Page Fiske and Tage Shakti Rai, in *Virtuous Violence* (2014), argue convincingly that, far from our social nature precluding us from having violent emotions that can spring into action, violence can be an important factor in maintaining sociality! It promotes ingroup togetherness. The most obvious example is parents chastising their children. This is the antithesis of killer-ape behavior. It is done to ensure that the children will be good ingroup participants. Likewise, conflict between adults. Males compete sometimes violently (as do the higher primates) for status. Killing each other would defeat the purpose. It is rather that a group with clearly delimited roles and status is going to function better than one without anything like this. And there are many other examples, for instance painful initiation rites. If you interpret him as saying, not so much that there is no violence—"a dog will bite the stone"—but that there is no systematic violence, of a warlike nature, Rousseau is right. But, so also is Hobbes, for if the circumstances change dramatically—agriculture—adaptations for one purpose, group harmony, might get diverted (perverted?) to other ends.

Original Sin Redivivus?

Having spoken to the critics, it is time to conclude the discussion by becoming critics. If the killer-ape hypothesis—we were innate killers from the first—is being rejected, why has it had such a hold on people's imaginations? The philosopher A. C. Grayling (2017), in an overall analysis like to mine—"war is an artefact of the political, economic and cultural arrangements that evolved when settled societies emerged into history about ten thousand years ago" (160)—puts his finger on the problem and its cause: religion (127). Dart (1953) gives the game away. He starts his piece with a theological reflection. "Of all beasts the man-beast is the worst, To others and himself the cruellest foe." Quoting *Christian Ethics* by Richard Baxter (1615–1691). Compare: Zechariah 8:10 "For before those days there was no wage for man or any wage for beast, neither was there any safety from the foe for him who went out or came in, for I set every man against his neighbor." Remember also: "this common bloodlust differentiator, this predaceous habit, this mark of Cain that separates man dietetically from his anthropoidal relatives." The fact is we are getting the wisdom of the Bible rather than the wisdom of the rocks. It is but a step to the Augustinian thesis of original sin. We are all tainted because first Eve, and then Adam, disobeyed God and ate that wretched apple. Even the most secular of us, living as we do in a Christian society, are prone to this kind of thinking. No need to go on to accept the second part of the Augustinian story: "Substitutionary Atonement." Jesus died in agony on the cross for our salvation.

As the paleoanthropologist Raymond Tuttle points out, Dart and Ardrey and others were writing at a time receptive to this kind of thinking. Second World War and later. "In the 1960s and 1970s, as the Vietnam conflagration raged and the Cuban missile crisis menaced the Northern Hemisphere with nuclear Armageddon, Robert Ardrey (1908–1980) and Konrad Lorenz (1903–1989) and other dramatists and writers of popular books, envisioned Dart's killer ape in every man, not just the ancient cave-dwellers" (Tuttle 2014, 5). Historian Erika Milam in her penetrating *Creatures of Cain* (2019) makes a similar case. This does not make the claim true. Nor does it mean that someone who rejects the killer-ape hypothesis is antireligion in general and anti-Christian in particular. Many Christians—the Eastern Orthodox Church for a start, together with Western Christians like Quakers—reject Augustinian original sin theory, opting instead for the older position of Irenaeus of Lyon, whose "Incarnational" theory sees the death of Jesus on the Cross, not as a sacrifice, but as an example of perfect love. We are made in the image of God, so why on earth would we be killer apes? Theology gives no support, nor does the empirical world. Witheringly, Tuttle points out that we are just not fitted out to be killers. "Indeed, given the lack of fearsome teeth and other morphological or technological means to kill one another, the arguable probability is that they lived consistently in groups with sizable cohorts of adult males under an omnipresent possibility that they might be confronted by carnivoran predators, which were more formidable in number and variety than modern ones" (593).

In short, the thesis of this chapter is confirmed. "Because there were fewer hominids in the Pliocene and Pleistocene, group migration away from agonistic groups would seem to have been an available option. Moreover, developing mutually beneficial relationships with them probably would be a better option for one or both parties, instead of having to plan and execute attacks in lieu of foraging and sustaining bonds within one's own group" (594). No more need be said.

2 | THE BIOLOGY OF PREJUDICE

Turn to prejudice. Like war it involves hatred of others, now of the individual as a member of a group. Gordon Allport, in his classic study of the issue—*The Nature of Prejudice*—defined it as "an avertive or hostile attitude toward a person who belongs to a group, simply because he belongs to that group, and is therefore presumed to have the objectionable qualities ascribed to that group" (Allport 1954, 8). Allport's emphasis is on hostility and dislike of the "outgroup." We are "ingroup"; they are outgroup. One hardly needs to look around to realize that Allport was on to something. Stressing that, in examining both war and prejudice, we are very much dealing with different sides of the same causal coin—as was hinted by the quotation from Hume in the Introduction—I shall begin with the conclusions of the last chapter. I shall then move to see what light the science throws on various forms of prejudice. I see continuity—identity—between the proper thinking on war and on prejudice; likewise, although I shall subdivide prejudice into categories, I see all the discussion as linked through the same theoretical background. Categories

Why We Hate. Michael Ruse, Oxford University Press. © Oxford University Press 2022.
DOI: 10.1093/oso/9780197621288.003.0003

overlap and connect causally. As with race and class: "many of the poor white Americans who would benefit from more generous welfare provisions oppose welfare, as they see it primarily benefitting African-Americans and not their own group" (Sobolewska and Ford 2020, 333). So common is this connection, it has its own name: "racialisation." "In the state of Tennessee, for example, [the physician Jonathan M. Metzl] found that restrictive health policies may have cost the lives of as many as 4,599 African-Americans between 2011 and 2015, but it also cost the lives of as many as 12,013 white Tennesseans, more than double the loss sustained by black residents" (Wilkerson 2020, 189). Note, as this example shows, increasingly in this chapter and those following, although the conceptual starting point is with prehistory, the focus moves toward humans and their attitudes today.

Ingroup–Outgroup

A basic outline suggests itself at once. The history of humankind, until the arrival of agriculture, was one of the hunter-gatherer—small groups on a large continent, going about their business. At times, one would come up against other bands, and, although you didn't want to go to war with them—people might get hurt—it made good sense to be wary of them. You didn't want them pushing you out of favored territory or learning your secrets. You didn't want people pinching your women, or (as happens) your women eager to be pinched. You didn't want your best young hunters thinking perhaps the grass is greener on the other side. Conversely, usually, there was little incentive to join forces and work together.

Sensible population size is a must for hunter-gatherers. If nothing else, you want the catch to go around the whole group. Wariness, prejudice, against others—the outgroup—was an obvious adaptation. Note that this is all very much pre-agriculture. With growth and the coming of a more ordered and stable society, these attitudes obviously transplanted perhaps a little too easily. Leave to one side the genes/culture issue, although one should be careful of making too much of the genes at this point. Social psychologist Jonathan Haidt stresses that being innate does not mean fixed once and for all. He quotes the neuroscientist Gary Marcus: "Nature provides a first draft which experience then revises," continuing " 'Built-in' does not mean unmalleable; it means *'organized in advance of experience'* " (Haidt 2012, 153, quoting Marcus 2004, 34, 40).

Thus far, we are missing a major element in the story. Increasingly psychologists and others are suggesting that ingroup relationships are primary and more fundamental: "because people care about cooperative alliances, they intuitively interpret the groups that they are assigned to as requiring their cooperation, trust, and support, which leads to behaving in ways that benefit the ingroup and are consistent with ingroup norms" (Roberts and Rizzo 2020, 9). Outgroup prejudices follow, but not necessarily every time. What is going on?

Since ingroup/outgroup distinctions do not always involve intense (or even mild) competition or conflict over scarce resources, there is need for a theory of the evolution of social groups that does not depend on intergroup conflict per se. Such a theory starts from the recognition that group living represents the fundamental survival strategy that characterizes the human species. In the course of our evolutionary history, humans abandoned most of the physical characteristics and instincts that make possible survival and reproduction as isolated individuals or pairs of individuals, in favor of other advantages that require cooperative interdependence with others in order to survive in a broad range of physical environments. In other words, as a species we have evolved to rely on cooperation rather than strength, and on social learning rather than instinct as basic adaptations. The result is that, as a species, human beings are characterized by obligatory interdependence. (Brewer 1999, 433)

This is music to our ears. "No tribe could hold together if murder, robbery, treachery, &c., were common; consequently such crimes within the limits of the same tribe 'are branded with everlasting infamy'" (Darwin 1871, 1, 93). The very evolutionary position we have been promoting. "Ingroup membership is a form of contingent altruism. By limiting aid to mutually acknowledged ingroup members, total costs and risks of nonreciprocation can be contained. Thus, ingroups can be defined as bounded communities of mutual trust and obligation that delimit mutual interdependence and cooperation" (Brewer 1999, 433).

This all makes such good sense. You are in a hunter-gatherer group. Remember, most of the time you are not interacting with other groups. You are getting on with your own business. And above all, that means relying on each other. As Darwin asserted, the chances are that you are all related, or you think you are. But related or not, you need to work together. Kin selection or reciprocal altruism—both are almost certainly at work. A lot of the time, you will have to work together to catch your prey. Or you will need to pass information to find and gather the best crops. You cannot afford to get a reputation for being shifty or not playing your role. As the philosopher John Rawls (1971) tells us, fairness is what it is all about. Think of children. It is not so much that they want it all, but that others do not get it all. They want their fair share. Ingroup adaptations. Note how nothing yet speaks to outgroup discrimination.

> The evolutionary argument for bounded social cooperation carries no implicit link between ingroup formation and intergroup hostility or conflict. In fact, in a context of limited resources, group differentiation and territory boundaries can serve as a mechanism to prevent conflict among individuals rather than promoting it. Discrimination between ingroup and outgroups is a matter of relative favoritism toward the ingroup and the absence of equivalent favoritism toward outgroups. Within this framework, outgroups can be viewed with indifference, sympathy, even admiration, as long as intergroup distinctiveness is maintained. (Brewer 1999, 434)

Douglas Fry gives a nice example supporting this point. He writes of groups, tribes, living under the tough conditions of Western Australia, where droughts are an ongoing threat. "In Australia's Western Desert, it would seem that a harsh environment with unpredictable rainfall creates mutual dependence among different groups." He continues: "This interdependence, in turn, facilitates peaceful intergroup relations that encourage the desert-dwellers to cooperate, offer assistance to each other in times of need, reciprocally share resources, and behave kindly toward others within and beyond the immediate group" (Fry 2014, 87).

This said, as argued above, it is easy to see how outgroup aggression—not necessarily violence—might be generated. Obviously, to those factors already mentioned, discrimination might come about as a byproduct of ingroup favoritism. "Ultimately, many forms of discrimination and bias may develop not because outgroups are hated, but because positive emotions such as admiration, sympathy, and trust are reserved for the ingroup and withheld from outgroups." As we move toward modern societies, as we get to that bottom corner picture of Figure 1.3, we can see that this process might be of increasing importance. "A direct relationship between intense ingroup favoritism and outgroup antagonism might also be expected in highly segmented societies that are differentiated along a single primary categorization, such as ethnicity or religion" (Brewer 1999, 439). But let us not anticipate. Rather, turn to specific types of prejudice.

Foreigners

The English do not much like foreigners. Read Charles Dickens and his great novel *Little Dorrit*, published in serial form between 1855 and 1857. He is writing of people in a working-class part of London, and of how it "was uphill work for a foreigner" to make any inroads to their confidence or genuine friendship.

In the first place, they were vaguely persuaded that every foreigner had a knife about him; in the second, they held it to be a sound constitutional national axiom that he ought to go home to his own country. They never thought of inquiring how many of their own countrymen would be returned upon their hands from divers parts of the world, if the principle were generally recognised; they considered it particularly and peculiarly British. In the third place, they had a notion that it was a sort of Divine visitation upon a foreigner that he was not an Englishman, and that all kinds of calamities happened to his country because it did things that England did not, and did not do things that England did. (Dickens 1857, 302)

This is but a start. "They believed that foreigners were always badly off" (302–303). "They "believed that foreigners were dragooned and bayoneted" (303). "They believed that foreigners were always immoral" (303). Combined with this was pitying condescension about people whose native language was other than their own. As English citizens born and bred, they were convinced that if you speak to foreigners in a loud voice, using baby language, all will be made clear. It is a question of having the right knack. "Mrs Plornish was particularly ingenious in this art; and attained so much celebrity for saying 'Me ope you leg well soon,' that it was considered in the Yard but a very short remove indeed from speaking Italian. Even Mrs. Plornish herself began to think that she had a natural call towards that language" (303). She was part of a long tradition. One hundred and fifty years after Dickens's parody, my late father, who knew not one word of a foreign language, was fully convinced that he was polylingual as he made his way across Europe after the fashion of Mrs. Plornish.

Avoiding, at least for now, the temptation to move to the present and from fiction to fact, let us delay our discussion of Brexit.

Turn to those foreigners who need the talents of Mrs. Plornish, immigrants who have come to our country, and take up the reactions of the English conservative politician Enoch Powell (Heffer 1998). Particularly active in the 1960s, he led the forces of opposition. After the Second World War, taking advantage of the open borders within the British Commonwealth, there had been an influx of immigrants to the Mother Country. Between 1948 and 1970, about half a million people came from the West Indies. In 1951 there were around 30,000 Indians living in Britain. In 1971, there were just under 400,000. (In 2011 there were a million and a half people of Indian ethnicity in Britain, about 2½% of the total population.) In 1951 there were about 10,000 Pakistanis. In 1971 there were about 120,000 and the numbers kept growing rapidly. (In 2011 there were rather more than a million people of Pakistani ethnicity, about 2% of the population.) By comparison, the total British population in Britain in 1950 was about 50 million, with 3% born elsewhere, and overwhelmingly white.

Enoch Powell spoke for many (white) people when on April 20, 1968, in Birmingham, he gave his notorious "rivers of blood" speech. "We must be mad, literally mad, as a nation to be permitting the annual inflow of some 50,000 dependents, who are for the most part the material of the future growth of the immigrant descended population. It is like watching a nation busily engaged in heaping up its own funeral pyre" (Powell 1969, 282). He called for action: "In these circumstances nothing will suffice but that the total inflow for settlement should be reduced at once to negligible proportions, and that the necessary legislative and administrative measures be taken without delay." Powell was a classical scholar, and in ending he made use of his knowledge of Latin literature. The references to the state of the United States will not be overlooked.

> As I look ahead, I am filled with foreboding. Like the Roman, I seem to see "the River Tiber foaming with much blood." That tragic and intractable phenomenon which we watch with horror on the other side of the Atlantic but which there is interwoven with the history and existence of the States itself, is coming upon us here by our own volition and our own neglect. Indeed, it has all but come. In numerical terms, it will be of American proportions long before the end of the century. (289–90)

Expectedly, ecumenical in his distaste for foreigners—at home or abroad—Powell was no lover of the European Community. He feared that by joining, Britain would "become one province in a new European superstate under institutions which know nothing of the political rights and liberties that we have so long taken for granted" (Strafford 2009, 10).

In the light of what we have learned so far, isn't this all a little bit surprising? The emphasis in the last chapter was on hunter-gatherers minding their own business and staying out of the way of strangers. You might be wary of them, but outright hostility seems unneeded. A couple of points. First, as in the case of war, we are looking for understanding from the pre-agricultural past. We are not searching for a gene, uniquely possessed by the British, which inclines them to think: "Wogs begin at Calais." We are looking for conditions that make it plausible that our ancestors might have a genetic substratum that can let slip strong emotions against others, which might then be activated by cultural changes and circumstances. If England were located in the present position of New Zealand, one doubts that this (intentionally offensive) phrase would have gained traction. (A "wog" is a "wily oriental gentleman." The phrase is attributed to George Wigg, a Labour politician, who used it in a parliamentary debate in 1949.)

A second point is whether, for all the space in pre-agricultural days, is there reason to think our hunter-gatherer ancestors might have found themselves sufficiently systematically having to compete for more restricted necessities of life that biology might have intensified the hostility to others? As the new technique of ferreting out ancient DNA reveals, there is such reason. Humans did not just hang around a patch of desert in Africa. They have been on the move. We know that for a very long time our ancestors had been leaving Africa for Europe and Asia—up to two million years ago. Such invasions continued, hardly that surprising since these already intelligent primates would always have been on the lookout for new opportunities and sources of food and shelter and the like. Move down to the most recent significant move out of Africa, some 50K years ago or a bit earlier. One group went east toward what we now call "Asia," and another west to what we now call "Europe." (See Figure 2.1.) Over time, always on the move, looking for better opportunities, which of course could involve getting away from others in their present surroundings. (In moving to Canada when I was twenty-two, I was part of a long tradition.) But then came an Ice Age, making much of northern Europe uninhabitable. People were squashed down to places like Spain, beyond the grip of the glacial ice. It hardly takes much imagination to see that, while you may not want to go to war with your

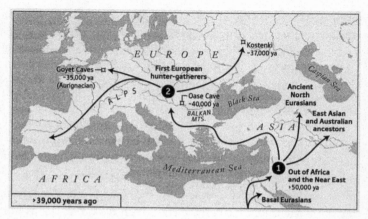

FIGURE 2.1 The history of European hunter-gatherers. (From Reich 2018, with permission)

competitors, there would be increasing pressure to keep your distance and not let others grab or move in on what you now had—and conversely. An edge against outsiders would be of selective value—clearly something that could persist as the ice receded and people could start to move north.

As noted, this does not imply hardline genetic forces dictating specific forms or kinds of hostility and wariness, but as it happens the DNA can bring us down to the present. Around five thousand years ago, there was a major invasion from the east into Europe, displacing the then-inhabitants. More efficient methods of agriculture were clearly a significant factor. This eventually pushed across to the extremes of the continent, specifically the British Isles. Named after their style of pottery, the "Bell Beaker culture" arrived rather more than four thousand years ago, and the genetic evidence is that the newcomers really pushed aside the established denizens of the isles. (See Figure 2.2.) With ongoing consequences in our heredity: "The genetic impact of the spread of peoples from the continent into the British Isles in this period was permanent. British and Irish skeletons from the Bronze Age that followed the Beaker period had at most about 10 percent ancestry from the first farmers of these islands, with the other 90 percent from people like those closely associated with the Bell Beaker culture in the Netherlands" (Reich 2018, 115). Since the initial

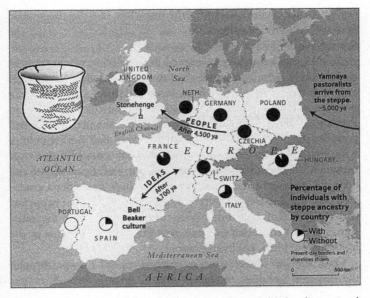

FIGURE 2.2 The spread of Beaker pottery to the British Isles. (From Reich 2018, with permission)

building of Stonehenge predates this invasion, it means that those who started it and those who today celebrate the Summer Solstice around it have very different ancestries. It takes little imagination to see why the different groups involved in this ongoing changing would have little love for each other. In come all of these strangers intent on pushing us to one side. They are not our friends.

Class

Talk on these topics segues naturally into talk about class. Most obviously, we have the prejudice of the upper classes, meaning particularly the educated, upper classes, toward the uneducated, lower classes. Victorian fiction again. *Tom Brown's Schooldays* is an incredibly popular novel, about a lad who goes to Rugby School—an English public school—in the 1830s, when Dr. Thomas Arnold (father of the poet Matthew Arnold) was headmaster. The follow-up novel, *Tom Brown at Oxford*, tells of the hero's time at university (Hughes 1861). At some point, as these things happen, Tom meets and falls in love with a barmaid. This, it is made clear to Tom (by an older fellow-undergraduate), is unacceptable. Tom and the barmaid are of different social classes and never the twain shall meet. Tom follows the advice and breaks the relationship.

"How do you feel yourself? What's your own instinct about it?"

"Of course, I must break it all off at once, completely," said Tom, mournfully, and half hoping that Hardy might not agree with him.

"Of course," answered Hardy, "but how?"

"In the way that will pain her least. I would sooner lose my hand or bite my tongue off than that she should feel lowered, or lose any self-respect, you know," said Tom, looking helplessly at his friend.

"Yes, that's all right—you must take all you can on your own shoulders. It must leave a sting though for both of you, manage how you will."

"But I can't bear to let her think I don't care for her—I needn't do that—I can't do that."

"I don't know what to advise. However, I believe I was wrong in thinking she cared for you so much. She will be hurt, of course—she can't help being hurt—but it won't be so bad as I used to think."

Note the hint that, although Tom is belittling himself, she is not entirely blameless because she is after a trophy from a class above herself. One is happy to say that the story ends well, when Tom marries a girl of his own social class. It is made clear that, although the couple are very young, it is better this way so that Tom is removed from further temptation.

These attitudes about class and its importance are ingroup attitudes. Aren't they antithetical to the harmony of the group? How can things work if one segment of the group looks down on other segments, and other segments get used by this first segment? Dig into causes. Why might class differences occur? The archaeologist Brian Hayden has done extensive research on and around the question, focusing especially—perhaps expectedly for one located at Simon Fraser University in Vancouver—on fishing communities in the American Northwest. The key issue is something we touched on earlier, "social complexity," which Hayden (2014) characterizes as "the development of hierarchical (and/or heterarchical) social, economic, and political structures that manifest themselves materially in a number of ways stemming from control over labour and produce beyond the immediate family" (644). Continuing that this will kick in, first "under conditions where it is possible to produce relatively reliable surpluses," and second, when "various individuals (aggrandizers) begin to develop strategies to use surplus foods to enhance their social, economic, and political self-interests. These ultimately result not only in significant reproductive and survival advantages for aggrandizers, but also in the concentration of power (or undue influence) and materials in their hands, which archaeologists think of as social complexity and social inequality" (644–45).

A number of points. First, note that this is an argument that (in principle) makes perfect sense from an individual-selection perspective but less so from a group-selection perspective. It must be backed by empirical evidence, but it is the sort of thing one might expect. Second, the emphasis is on "relatively reliable surpluses." This means one looks for such complexity in situations where this might obtain. "I would like to emphasize . . . that there is a strong relationship between certain Upper Paleolithic [50K to 12K years ago] geographical areas that were at least seasonally rich in resources, and the development of more complex societies" (Hayden 2020, 2–3). Continuing:

Ethnographic foragers such as the Western Desert Australian Aborigines typically inhabited resource-poor areas or have limited technologies for extracting resources. As a result, population levels were very low (< 0.2 people per square km), mobility was high, group sizes were relatively small (<20), sharing of food and most personal items was mandatory, competition involving food was prohibited, private property was very limited, and the interest of the entire group was far more important than individual interests (Testart 1982; Hayden 2019). They were the closest approximation to socio-economically egalitarian societies that are known. (3)

Conversely, the point made about Hayden working out of Vancouver starts to become relevant, because many Northwestern hunter-gatherers got much of their catch from the sea, a reliable source of prey, namely fish of various kinds, including salmon and shellfish. Such hunter-gatherers, living as they did "in regions with abundant resources such as the American Northwest Coast, had high population levels (>0.2 people per square km), were at least seasonally sedentary and sometimes fully sedentary, had family and personal private property including ownership of resource locations, exhibited reduced food sharing, used surplus food in a competitive fashion (e.g., in feasts, marriage payments, alliance formations), and often prioritized individual self-interests over group interests using a variety of strategies, including feasts, marriages, conflicts, prestige items, and other means" (3–4).

Third, if you are going to build up surpluses, you almost certainly need some way to preserve and store your surplus food. This points to ever-more-sophisticated tools and practices. A rotting salmon caught a week ago is not much of a surplus. The need of these kinds of tools and practices suggests later rather than sooner, and it does seem that social complexity starts to kick in around 50K years ago, not back another 100K years or more, when hunter-gathering was already the norm. Fourth, one would like some archaeological evidence to back all this supposing. Most revealing are the ornamental artifacts that start to appear, suggesting sophisticated abilities to manufacture such artifacts as well as the freeing up of artisans for considerable time as they are fashioned. Burial sites are rich sources of information. The average hunter-gatherer left few, if any, remains. There were exceptions. "The hundreds or thousands of ivory beads, shell beads, pendants, disks, fox canines, stag canines, sculptures, and other objects buried with these individuals attest to inordinate inequalities in wealth, status, and political power that tend to typify the more complex transegalitarian societies ethnographically" (14).

This final point shows how, conversely, it is difficult if not impossible to assess the attitudes of the non-haves, the proto-lower classes. They are precisely the sorts of people who will not leave "hundreds or thousands of ivory beads." Digging out this sort of information requires that we turn back to the present, assuming that the pattern today was not unknown in the past. Are they satisfied with their lot or are they discontent? Not an easy question to answer. In America today, there are huge class tensions, with serious societal issues about the resentment of the less-fortunate toward the fortunate, especially when it comes to education. All too typical was the reaction in Arkansas to the thought of paying a librarian above poverty wages. '"Call me narrow-minded but I've never understood why a librarian needs a four-year degree,' someone wrote. 'We were taught Dewey decimal system in grade school. Never sounded like anything too tough'" (Potts 2019).

Nothing too ingroup-harmony promoting going on here. The last thing one expects selection to promote.

For the moment, let us shelve this worry, intending to return to it and to speak to it in detail. Here, I want to stress—if the most class-ridden society ever known is any guide—it is not necessarily the case that the lower-classes will resent their status. Judging by the British, they can be happy with it. Boastful, even. In George Bernard Shaw's play, *Pygmalion*, Eliza's father, the dustman Alfred Doolittle, is a parody, but funny precisely because what he is saying has an odor of authenticity. I am what I am and I am proud to be what I am. "What am I, Governors both? I ask you, what am I? I'm one of the undeserving poor: that's what I am." So, big deal, I still must pay my way. And it certainly isn't going to be by resenting the rich or striving to be one of them. I just want my cut. "I ain't pretending to be deserving. I'm undeserving; and I mean to go on being undeserving. I like it; and that's the truth." Fast forwarding, growing up in the 1950s in England, when good jobs were abundant, a significant portion of the working class voted conservative. Let the nobs rule. This goes back to Benjamin Disraeli and the Reform Act of 1867, when many more (male) people were allowed to vote. Disraeli quipped: "now we must educate our masters," and it has always been part of Tory policy to appeal to the conservative nature of the working class—something that exists in abundance. The working class was hugely enthusiastic about Enoch Powell's "rivers of blood" speech. A thousand dock workers marched on Westminster (the home of the British parliament) in his support: "Enoch here, Enoch there, we want Enoch everywhere" (Heffer 1998, 462).

Note the underlying worry here—jobs! Immigrants might undercut our established way of life. That is precisely why the conservatives appeal (as they still do today) to so many of the lower classes. Whether or not it is true—and, to be honest, it is not always entirely true—the conservatives promise stability. That is what being a conservative is all about. Minimal change. Comforting. Little surprise that, with respect to group harmony, the class system can help rather than hinder. It can promote ingroup solidarity. One has only to think of the First World War and the bonds between those commanding and those commanded. However inexperienced and junior the officers might have been—subalterns, mostly—they represented the class above and hence got respect and obedience. It worked the other way too. With privilege comes obligation. The upper classes did not despise the lower classes. They appreciated them for their intrinsic worth. Remember, these officers put their lives and souls where their convictions lay. Over twice as many commissioned, as opposed to noncommissioned, soldiers died in battle. Appropriately, in the huge war cemeteries of Flanders, all have the same headstone and are buried without regard to rank—officers next to privates (Figure 2.3). When it comes to the important things, in death as in life, ingroup solidarity is what counts. Reaffirming this, the same courtesy was not extended to non-European troops from the Empire: "The average native of the Gold Coast would not understand or appreciate a headstone" (Syal 2021).

Race

In 1955, Emmett Till was a fourteen-year-old black boy from Chicago spending the summer with relatives in Mississippi. One

FIGURE 2.3 World War I graves. Note the captain buried next to the private.

Sunday morning he went to a local grocery store, where supposedly he made sexual advances on a young white woman (aged twenty-one)—whether they were physical or just verbal was, at the time, a matter of dispute. (Years later the woman admitted the physical claims were fabricated.) Several days after, the woman's husband and a half-brother abducted Till, beat him, mutilated him, shot him, and dumped his body into the Tallahatchie River. Three days later, the body was recovered and returned to Chicago, where the boy's mother insisted on an open-coffin funeral that the world might see what was done to her son. The miscreants were arrested and went to trial. After a sixty-seven-minute deliberation, they were acquitted by an all-white, male jury—women and blacks had been barred. "If we hadn't stopped to drink pop, it wouldn't have taken that long" (Robbins 2020). A year later, the open-coffin funeral, as intended attracting worldwide attention, paid dividends. Protected by the rule against double jeopardy, the exonerated men made several thousand dollars, cashing in on their experiences, and admitting in an interview for a magazine (*Look*) that they had indeed done it. Justice was done in the State of Mississippi.

What of the general relationship between whites and blacks? How well does our theoretical analysis apply? In the United States, and no doubt elsewhere, the fear that even one drop of black blood would contaminate the group shows that identification with the white group was hugely important. However friendly one may be with black people, and there are countless tales of people being devoted to the black servants who raised them, white is white and black is black. With the need to affirm one's whiteness went the almost inevitable fear of the other, of the black, even though politically and socially blacks were in a subservient position. In our ingroup/outgroup language, insecurity about one's standing as an ingroup member could lead to ever-more ferocious attitudes to outgroup individuals. *Absalom, Absalom!*, by the Nobel Prize–winning, Southern author William Faulkner, tells the story of a poor man from West Virginia who moves south to make his fortune, having first been to Haiti, where he has a son with a woman who is one-eighth black. Rejecting his son—"tainted and corrupt"—because of those few drops of black blood, he moves back to the United States, where he gets a gang of negro slaves to work for him. Despite the fact that he lives with them, has sex with the females, raising the children in his own house, the contempt and fear oozes out. He speaks of his gang as a "band of wild niggers like beasts half tamed to walk upright like men"—"half tamed," but ever ready to strike out against their master. He marries a white woman and has two children, a boy and a girl. The son from Haiti turns up and wants to marry the girl, his half-sister. The son has no objection until he learns of his half-brother's black blood. The former then shoots the latter (it's that kind of novel!), at which the father remarks (truly): "So it's the miscegenation, not the incest, which you can't bear" (Faulkner 1936, 285).

There is more along the same lines. It turns out that the son from Haiti had already married a black wife, described as a "coal black and ape-like Woman" (166). This son takes pride in the "ape-like body of his charcoal companion" (167), who is a "black gargoyle" (170) resembling "something in a zoo" (169). Contempt and yet that undercurrent of fear. What gives the novel added significance is that at the center of the story is the Civil War, and it is made clear that attitudes are totally unchanged after the War from before the War. A half-black family member puts her restraining hand on the arm of a woman whose father killed himself rather than fight for the South. Appalled by the fact that the negro woman had the temerity to address her by her first name, the contaminating hand was beyond horror: "that black arresting and untimorous hand on my white woman's flesh" (111). Ingroup affirmation; outgroup rejection, hostility, fear. So often predicated on just the kinds of factors we see in the case of class. The desperate need to belong.

What of the biology? Famously, our species *Homo sapiens* had variants, subspecies. There are humans living today (*H. s. sapiens*); there are the already-mentioned (in the Introduction) Neanderthals (*H. s. neandertalis*), known from the middle of the nineteenth century; and then, a much more recent find, the Denisovans (*H. s. denisova*). The divide came about half a million years ago, the two rival subspecies lasting right down to about 50K years ago, give or take. Focusing on the better-known Neanderthals, the automatic assumption in Victorian times was that they really were primitive. One writer, shortly after the *Origin*, compared Neanderthals to the now almost-extinct Andamaner islanders. The latter have no conception of God or of morality or anything else much. "Psychical endowments of a lower grade than those characterizing the Andamaner cannot be conceived to exist." Given that the Neanderthal skull "more closely conforms to that of the Chimpanzee," it follows that "there seems no reason to believe otherwise than that similar darkness characterized the being to which the fossil belonged" (Zilhão 2014, 192, quoting King 1864).

General opinion today seems hardly less favorable. "A full-grown Neandertal must have been a peculiar sight. Envision a relatively short, thickset body with a barrel-chest, wide trunk, and short, muscular limbs, topped with a large, elongated head." This is complemented by "a forward-thrust, beetle-browed, and chinless face adorned with an enormous protruding nose." To us today, "the overwhelming visual impression would be one of a creature squat, stocky, and strange. Even shorn, shaved, bathed, and suitably attired, I think a Neandertal would still turn heads on a New York City subway" (Churchill 1998, see Figure 2.4). Yet, to stop there would be deeply misleading, starting with the fact that Neanderthal brains, at around 1500cc on average, are two or three hundred cc bigger than our brains! There have been many supposed or hypothesized differences between humans and

Neanderthals. The Neanderthals were scavengers unlike us, or conversely they just went in for top-of-the-food-chain big mammal hunting. They didn't have the same division of labor—men hunting, women foraging—as us. They didn't go in for ornaments like us. Nope. None of them work. There is overlap down the line. For instance, someone was eating oysters rather than buffalo or whatever large animal was on hand. Someone was giving hunting a miss as they made very sophisticated and functional clothing to keep themselves warm in bitter winters. Someone was into the carving and painting of subtle artifacts for decoration and the like. "In short, there is no such thing as 'Neandertal behavior'" (Zilhão 2014, 196). See Figure 2.4.

Why then did they go extinct, 40K or so years ago? Various suggestions have been made, such as our outbreeding them. A recent idea has them suffering from chronic earache.

Results showed Neanderthal adults exhibiting primitively tall and narrow nasopharynges with infant-like horizontal CET [cartilaginous Eustachian tube, a vital component of the upper respiratory tract and nexus for the middle ear and postnasal airway] and choanal orientation. As horizontal CET orientation is associated with increased OM [middle ear disease, otitis media] incidence in infants and children until around age six, its appearance in Neanderthal adults strongly indicates persistence of high OM susceptibility at this time. This could have compromised fitness and disease load relative to sympatric modern humans, affecting Neanderthals' ability to compete within their ecological niche, and potentially contributing to their rapid extinction. (Pagano, Mirquez, and Laitman 2019, 2109)

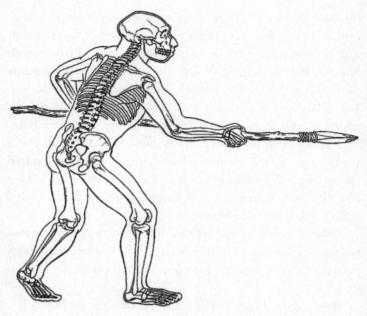

FIGURE 2.4 Neanderthal.

Apparently, this is all connected with "hearing loss, meningitis, and pneumonia." As one who, as a child, suffered dreadfully from ongoing earache, I can sympathize. I pride myself on having the appropriate brain size.

The point is that while, given their looks, one can understand why our ancestors might sheer away from Neanderthals, pushing ingroup/outgroup distinctions, there is no reason to think that, with respect to things we value like intelligence, they were adaptively that inferior to us, or that we wiped them out physically.

And the same applies when we stay in our own subspecies and consider the clear genetic differences. Different skin colors, a function of the distribution of pigment melanin, make perfectly good Darwinian sense. A darker skin protects from UV radiation, a bigger problem in Africa. White skin does a better job of Vitamin D synthesis, in the absence of strong sunlight. Just the ticket for northern Europe. Whatever later cultural overlays there may be, and we have just seen in fact and fiction that these certainly did exist, we are not talking here about brute intelligence or anything like that.

What about interracial breeding? As we all know, that certainly existed. Thomas Jefferson, author of the Declaration of Independence, is a prime example of the complexity—hypocrisy, one is inclined to say. The man who declared that "all men are equal" was a slave owner, and, after his wife's death, took as a concubine one of his female slaves, a half-sister of his wife—the women shared a (white) father—and he and Sally Hemmings had no less than six children, all his slaves, despite their being seven-eighths European. Sufficient that, in adulthood, several passed as white. The only family that Jefferson ever freed. Going back in time, we now know the hitherto-much-denied fact (Karl Popper once assured me that it was completely impossible) that there was interbreeding with Neanderthals and with Denisovans. The attached figures show distributions and percentages. Expectedly the carriers of the outgroup genes today are the ancestors of those that left Africa and not generally found south of the Sahara. (See Figures 2.5 and 2.6.)

It all fits. Ingroup/outgroup has huge effects. Yet, we do not necessarily expect and, predictably, do not find that it is always an

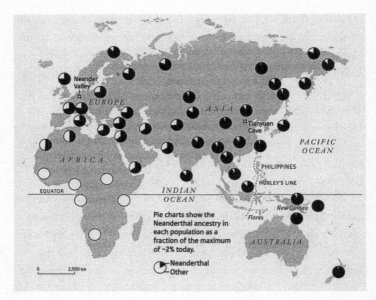

FIGURE 2.5 Neanderthal ancestry in today's humans. (From Reich 2018, with permission)

absolute. Sexual imperatives can smash through some very powerful social barriers.

Sexual Orientation

On February 18, 1895, the Marquess of Queensberry left his calling card at one of the posh London clubs, the Albemarle. It was inscribed: "For Oscar Wilde, posing somdomite." The Marquess could have benefited from the use of Spell Check, but the intent was clear. What made this more than a now-forgotten brush

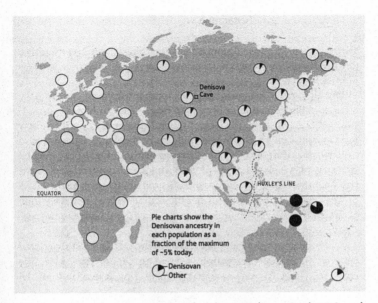

Denisova Cave

EQUATOR

HUXLEY'S LINE

Pie charts show the
Denisovan ancestry in
each population as a
fraction of the maximum
of ~5% today.

Denisovan
Other

FIGURE 2.6 Denisovan ancestry in today's humans. (From Reich 2018, with permission)

between two Victorians was that Oscar Wilde was one of the best-known figures of his day. He was the author of the brilliant farce, the best in the English language, *The Importance of Being Earnest*. It is still a staple of high-school performances in Britain, starring the pupils' English master in drag playing Lady Bracknell (Figure 2.7). A dowager with an eligible daughter, Gwendolyn Fairfax, her classic reaction comes when she discovers that Gwen's suitor, Jack Worthing, had been found as a baby in cloakroom at Victoria Station. "To be born, or at any rate bred, in a hand-bag, whether it had handles or not, seems to me to display a contempt for the ordinary decencies of family life that reminds one of the worst excesses of the French Revolution." Fortunately, all ends well when it is discovered that Jack is truly the offspring of a suitably high-status family.

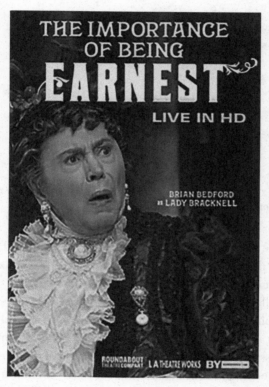

FIGURE 2.7 Well-known Shakespearean actor Brian Bedford playing Lady Bracknell.

Wilde was already well known as a leading figure in the "aesthetic movement," a group of poets and others, given to flamboyant dress and theatrical public behavior—velvet clothes sort of thing. The movement is immortalized in the Gilbert and Sullivan operetta *Patience*, where the leading figure, the poet Reginald Bunthorne, is often taken to be a caricature of Wilde, although that is probably a retrospective assessment. By the time of the Marquess's note, it was well known that Wilde was in a homosexual relationship with Lord Alfred Douglas, the son of the Marquess. Foolishly, although entirely in character, Wilde sued the Marquess for libel and, although, on cross examination, he got in some good lines—works of art are neither moral nor immoral, only well or badly done—predictably the case collapsed. At once, Wilde was arrested on charges of homosexual behavior—a new law prohibiting "gross indecency" had been passed in 1885—found guilty and sentenced to two years in jail. On release, a broken man, he fled to France, where he died at the age of forty-six. He is buried in the cemetery of Père Lachaise in Paris, lying not far from another whose sex life led to misfortune, Pierre Abelard, sans genitalia. For thousands, including me, Wilde's grave has long been a place of pilgrimage; the tomb defaced by the lipstick marks left thanks to the kisses of many admirers, male and female, not including me.

Unsurprisingly, there is little evidence, anthropological or archaeological, for or against same-sex behavior. There is some suggestion that, with the coming of agriculture, homosexuality may have become more prevalent in "agropastoral" societies than in hunter-gatherer societies. In the former, arranged marriages were the norm and hence you were likely to reproduce whatever your sexual orientation, whereas, in the latter, there would have been selection pressure against same-sex activity. "Homosexual individuals in a free-mate context may face difficulties in attracting and retaining opposite-sex partners, but in arranged-marriage societies these mates are supplied by their parents, and they can choose to stay with them in order to have children" (Apostolou 2017). Be this as it may—and note the (later-to-be-discussed) assumption that sexual orientation has a biological foundation— in human history, male homosexuality particularly is a well-known phenomenon, tolerated or not according to its nature and to the age. Ancient Greeks accepted homosexuality. Not a free-for-all, as in San Francisco bathhouses in the years before HIV. Homosexual yearning and behavior was highly stylized, masturbation occurring in the middle or upper classes between a young man and his adolescent lover (Dover 1978). (See Figure 2.8.) Anal intercourse was considered as womanly and degrading. One suspects that much that happened was encased in and a function of the all-male environments in which young Greek men of their classes were raised. As today, with prisons and single-sex boarding schools, these sorts of practices are almost inevitable.

With the appearance of Christianity, despite the somewhat dodgy relationship between David and Jonathan—"Jonathan was knit to the soul of David, and Jonathan loved him as his own soul" (Samuel 18:1)—homosexuality, male or female, was put firmly beyond acceptability. To this day. Pope Francis, who has a deservedly justified reputation for tolerance and understanding, has made it clear that homosexuality is sinful. Priests may not bless homosexual unions. Although the inclinations are understood and find sympathy, the behavior does not. It is "illicit" and "not

FIGURE 2.8 Greek homosexual activity.

ordered according to the Creator's plans" (Mellen 2021). This last phrase helps us to dig more deeply into the state of play. Catholic moral teaching is based on natural law theory, which argues that we should obey God's will where God's will is doing what is natural. Caring about young children is natural and good. Killing for kicks is unnatural and bad. Is homosexual behavior unnatural? One suspects that many, if not most, people are not too bothered, either way. Britain in the fifties was typical. Everyone knew people who were "nature's bachelors," often chumming up together. Even though male homosexuality was against the law, no one was much troubled. As a Kinsey report makes clear, realtors loved having (male) homosexuals in the district. They kept up their houses and were typically good neighbors (Bell and Weinberg 1978). However, one could easily imagine, in hunter-gatherer societies, too much overt behavior might be disrupting, putting the group out of balance. Not working as were others to support a family and so forth. It was not the norm.

This said, importantly, such behavior was almost certainly readily associated with outgroup hostility—especially with the growth and influence of religions, which are notable for laying down moral restrictions. What better way of building up barriers than suggesting that outgroups are guilty of unnatural practices? The Old Testament makes it very clear that outgroups are given to homosexual behavior and hence to be shunned and condemned. Lot is entertaining a pair of visiting angels. "Before they had gone to bed, all the men from every part of the city of Sodom—both young and old—surrounded the house. They called to Lot, 'Where are the men who came to you tonight? Bring them out to us so that we can have sex with them'" (Genesis 19:5). They were about to be sorry. Especially since they turned down Lot's offer of his virgin daughters as substitutes for the angels. "Then the Lord rained down burning sulfur on Sodom and Gomorrah—from the Lord out of the heavens. Thus he overthrew those cities and the entire plain, destroying all those living in the cities—and also the vegetation in the land" (19:24–25).

Back to the present and think of how readily religions presume to lecture on all forms of sexual behavior. Ingroup good. Outgroup bad.

Religion

The god Cronos was into the business of eating his own children. Religions are good at that. Persecuted by their own kind, most if not all religions have been the subject of prejudice at one time or another. Hard to imagine the inoffensive Quakers to have been the target of hatred, but such was the case in early New England. "In 1659 alone, over forty Quakers were whipped, sixty-four imprisoned, forty banished, one branded, three had ears cut off, and four killed. One victim's flesh was recorded as 'beaten Black, and as into Gelly, and under his Arms the bruised Flesh and Blood hung down, clodded as it were in bags'" (Perlmutter 1992, 68). More recently, and better known, is the prejudice against Catholicism. In the nineteenth century, immigrants from Ireland, Italy, and East Europe, in search of better lives in the New World, streamed across the Atlantic. At times, the reaction is hair raising. "Catholic immigrants were charged with plotting to seize the country, undermine Protestantism, and destroy religious freedom. Anti-Catholic books, pamphlets and magazines proliferated. Differences over state aid to parochial schools and over whose Bible should be read in public schools also helped trigger mob attacks and burning of Catholic churches and convents." Little wonder that "Boston's *Atlas* urged every 'true American' employer to immediately 'refuse to employ the miscreants, on any terms,' forcing them to return 'to their own benighted and miserable country'" (121).

Atheists also come into their fair share of prejudice. From the time of the ancient Greeks, questions of belief and nonbelief have rarely been purely epistemological, matters of right and wrong, but nearly always bring in moral issues (Ruse 2015). Can one, should one, be a nonbeliever? You might think this could hardly be a simple matter of morality. Either the earth is flat or it is not. Either God exists or He does not. But, whereas you have a reasonable chance of proving the Earth question once and for all—like photos of it from a satellite—there is always room for doubt about the God question. Even Richard Dawkins allows his chances of being right are probably no more than 99.9%! Plato certainly thought it was a moral issue and that atheism could lead to social unrest—nothing like a god, or two or three, for keeping people in line. He wanted atheists locked up, fed only by slaves, and after death buried outside the city walls. The same kind of mentality persists down to the present. Many countries in the West today could not care less about a politician's personal religious beliefs. Others, Muslim countries particularly, monitor the beliefs of everyone. And in some, while nonbelief may not be illegal, it is not a recipe for societal success. An avowed atheist would never get elected president of the United States of America.

Is religion just a way to be nasty to our fellow human beings? Obviously not. The list of those, guided by their religious beliefs, who have given—given their all—to their fellow human beings is endless. Think of twenty-one-year-old Sophie Scholl, Lutheran, who (with her brother Hans) died on the guillotine on February 22, 1943, for her active membership in the White Rose group, opposing the Nazis and crying for an end to war. "It is such a splendid sunny day, and I have to go. But how many have to die on the battlefield in these days, how many young, promising lives. What does my death matter if by our acts thousands are warned and alerted?" (Newborn 2006) Truly, though, it is distorting to pick out exceptional people, whatever their religion. Better to remember the countless people, present and past—teachers, doctors, shop keepers, house cleaners, garbage men—whose lives have been shaped by religion, not just Christianity, and have given so much to their fellow humans. I paid my respects in my dedication to just such people.

The questions become: Why religion?, and Does the ingroup/outgroup division help in our understanding? David Hume (1757) suggested that religion all started with animism, basically a mistake of understanding.

> There is a universal tendency among mankind to think of all things as being like themselves, and to transfer to every object the qualities they are familiarly acquainted with and intimately conscious of. We find human faces in the moon, armies in the clouds; and, if not corrected by experience and reflection, our natural tendency leads us to ascribe malice or good-will to everything that hurts or pleases us.

Modern thinkers accept something similar. A recent study of the origins of religions in hunter-gatherer societies concluded that "the oldest trait of religion, present in the most recent common ancestor of present-day hunter-gatherers, was animism, in agreement with long-standing beliefs about the fundamental role of this trait. Belief in an afterlife emerged, followed by shamanism and ancestor worship. Ancestor spirits or high gods who are active in human affairs were absent in early humans, suggesting a deep history for the egalitarian nature of hunter-gatherer societies" (Peoples, Duda, and Marlowe 2016). Clarifying, they define "shamanism as the presence in a society of a 'shaman' (male or female), a socially recognized part-time ritual intercessor, healer, and problem solver." Note, we are talking a long time here. "The archaeological record indicates that [religious] rituals have been part of human culture since the Lower Paleolithic (over 100,000 years ago), so that they have persisted for long periods of time" (Hayden 1987, 82).

Does this then mean that religion is little more than an accidental add-on, brought on by misconceptions of the world around us? Highly unlikely when one thinks of the costs of religions. Tithing has a long tradition. What may have started as an accident will not persist unless it gives reasons to be picked up and cherished by natural selection. Ingroup/outgroup thinking is clearly pertinent here. If one thinks in terms of proximate causes, Robert Bellah suggests that animism—seeing the world around us as in some sense living and human-like—can provide a sense of security needed by humans given their vulnerabilities, such as needing child care way beyond that needed by other mammals: "there is a deep human need . . . to think of the universe to see the largest world one is capable of imagining, as personal" (Bellah 2011, 104). At the more ultimate cause level, again and again, the response comes: "cooperation." Promotion of the ingroup. "We view shamans as a general category of individuals often found in hunter-gatherer societies who mediate between the earthly and spirit worlds to promote cohesion and physical and mental well-being in the society."

And: "Shamanism acts as a mechanism to reinforce social norms, encouraging group cooperation through ritual and social bonding, and calming anxiety during times of resource stress." In our terms, as stressed by one of the fathers of sociology, religion promotes ingroup harmony and strength of bonds: "We now see the real reason why the gods cannot do without their worshippers any more than these can do without their gods; it is because society, of which the gods are only a symbolic expression, cannot do without individuals any more than these can do without society" (Durkheim 1912, 347). A telling study found that, comparing nineteenth-century communes, those with a religious foundation outlived by four to one those with a secular foundation (Sosis and Alcorta 2003, 269; see also Sosis and Bressler 2003, and Figure 2.9).

We start to move toward outgroup thinking and why religionists so often treat deviants harshly. Michel Servetus, a Spanish physician and theologian, denied the Trinity, seeing Jesus as more a manifestation of God rather than God Himself. He escaped to Switzerland from France, and to Jean Calvin's Geneva, home of the "Reform" version of Protestant Christianity. Literally, out of the frying pan and into the fire. Servetus was condemned and burned at the stake. Calvin, merciful to the end, wanted him executed by the less painful, decapitating sword. He agreed however with the verdict. It was a classic case of "virtuous violence." Servetus was a threat to the Protestant Christianity that Calvin represented. And more generally we can see why condemning the outgroup—Protestants against Catholics, Christians against Muslims—is the obverse side to the ingroup ties of religions. Read the Old Testament if you find this implausible.

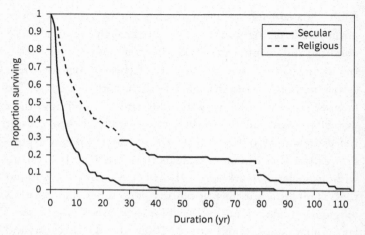

FIGURE 2.9 Duration of secular communes as against religious communes. (From Sosis and Bressler 2003.)

When the Lord your God thrusts them out before you, do not say to yourself, "It is because of my righteousness that the Lord has brought me in to occupy this land"; it is rather because of the wickedness of these nations that the Lord is dispossessing them before you. It is not because of your righteousness or the uprightness of your heart that you are going in to occupy their land; but because of the wickedness of these nations the Lord your God is dispossessing them before you, in order to fulfill the promise that the Lord made on oath to your ancestors, to Abraham, to Isaac, and to Jacob. (Deuteronomy 9:4–5)

So much for the Canaanites.

Disability

Franklin D. Roosevelt was four-times elected president of the United States of America, from 1932 until his death in 1945. He is generally and rightfully considered one of the very greatest of the presidents, bracketed with George Washington and Abraham Lincoln. He was also most dreadfully handicapped. In 1921, he caught poliomyelitis (also then known as infantile paralysis) and was paralyzed permanently from the waist down. He did not let this get in the way of his ambition. He could never walk but learned how to hobble with sticks and would always stand in public, often with the aid of those beside him. He would not refer to his disability, but in 1938 he founded the National Foundation for Infantile Paralysis, which as is well known was instrumental in the eventual finding in the 1950s of a vaccine against polio. The Franklin Delano Roosevelt Memorial in Washington was dedicated in 1997 by President Bill Clinton. The first statue of Roosevelt had him sitting on a chair next to his beloved Scotty dog, Fala. He was wearing a cloak that concealed his disability. Following protests, money was raised, and now at the entrance there is a statue of Roosevelt in a wheelchair, openly acknowledging his disability. (See Figure 2.10.) There we have a cameo of disabilities and of attitudes—changing attitudes—toward them. No one is going to criticize Roosevelt for wanting to conceal, or at least play down, his disability. However, his very life of doing what he did while disabled was a testament to the need and ability to overcome prejudice.

Traditionally, disabled people of all kinds have been regarded with fear and contempt—classic objects of prejudice. Numerically,

FIGURE 2.10 Franklin Roosevelt in wheelchair. From the Franklin Roosevelt memorial, in Washington, DC.

prejudice against the disabled has been and still is one of the great instances of hatred toward fellow human beings. Today, there are just under 8 billion people on this planet and it is estimated that at least 500 million are disabled. What exactly qualifies as disabled is, to some extent, a judgment. In a country with expected literary skills, there might be harsher judgments than in a country where such skills were not at a premium. It is estimated that one in seven Americans is disabled. This covers a wide range of handicaps. These include visual and hearing and speech disabilities. Then, obviously, mental incapacities. Loss of body parts, restricted mobility, and spinal injuries. Various crippling diseases like muscular dystrophy, which entails the gradual wasting away of the muscles and the consequent restrictions and inabilities that this entails, and cystic fibrosis, which entails difficulties in breathing because of the accumulation of mucus. The list can go on.

No one is saying—no one should be saying—that all afflictions are equally disabling. Having difficulties with reading and writing can be dreadful, lifelong problems. One doubts, however, that they are usually problems of the magnitude of a child struck down by polio and unable to use any of its limbs. This does however point to one thing, namely there is a tendency to regard all disabilities at the same level and often equally threatening, frightening, disgusting, or—the list of negative emotions is nigh endless. Those who make the distinctions are often only those who are themselves disabled or who have family members or friends who are disabled. Failure to do so can lead to hurtful and often ludicrous situations. Some forty years ago, my ten-year-old son joined a local pack of cub scouts and I got roped in as an adult helper. We learned that there was one pack in town, made up of, restricted to, boys with handicaps, of all kinds—blind, Down's syndrome, wheelchair bound, and more. Why one should assume a likeness, an identity, between these children is totally without foundation. A child who is blind has nothing especially in common with a child with Down's syndrome, and one suspects that treating such a child in this way is hurtful, if not significantly soul destroying. Many blind or deaf or physically handicapped children overcompensate by working particularly hard at school tasks, and then to be categorized with those who cannot do much of this at all must be devastating. It works the other way too. Fortunately, people realized that something was wrong and the children were distributed among all the packs in town. We got two kids with Down's syndrome. It turned out that one was rather quiet and shy, whereas the other was loud and cheeky—too much at times. Within a week, no one, children or helpers, saw there was anything different about our newcomers. They were a bit slow, but they were not physically handicapped and to treat them as equivalent would have been equally hurtful if not soul destroying. They could play to their strengths—a true gentleness—and they did. They became human beings. And one suspects, one hopes, that for the rest of their lives their fellow pack members think in new ways about mental handicaps. I do.

Let us not pat ourselves too quickly on the back. It is only too well known that, in the past, the treatment of the handicapped has ranged from the inadequate to the truly appalling. Notorious, even today, in part because of the etching by William Hogarth of the last stage of the "Rake's Progress," was the mental hospital or lunatic asylum founded in London in 1247 as a hospital sponsored by a military body, the New Order of our Lady of Bethlehem (Figure 2.11). It was not originally intended as a place especially for the mentally handicapped, but by the seventeenth century that was its role under the better-known name of "Bedlam." To say that conditions were horrific would be one of the understatements of all time. The inmates were ignored, fed inadequately, given no treatment systematic or otherwise at all. Even more appalling it

FIGURE 2.11 *In Bedlam* (William Hogarth, "The Rake's Progress").

had turned into a cash-generating operation, opening its doors to the public, who would come along to look and jeer at the unfortunates within the walls. From an account of a tour in 1725: "you find yourself in a long and wide gallery, on either side of which are a large number of little cells where lunatics of every description are shut up, and you can get a sight of these poor creatures, little windows being let into the doors. Many inoffensive madmen walk in the big gallery." Upstairs things are worse: "On the second floor is a corridor and cells like those on the first floor, and this is the part reserved for dangerous maniacs, most of them being chained and terrible to behold." Terrible, but entertaining too: "On holidays numerous persons of both sexes, but belonging generally to the lower classes, visit this hospital and amuse themselves watching these unfortunate wretches, who often give them cause for laughter." On leaving, you were expected to tip the porter. And then on to the Tower of London or Westminster Abbey and other sights of London (Saussure 1902).

It is all too easy to sneer at the past and feel smug because we live in modern times. Perhaps so, but if one looks at the treatment of the handicapped, particularly the mentally handicapped, in both Britain and America during the nineteenth and twentieth centuries, there is reason for deep shame. Asylums for the "deaf and dumb" were a commonplace. An institution founded for "Idiotic and Feebleminded Youth" in Massachusetts in 1859— the same year as the *Origin*—caused no raising of eyebrows. And the proposed cures and solutions were often even worse than those of the seventeenth and eighteenth century. Most popular was the attempted elimination of the problem: eugenics. Influential were such works as the psychologist Henry Goddard's book *The Kallikak' Family: A Study in the Heredity of Feeble Mindedness* (1912), which purported to show that mental disability was not a one-off but a heritable condition. Actions followed. It was proposed to sterilize Carrie Buck, an eighteen-year-old with a supposed mental age of a nine-year-old, confined in the Virginia State Colony for Epileptics and Feebleminded. Ruling 8–1, the Supreme Court upheld the constitutionality of the sterilization order. Justice Oliver Wendell Holmes wrote the Court's opinion. He is credited with saying: "three generations of idiots is enough."

By 1929, twenty-three states had legalized "eugenical" sterilization of the mentally defective. In some states, the laws were on the
books until the 1970s.

The story is no less depressing when one spreads out from the
mental to the physical. One of my most horrific early experiences
was venturing out on afternoons, from my comfortable, middle-
class, English, boarding school, to cross town and help children at
a school for the blind during their crafts hour. It was like walking
from a novel by Jane Austen to walking into *Oliver Twist*. I con-
fess I lasted only three or four afternoons, a cowardice that still
brings a blush. One shudders, even today, at the thought of having
to negotiate the typical academic establishment in a wheelchair.
Leave things at that for the moment. The point is made. "All disabled people share one common experience—discrimination."
And it is surely gilding the lily to point out that discrimination
against the disabled fits comfortably—if that is the right term—
into the ingroup/outgroup theory. One can indeed well imagine
that, within the ingroup, there would be dislike of and hostility toward the handicapped. Not necessarily; not always. Family
bonds are tight, and some handicapped can survive and contribute
(Dettwyler 1991). But overall, especially in the early years, before
bands had developed more sophisticated tools and the like, not to
mention environmental challenges like the last Ice Age (about two
and a half million years ago), there would be negative feelings. It
is hard enough as it is living the life of a hunter-gatherer, without
having the added burdens of group members who, for various reasons, cannot pull their weight. Natural selection is not a friend of
the weak and helpless.

Jews

In 1954, my mother having died, on the rebound my father married a young German woman. The next year, our family crossed the (English) Channel and drove to my stepmother's parents, in the spa Bad Soden am Taunus, just outside Frankfurt am Main. Expectedly, Bad Soden has many parks and, one day, walking through one of them, my stepmother pointed across to an empty space among the trees and said: "That's where the old people's home used to be." On asking, I learned that the home was for old Jewish people and, one night in 1938, the authorities, my stepmother did not know which authorities, came and emptied the home, making the inhabitants seek shelter elsewhere. I asked: "Didn't you folks do anything about it? Complain at least." "What good would it have done? We would only have got ourselves into trouble." "Couldn't you have offered some space in your home?" "They wouldn't have felt comfortable." My personal introduction to the Jewish Question. I was a johnny come lately, because persecution had long been going strong, back at least to the founding of Christianity. Read the Gospel of John. Prejudice against Jews was one of the huge marks of the Middle Ages, as Jews were accused of all sorts of vile sins, often including the eating of Christian babies. At the same time, hypocritically, they were used as needed. Christians were forbidden to lend money for a profit. So, Jews stepped in and performed that role. Shakespeare's *Merchant of Venice*, with Shylock a money lender a main character, gives a good idea of their then image.

Move to the age of evolution. There were no Jews in the Pleistocene. No gentiles either, for that matter. Even if there are biological differences, one would expect them to be as superficial as skin color. Darwin saw that. Biologically, he simply saw no reason to pick out the Jews as different. "The singular fact that Europeans and Hindoos, who belong to the same Aryan stock and speak a language fundamentally the same, differ widely in appearance, whilst Europeans differ but little from Jews, who belong to the Semitic stock and speak quite another language, has been accounted for by Broca through the Aryan branches having been largely crossed during their wide diffusion by various indigenous tribes" (Darwin 1871, 1 240). Hitler begged to differ. He came to power early in 1933, and the Third Reich came into being (Evans 2005). At once began the persecution of the Jews—about 525,000, 0.75% of the total German population. Exclusion from government jobs was followed by exclusion from the military, and then expulsion from professional employment, including university posts. The enacted "Nuremberg Laws" became ever-more oppressive, with males with non-Jewish names having to add "Israel" and females "Sarah." Jewish children were forbidden to go to state schools, and Jewish doctors were forbidden to treat non-Jewish patients. Violence increased, culminating in *Kristallnacht*, November 9–10, 1938, when, following the shooting in France of a German diplomat by a young Polish Jew, Jewish shops were smashed up, 91 Jews were killed, and 30,000 Jews were arrested and sent to concentration camps. I suspect it was then that the old folks in the Bad Soden park were kicked out of their home. "While the overwhelming majority of Germans deplored the wanton destruction of Jews' property and resented boycotts, they gradually came to accept the pariah status of Jews as inevitable" (Koonz 2003, 1930).

This was just the beginning. Hitler was already into prejudice against the disabled, promoting eugenics—*Rassenhygiene*
or "racial hygiene"—of the most horrendous kind. More than
400,000 people were sterilized against their will, while up to
300,000 were killed as inadequate. This was practice. Jews were
forced into ghettos, often far from home in the East. Then, the
killings began in serious. During the length of the war, paramilitary death squads (*Einsatzgruppen*) killed upward of a million
and a half Jews, usually by lining them up before trenches (that
the Jews themselves had dug) and shooting them. After the so-
called Wannsee Conference in January 1942, when the "Final
Solution" was decided upon, Jews were shipped to death camps,
many like Auschwitz in Poland, where killing large numbers was
an assembly-line process, rather like the Ford Motor Company.
(A bit of an unfair dig, but not entirely unfair, given Henry Ford's
extreme and vocal anti-Semitism.) Arriving at the camps, dividing those destined for instant death from those for arduous labor
merely postponing death, the victims were made to strip naked,
forced to give up their possessions, and herded into the gas cham-
bers, and Zyklon-B was dropped in through vents. Within twenty
minutes, everyone in the chamber was dead. Then came the haul-
ing to the ever-burning ovens, and mass cremation. In all, about
6 million Jews—not just from Germany but from occupied other
countries like France—died, with rather more than half killed in
the death camps.

Prejudice run riot. And a nigh paradigmatic example of the
significance of ingroup/outgroup thinking. There was a German
tradition of anti-Semitism going back in time, especially to
Martin Luther. "They are our public enemies. They do not stop

blaspheming our Lord Christ, calling the Virgin Mary a whore, Christ, a bastard, and us changelings or abortions. If they could kill us all, they would gladly do it" (Luther 1955–, 58: 458–59). They are rats. They are vermin attacking the organic whole, the Reich. Speech after speech affirmed this. Cartoon after cartoon told of this. (See Figure 2.12.) Films too. On the orders of Dr. Goebbels, the hugely popular *Jud Süss* was made in 1940. (See Figure 2.13.) Based at least in part on a true story, it tells the tale of a Jew who (through judicious loans) gains much control over the state of Württemberg. Long barred from the state, Süss convinces his patron to allow Jews to return. Perhaps the most dramatic episode of the whole movie is that of a column of Jews entering the city, to the horror and fear of the populace. They are not an orderly file, but a carnival of leering jesters and clowns, showing no restraints or bounds to their behavior. Rats entering the clean and tidy bourgeois home of a decent citizen, bringing filth and disease with them. At the end of the film, Süss gets his well-merited comeuppance. He is hanged in graphic detail; although, interestingly, less for what he has done to the town and more for having had sex with a Christian woman. Rightfully, the Jews are given three days to leave the city, as one citizen observes having taught everyone a lesson. Hatred of the outgroup by the ingroup.

Women

TRUMP: You know I'm automatically attracted to beautiful—I just start kissing them. It's like a magnet. Just kiss. I don't even wait. And when you're a star they let you do it. You can do anything.

Das Ungeziefer

Das Leben ist nicht lebenswert,
Wo man nicht dem Schmarotzer wehrt,
Als Nimmersatt herumzukriechen.
Wir müssen und wir werden siegen.

Life is not worth living,
When one does not resist the parasite,
Never satisfied as it creeps about.
We must and will win.
(*Der Stürmer*, 28 September 1944)

FIGURE 2.12 Jews as vermin cartoon, from *Der Stürme*.

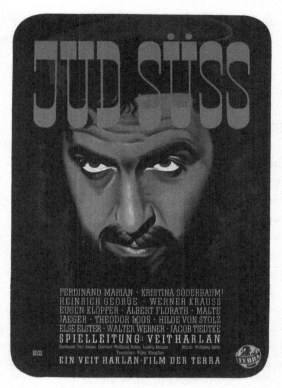

FIGURE 2.13 Poster for *Jud Süss.*

BUSH: Whatever you want.

TRUMP: Grab them by the pussy. You can do anything.

This is not quite true. On at least one occasion, he was not able to do anything.

TRUMP: I moved on her, actually. You know, she was down on
    Palm Beach. I moved on her, and I failed. I'll admit it.
UNKNOWN: Whoa.
TRUMP: I did try and fuck her. She was married.
(TRUMP 2016)

Donald Trump talking to the TV personality Billy Bush, a month
before, over his rival, Hillary Clinton, he was elected president of
the United States of America. Prejudice against women. Leaving
them until last is not a sign of disrespect. The very opposite. More
a sign that prejudice against them may not be entirely typical.
Significant perhaps is that Allport does not have much to say
about the issue. But it is so obvious that they are discriminated
against. Prejudice against them presuming to take male roles;
although, interestingly, one of the first to write on the subject,
Plato, was prepared—at least in theory—to give women roles
equal to men in ruling his ideal state, as sketched in his *Republic*.
"Women and men have the same nature in respect to the guard-
ianship of the state, save insofar as the one is weaker and the other
is stronger" (*Republic* V; Cooper 1997, 1079). Physical attributes
are irrelevant when it comes to talent and ability. It is all a matter
of education. "If women are expected to do the same work as men,
we must teach them the same things." Aristotle was more conventional. "The relation of male to female is by nature a relation of
superior to inferior and ruler to ruled." Well, that tells it like it is.
Is there anything to back up this judgment? How about: "the male
is more courageous than the female, and more sympathetic in the
way of standing by to help. Even in the case of cephalopods, when
the cuttle-fish is struck with the trident the male stands by to help

the female; but when the male is struck the female runs away" (*History of Animals*; Barnes 1984, 949). Christian theologians lapped up this sort of thing. Although, admittedly, they did have sources of their own. There is a proper ordering and women are not first. "As in all the congregations of the Lord's people. Women should remain silent in the churches. They are not allowed to speak, but must be in submission, as the law says. If they want to inquire about something, they should ask their own husbands at home; for it is disgraceful for a woman to speak in the church" (1 Corinthians 14: 33–35).

St. Paul notwithstanding, this cannot be the whole story. We are talking here about groups and what leads to their success. If half the members are doing nothing, or at best performing at an inferior level, this is not a potential strategy. Females must be part of the whole. Otherwise, natural selection will produce group after group of Jesuits and nothing else. St. Ignatius Loyola might be delighted. I doubt others will be. We have seen the snares of uncritical analogies from the primate world, but—"social grace"!—everyone knows how Franz de Waal (2007) showed that, in troops of chimpanzees, with males strutting around like they were pop stars before groupies, it is in fact the older females who control the strings of power. Save the males make appropriate alliances with these troop members, they are going to remain at the level of your average philosopher. Not a recipe for a glorious future.

Fears are misplaced. The evidence both from present-day groups and from archaeology—health, tooth wear, artifacts—is that females did indeed play an active role. For a start, the typical *National Geographic* picture of dominant males, clad only in athletic supports, armed with spears for the hunt, with the little bare-breasted woman staying home and looking after babies, is simply not true. A huge amount of hunting by humans relies on artifacts—traps and the like—as well as the knowledge of how best to use them. Women can and do play full roles here. Again, when it comes to food processing and the like, males and females both have stakes in working efficiently. Most importantly, however dominant males may seem, as with the chimpanzees, they need female support: "women are not accorded a lower status due to their childbearing, childrearing, and lactating functions, but rather, are honoured by men for these contributions" (Jarvenpa and Brumbach 2014, 1253). Ongoing rape is simply not the best way of getting sexual favors and thus producing children, especially sons. Getting along and being welcome is a much better strategy. Also, this is not to mention the power that women have over their children. Freud knew whereof he spoke when he talked about the importance of mothers for sons. Treating them as dirt is simply not human practice. In short, groups must have females, and natural selection is going to promote their value—as producers of more group members and as contributing to the whole (Hrdy 1999).

Female inequality apparently is not typical. It should not exist. How then do we get the kinds of forces that led to Donald Trump? Fitting with much of already-encountered theory, much inequality is a function of the move to agriculture.

A possible clue for the evolution of sex equality in the hominin lineage was the increase in the cost of human reproduction associated with larger brain sizes in early Homo. Higher offspring costs would require investment from both mothers and fathers, as seen among extant hunter-gatherers. The need for biparental investment predicts increased sex equality, which is reflected in the high frequency of monogamy and the reproductive schedules of male hunter-gatherers who typically stop reproducing early and exhibit long life spans after their last reproduction. (Dyble et al. 2015, 798)

Among farmers, these pressures are off and males can more readily manipulate themselves into power. The hunter-gatherer "pattern contrasts with that of male farmers and pastoralists, whose reproductive spans extend well into late life. The recognition of affinal ties throughout our long life span has been argued to be an important step in human social evolution." If, thanks to agriculture, women go on having kids—many more kids—then obviously they are going to be tied down to the basic needs of infants and small children. Men do not breast feed. And so gender differences will appear and be accentuated. Men have a dimension of freedom that women did not have. "With more pregnancies, women had to spend more energy on nurturing zygotes, fetuses, and helpless babies—a costly enterprise indeed" (Adovasio, Soffer, and Page 2007, 269–70).

Last Thoughts

Time to conclude: "the very factors that make ingroup attachment and allegiance important to individuals also provide a fertile ground for antagonism and distrust of those outside the ingroup boundaries. The need to justify ingroup values in the form of moral superiority to others, sensitivity to threat, the anticipation of interdependence under conditions of distrust, social comparison processes, and power politics all conspire to connect ingroup identification and loyalty to disdain and overt hostility toward outgroups" (Brewer 1999, 439).

Rudyard Kipling told us what it is all about.

> The Stranger within my gate,
> He may be true or kind,
> But he does not talk my talk—
> I cannot feel his mind.
> I see the face and the eyes and the mouth,
> But not the soul behind.
>
> The men of my own stock,
> They may do ill or well,
> But they tell the lies I am wanted to,
> They are used to the lies I tell;
> And we do not need interpreters
> When we go to buy or sell.
>
> The Stranger within my gates,
> He may be evil or good,
> But I cannot tell what powers control–
> What reasons sway his mood;
> Nor when the Gods of his far-off land
> Shall repossess his blood.

The men of my own stock,
Bitter bad they may be,
But, at least, they hear the things I hear,
And see the things I see;
And whatever I think of them and their likes
They think of the likes of me.

This was my father's belief
And this is also mine:
Let the corn be all one sheaf—
And the grapes be all one vine,
Ere our children's teeth are set on edge
By bitter bread and wine.

3 | THE CULTURE OF WAR

On March 16, 1968, during the Vietnam War, in the village of My Lai, between 347 and 504 people were killed by US Army soldiers from Company C, 1st Battalion, 20th Infantry Regiment and Company B, 4th Battalion, 3rd Infantry Regiment, 11th Brigade, 23rd (American) Infantry Division (Hersch 1972). The victims, mainly women and children, were unarmed. Some of the women were gang-raped before death, their bodies left mutilated, as were those of some children no more than twelve years old. The leader of the Americans, Lieutenant William Calley Jr., claimed he was following orders. My hypothetical example of chapter 1 turned out to be not so hypothetical. But why should we care or remark on this? Why, fifty years later, should this episode still be the memory of the war that, above all, causes anger, disgust, shame (Jones 2017)? After all, the United States was at war, and war means killing people.

Our science gives us very good reasons why My Lai stands out in the annals of human immoral behavior. First, above all, humans are not killer apes. Behaving like the soldiers in My Lai

Why We Hate. Michael Ruse, Oxford University Press. © Oxford University Press 2022.
DOI: 10.1093/oso/9780197621288.003.0004

goes, in some very deep sense, against human nature. As we have seen, if anything the average person—and there is no reason to think those US soldiers other than average—finds it very difficult to kill other human beings. No surprise. This is precisely what one would expect from natural selection. Fighting means that people get hurt, and that could be you. As pointed out, we simply have not evolved in the direction of murdering machines. As weapons of attack, our teeth are pathetic and the same goes for other human features. In a matchup, you would be a fool if you did not back your average gorilla against Muhammad Ali.

Second, notwithstanding our pacific nature, humans do commit violent acts. But they are, as we have seen, "virtuous." You are in a group and for various reasons—changing climate perhaps—food supplies are increasingly scarce. It is hard to support all the members of the group. You have two adult males, neither of whom is a particularly good hunter. One is totally selfish, always getting into rows, unsafe around the wives of other men, first to grab scarce supplies. The other, conversely, is totally generous. On the principle of "if you can do, and if you can't teach," he devotes his time to training the young people in the group, fishing and hut building and the like. Whom are you more likely to kill, perhaps by leaving them isolated without help? There is no contest, confirming the point that, while violence almost inevitably is going to occur, it is going to be strictly regulated. Morality will be brought into play here with a force unequaled elsewhere. It was morally right to protect the generous member; it was morally right to expel or kill the selfish member.

Third, ingroup/outgroup. Our first urges, fully developed and backed by natural selection, will be toward the well-being of our own group. United we stand, divided we fall. Nothing mysterious and nothing that is not totally ruled by individual selection. Even if I do not benefit, my brother or sister might make gains. As far as outgroups are concerned, if they don't bother us, then we will not be inclined to bother them. However, if we do find ourselves in conflict, brought on by agriculture and its effects, we are still going to be working according to our human nature and governed by the kinds of rules that govern violence within the group. After all, the question is: what best can help our ingroup? The answer is: avoid undue violence toward outgroup; it is unneeded and could rebound. Leading to the obvious conclusion that a general code of conduct toward the enemy is no bad thing. As Darwin said: "as the reasoning powers and foresight of the members [of a tribe] became improved, each man would soon learn from experience that if he aided his fellow-men, he would commonly receive aid in return" (1, 163). The enemy are fellow-men, and hence there is good reason not to relinquish the kinds of moral rules that govern ingroup violence. After all, you may be a loser and very grateful for the rule of morality.

The expectation is that cultures will have developed rules, implicit and explicit, that govern war. My Lai was—is—so appalling because, by any measure, such rules were being violated. You do not kill unarmed civilians; you do not rape women, even if they are of the enemy; and, especially, you cherish the well-being of children—all children, regardless of race, color, sex, or whatever. Rules pertinent to warfare. The Japanese bombing the American fleet at Pearl Harbor, on Sunday, December 7, 1941, was immoral. Those pilots defending Britain in the summer of 1940, against the would-be-invading Germans, were moral exemplars. We cannot thank them enough for their sacrifices. So now the question becomes, as in our discussion of war we turn from the contribution of the sciences to the contribution of the humanities, what has culture had to say about proper and improper warfare? Expectedly, it has had much to say. Although I shall here focus on Western culture, I do stress that this is not an idiosyncratic enterprise of Europeans. Islam, for instance, has from the first worked to articulate rightful occasions for war—"Those that have been attacked are permitted to take up arms because they have been wronged"—and to address issues of proper conduct—"But do not exceed the bounds. God does not approve the transgressors" (Kelsay 2007, 24, 107).

In the West, most importantly, there is "Just War Theory," subdivided into *jus ad bellum*—the conditions under which one can go to war—and *jus in bello*—the conduct of behavior while at war. Let us use this to structure our discussion. First, presenting the philosophical/theological reasoning that goes into Just War Theory. Then, seeing how the theory does, or does not, seem relevant and help understanding in looking at actual examples of war. Rather than a general survey, I shall focus in depth on the two world wars of the last century, and then a more limited war fought by American troops toward the end of the century.

Just War Theory: Cicero to Aquinas

It was the Roman statesman Cicero (106–43 BC) who formulated the problem and began the search for answers. He thought in a remarkably proto-Darwinian way about the nature of humans.

Nature likewise by the power of reason associates man with man in the common bonds of speech and life; she implants in him above all, I may say, a strangely tender love for his off-spring. She also prompts men to meet in companies, to form public assemblies and to take part in them themselves; and she further dictates, as a consequence of this, the effort on man's part to provide a store of things that minister to his comforts and wants—and not for himself alone, but for his wife and children and the others whom he holds dear and for whom he ought to provide; and this responsibility also stimulates his (courage) and makes it stronger for the active duties of life. (*De Officiis*, in Holmes 2005, 26)

The question is how we are to behave. For Cicero, there are external rules of moral conduct laid on us all, whoever we are, unchanging and unbreakable. Cicero puts God behind them, but one senses almost as a secondary thought. Like the rules of mathematics, they exist independently. "There is indeed a law, right reason, which is in accordance with nature; existing in all, unchangeable, eternal. Commanding us to do what is right, forbidding us to do what is wrong." Adding: "It is not one thing at Rome, and another thing at Athens: one thing to-day, and another thing to-morrow; but it is a law eternal and immutable for all nations and for all time. God, the sole Ruler, and universal Lord, has framed and proclaimed this law" (*De Republica*, in Holmes 2005, 25).

Within this context, we can start to think about war, and the possible reasons—or rather, the possible moral reasons. Above all, offensive war is ruled out. It is defensive war or nothing: "wars are unjust which are undertaken without provocation. For only a war waged for revenge or defense can actually be just" (*De Republica*, in Holmes 2005, 25). Of course, part of the question is what constitutes "without provocation." More generally, as we saw in our reference to the Crimean War, there is the problem of pigeonholing wars into the categories. The 1066 invasion of Britain was offensive, and yet was William truly "without provocation" when he invaded England to claim the crown he thought was rightfully his? Conversely, does provocation at once translate into defense? In 1982, Argentina invaded the Falkland Islands, about 300 miles from the coast of South America. The islands were under British rule, and Argentina claimed them for its own. In response, Britain at once sent a military force south and retook the islands. Argentina was being provocative in a way not true of William at Hastings. The islands had been unoccupied until Europeans settled them in the eighteenth century. The invasion had little to do with sovereignty and was essentially a function of Argentina's military government trying to distract the nation from internal problems. However, as the British prime minister at the time, Margaret Thatcher, admitted openly, the response had little to do with defense. At least, not of people or property. It was ideological. "We were defending our honour as a nation" (Thatcher 1993, 173). Questions like these have given rise to two thousand years of debate.

Cicero slides easily back and forth between *jus ad bellum* and *jus in bello*. Going to war without provocation falls under *jus ad bellum*. But then, conduct in the war, *jus in bello*, is equally important. "Not only must we show consideration for those whom we have conquered by force of arms but we must also ensure protection to those *who* lay down their arms and throw themselves upon the mercy of our generals, even though the battering-ram has hammered at their walls" (*De Officiis*, in Holmes 2005, 29). Notice that what we are saying clearly has implications for hatred. It is right to hate aggressors, Hitler for instance. But it is not obvious that we are going to hate everyone against whom we are fighting, even though we may feel that we should fight them. To the extreme disapproval of leaders on both sides, the first Christmas of the Great War, December 25, 1914, German and British troops left their trenches and fraternized, playing soccer and exchanging gifts. Not only did they not hate each other, most then and now would tend to commend them—at least, understand them—rather than condemn. Analogously, in the North African fighting in the Second World War, the German commander, Erwin Rommel—the "Desert Fox"—elicited admiration from both sides, and he is rightly known for his phrase, "war without hate" (Bierman and Smith 2004). Take note of the very important point underlying the discussion here. The basic premise of Just War Theory is that in war we are fighting fellow human beings. We need Just War Theory precisely because we are human beings and so are our opponents.

The two thousand years, subsequent to Cicero, have been variations on and extensions of his thinking about war. The important new factor being that it was conducted in a Christian context. There are difficulties here. Jesus Christ leaves no room for doubt or equivocation. Killing another human being under any and all circumstances is wrong. "You have heard that it was said, 'Eye for eye, and tooth for tooth.' But I tell you, do not resist an evil person. If anyone slaps you on the right cheek, turn to them the other cheek also" (Matthew 5:38–39). The Sermon on the Mount is

categorical. The Christian must be a pacifist. This was the thinking of the Alexandrian Church Father, Origen (ca. 185–ca. 254).
If you object that this is wildly impractical, remember, in those
early centuries after Jesus, Christians were very much a minority, not really part of the big societal picture. They could think in
apocalyptic terms. The Day of Judgment is immanent, and God
will put all right when He returns.

As the centuries went by, and Christianity gained strength
and powerful backers, this increasingly was not an option (Brown
1967). Some way had to be found to make the Christian approach
to war into one that could function in a modern state. A modern state with an army that may have to go to war. This was the
key role of St. Augustine, who started off by pointing out that the
Bible is by no means unequivocal on the subject of war and killing.
King David was a warrior and yet no one was more loved by God,
at least as much for his skill and success in war as for his versifica-
tion producing the Psalms. In the New Testament, Jesus did not
turn away the centurion but praised him. The soldier came asking
Jesus to heal his servant. The centurion tells Jesus that his power
is enough to do the task at a distance. "Lord, I do not deserve you
to come under my roof" (Matthew 8:8). Jesus is touched. "When
Jesus heard this, he was amazed and said to those following him,
'Truly I tell you, I have not found anyone in Israel with such great
faith'" (8:10).

Theologically, Augustine started from his interpretation of the
meaning of the Adam and Eve story. Thanks to their sin of disobe-
dience, we are all tainted by original sin. This does not mean we
are born sinners but that we have a tendency to sin and, given time,
we will sin. Until the Day of Judgment, we are stuck with people

being sinners. We are going to hurt and kill each other. That is a fact that we cannot change. Hence, we must accept and deal with it. Love may and should work at the individual level. At the group level we need rules to regulate the violence. Christianized Just War Theory. "What is the evil in war? Is it the death of some who will soon die in any case, that others may live in peaceful subjection? This is mere cowardly dislike, not any religious feeling. The real evils in war are love of violence, revengeful cruelty, fierce and implacable enmity, wild resistance, and the lust for power, and such like" (*Reply to Faustus the Manichean*, in Holmes 2005, 64).

Where Augustine made his major contribution was in picking up and elaborating the thinking of Cicero. *Jus ad bellum*. "Peace should be the object of your desire; war should be waged only as a necessity, and waged only that by it God may deliver men from the necessity and preserve them in peace. For peace is not served in order to the kindling of war, but war is waged in order that peace may be obtained" (*Letter to Boniface*, in Holmes 2005, 62–63). Wars are to be sanctioned by the right and appropriate authority. "The act, the agent, and the authority for the action are all of great importance in the order of nature. For Abraham to sacrifice his own son is shocking madness. His doing so at the command of God proves him faithful and submissive" (*Reply to Faustus the Manichean*, in Holmes 2005, 63). Sliding then to *jus in bello*: "Let necessity, therefore, and not your will, slay the enemy who fights against you. As violence is used against him who rebels and resists, so mercy is due to the vanquished or the captive, especially in the case in which future troubling of the peace is not to be feared" (63). Like Cicero, Augustine is appealing here to natural law, established and sanctioned by God. The rules of war, getting into it and conducting it are not made up or our decision. They are there for us to follow. With one great end. Say it again. Peace! And not just peace for us. Peace for all. "This heavenly city, then, while it sojourns on earth, calls citizens out of all nations, and gathers together a society of pilgrims of all languages, not scrupling about diversities in the manners, laws, and institutions whereby earthly peace is secured and maintained, but recognizing that, however various these are, they all tend to one and the same end of earthly peace" (*City of God*, in Holmes 2005, 79).

Moving forward a millennium, St. Thomas Aquinas was he who put the stamp of approval on Augustine's approach to the ethics of war. First, all is to be set within God's eternal law. "Now it is evident, granted that the world is ruled by Divine Providence, . . . that the whole community of the universe is governed by Divine Reason. Wherefore the very Idea of the government of things in God the Ruler of the universe, has the nature of a law" (*Summa Theologica*, in Holmes 2005, 93). Then the three conditions for a Just War. "First, the *authority* of the sovereign by whose command the war is to be waged. For it is not the business of a private individual to declare war, because he can seek for redress of his rights from the tribunal of his superior" (107). Note that this rules out a private war such as that waged by Osama bin Laden. Second, a *just cause* is required, namely that those who are attacked, should be attacked because they deserve it on account of some fault. Quoting Augustine: "A just war is wont to be described as one that avenges wrongs, when a nation or state has to be punished, for refusing to make amends for the wrongs inflicted by its subjects, or to restore what it has seized unjustly" (107–108). This does seem to squeeze in some offensive wars. I suspect that William the Conqueror might have made such a case. The throne of England was right-fully his. Third, it is necessary that the belligerents should have a *rightful intention*, so that they intend the advancement of good, or the avoidance of evil. Augustine says: "True religion looks upon as peaceful those wars that are waged not for motives of aggrandize-ment, or cruelty, but with the object of securing peace, of punish-ing evil-doers, and of uplifting the good" (108). I would suspect that Margaret Thatcher would think this justifies the Falklands War. I doubt all would agree. The focus is on *jus ad bellum*, but by the time we get to the third reason, we are starting to move into the realm of *jus in bello*. The heavy lifting here was left for others later.

Just War Theory: Grotius to the Present

Hugo Grotius, the early-seventeenth-century Dutch humanist, in his *The Rights of War and Peace* (1625), gave the most detailed discussion of this issue. Quoting Cicero, he gave the general phi-losophy. "There are certain Duties to be observed even toward those that have wronged us, for there is a Moderation required in Revenge and Punishment" (3, XI, 1). Adding: "Even where Justice does not demand it, yet it is often agreeable to Goodness to Moderation, and a great Soul to forgive" (3, VII, 1). He then launched into a list of people and issues where moderation is called for. "If not for Justice, yet for Pity, we must not attempt any Thing which may prove the Destruction of Innocents, unless for some extraordinary Reasons, and for the Safety of many" (3, VIII). Hence: "Tender Age must excuse the Child, and her Sex the

Woman" (3, IX, 1). Priests are off the hook, as are those who "also have justly this same Privilege, as the Priests, who have embraced a like Sort of Life, as Monks, and Lay-Brothers, that is, Penitents, whom the Ecclesiastical Canons, according to natural Equity, would have spared equally as Priests. To these we may justly add those who apply themselves to the Study of Sciences and Arts beneficial to Mankind" (3, X, 2).

Going back to the war itself: "Honour, that is, a regard to Equity, does not permit us to take away the Life of a Prisoner" (3, XIII, 1). Grotius adds: "The same Equity commands us to spare those, who surrender to the Conqueror without Conditions in a suppliant Manner. To kill those that have yielded, (says Tacitus) is barbarous" (3, XV). Grotius does not think these rules—that is the principle behind these rules—is capricious and arbitrary. Cicero showed the way. It is given by God, it is eternal and binding on all, and above all it appeals to that which is natural. Often, in these sorts of discussions, the Euthyphro problem is raised. Does God want us to do what is (independently) Good—in which case, He seems not to be all-powerful—or is that which is Good that which God wants us to do—in which case, God can seem capricious? The move Cicero makes is to argue that God wants us to do that which is "natural," meaning proper function of the way he has created us. "Our forefathers have given us another striking example of justice toward an enemy: when a deserter from Pyrrhus promised the senate to administer poison to the king and thus work his death, the senate and Gaius Fabricius delivered the deserter up to Pyrrhus." Why? Because they disapproved strongly of "the treacherous murder even of an enemy who was at once powerful, unprovoked, aggressive, and successful." Using a traitor to poison your opponent, however awful he may be, is not playing the game. It is not what real men do. It is not natural. Don't do it. Kant agrees: "No state at war with another shall countenance such modes of hostility as would make mutual confidence impossible in a subsequent state of peace: such are the employment of assassins (*percussores*) or of poisoners (*venefici*), breaches of capitulation, the instigating and making use of treachery (*perduellio*) in the hostile state" (Kant 1795, 114).

Aquinas's influential theory of natural law is much in the tradition of Cicero, although, as always with Aquinas, the Aristotelian element infuses his thinking: "Now among all others, the rational creature is subject to Divine providence in the most excellent way, in so far as it partakes of a share of providence, by being provident both for itself and for others. Wherefore it has a share of the Eternal Reason, whereby it has a natural inclination to its proper act and end: and this participation of the eternal law in the rational creature is called the natural law" (Aquinas 1981, I-IIae, 91, 2). This is Grotius's position entirely. What He tells us to do, where He lays down the law, is given by what is natural for us as human beings. It is not natural to kill women and children. So, don't do it. It is obviously natural in the heat of battle to grab your opponents' possessions, to stop them being used against you and perhaps to use them against the opponent. But once the fighting is over, you don't need them. They are not yours. Give them back. Equally, it is totally unnatural to go after "those who apply themselves to the Study of Sciences and Arts beneficial to Mankind"—even philosophers. Don't do it.

We can move forward quickly. Both Luther and Calvin were ardent Augustinians, and, as is so often the case with disciples, they tended in respects to be more Augustinian than St. Augustine himself. Few have relished the concept of original sin more than Jean Calvin. Expectedly, both Luther and Calvin accepted the legitimacy of war, and Augustine was their backup. Jesus was talking about the spiritual life of the individual, not how we should act in the world at large. Worrying about an attack by the Catholics: "if war breaks out—which God forbid—I will not reprove those who defend themselves against the murderous and bloodthirsty papists, nor let anyone else rebuke them as being seditious, but I will accept their action and let it pass as self-defense" (Luther 1955–, 47: 19). Calvin, trained as a lawyer, was strong on rules and regulations. If you give monarchs or governments the power to rule, and "to maintain the tranquility of their subjects, repress the seditious movements of the turbulent, assist those who are violently oppressed, and animadvert on crimes, can they use it more opportunely than in repressing the fury of him who disturbs both the ease of individuals and the common tranquility of all; who excites seditious tumult, and perpetrates acts of violent oppression and gross wrongs?" (Calvin 1536, IV, 20, 12).

Those on the more radical side of the Reformation—Mennonites and the like—took the Jesus of the gospels as totally binding. They wanted little to do with wriggling one's way out of the direct words of the Savior. This tradition has continued down to the present. Quakers tend to be pretty accommodating to interpretations of most of the Bible. We saw that they have never, for instance, been hung up on Augustinian original sin, opting rather to go with the earlier tradition of Irenaeus of Lyon, whose Incarnational theory says that God on the Cross was not a sacrifice but an exemplar of perfect love, a model and ideal for us all. However, when it comes to the Sermon on the Mount, as we learned in the Preface, the most rabid American biblical literalist—Fundamentalist or Creationist—has nothing on the literal reading of Matthew 5–7 by members of the Religious Society of Friends (Quakers).

The basic thinking behind Just War Theory now laid out, the discussion must move on to demonstration of Just War Theory in action—or not. How it structured and governed conduct in war—or not. This is no idle or dated inquiry. There are those today who argue that Just War Theory is a sham, a cover for behavior of the most callous and wicked kind. One such critic records a conversation with a former captain in the US Marines, who had served in Iraq: "he argued that any serious critique of war—past, present, or future—was and is and will be undermined before it starts by the unthinking and all but universal acceptance of just war doctrine. He went on to say that the just war theory has to be taken down, discredited, revealed for the lie that it is" (Meagher 2014, xvi). This is a matter we must decide for ourselves. There are two questions to be answered. Did the war conform or not to the criteria of Just War Theory? Did the participants let themselves be guided (consciously or not) by the criteria of Just War Theory?

These are separate questions, and truly it is the first question that is our main concern. But answering the second question has value insofar as it will help us judge the truth of our answer to the first question. For instance, if we judge a war to fail to meet one of the criteria but the participants thought that they had met the criterion, we want to know why they were mistaken—or, perhaps it is we who are mistaken. Note once again the point made at the beginning of this chapter how this whole discussion meshes with the empirical findings and claims of Fiske and Rai on the role of violence in human interactions. Far from it precluding or denying morality, their fundamental thesis is that violence is almost always taken in a moral context. Humans are violent because they think it is a good thing. "Violence is often taken as the antithesis of sociality—people think that violence is an expression of our animal nature, breaking through when learned cultural norms collapse. Violence is considered to be the essence of evil; it is the prototype of immorality." This is a very one-sided perspective. Of course there are going to be psychopaths and people who are just plain immoral, prepared knowingly to do the wrong thing. However, in any kind of systematic or societal way, this is just not the norm: "an examination of violent acts and practices across cultures and throughout history shows just the opposite. When people hurt or kill someone, they usually do so because they feel they ought to: they feel it is morally right or even obligatory to be violent" (Fiske and Rai 2014, xxii). The existence of something akin to Just War Theory was almost predetermined.

The Great War

The two World Wars are an interesting contrast. In the First, there was little or no attention to Just War Theory, and, in the Second, there was such attention, albeit imperfect. With respect to proximate causes, the belligerents rather stumbled into the First World War. On June 28, 1914, Archduke Franz Ferdinand, presumptive heir to the throne of the Austro-Hungarian empire, and his wife were shot dead in Sarajevo by a Serbian assassin, Gavrilo

Princip. Austro-Hungary issued an ultimatum to Serbia, which caused Russia, Serbia's ally, to start mobilizing. Austro-Hungary sought backing from Germany, which it received. Meanwhile, France signed a pact with Russia. Austro-Hungary went to war with Serbia, Germany struck out against Russia and France, and the war was on. Britain supported Belgian neutrality and, when Germany invaded Belgium as part of the so-called Schlieffen Plan to get at France from the top, and to deal with the West before turning to Russia in the East, Britain declared war on Germany (MacMillan 2014).

Ultimate causes were several. The French were still sore after their defeat in the Prussian-Franco war of forty years earlier. British foreign policy, since at least the time of Elizabeth, was aimed at making sure not one single nation dominated the continent—as had been the aim of Napoleon. Above all, there were Germany's insecurities. Until 1871, Germany as we know it did not exist. There were many, many independent states. Then, all was unified under the "Iron Chancellor," Otto von Bismarck (Clark 2009). For all that they had defeated the French, Germany was still pain-fully aware that they were poor cousins at the European table, particularly when it came to grabbing real estate around the world to be part of their foreign empire. Something had to be done and what followed was nigh foreordained. Prussia dominated the new union, with the former ruler of Prussia—the Kaiser—as the monarch. Prussia was above all a militaristic society, and this was reflected in the new Germany, which at once started to arm itself—for instance, engaging in an ever-quickening naval arms race with the British, whose ships ruled the world. Combine this with the total inadequacy of the Kaiser from 1888, Wilhelm II, and the pot was ready to boil over. Germany must have more than it has.

The actual outbreak was a surprise. The Canadian author Lucy Maud Montgomery, author of *Anne of Green Gables*, wrote a series following that success, including one that takes place, on Prince Edward Island, during the war. At the beginning of *Rilla of Ingleside* (1921), the assassination is mentioned but hardly noted. "Susan tarried not over uninteresting, immaterial stuff like that." A month later, when the war breaks out—a war that was to come at terrible cost to Canada (and the rest of the Empire)—another character says equally conversationally: "Do you think a war for which Germany has been preparing for twenty years will be over in a few weeks?" Everyone knew it was coming. And this points to the difficulty of making easy judgments about the justice of the war. You might say that Germany was offensive; but, in a way, they rather backed into it, as did everyone else. Conversely, one might say that Britain and France were defensive, but they were really pursuing their own interests and policies, rather than simply acting to right the wrongs inflicted on others.

If we have trouble making judgments, the actual participants were no better off. To be honest, in Britain particularly, there had never been much interest in Just War Theory, a continental idea at the best of times. Cicero, Augustine, Aquinas, Grotius were foreigners, after all. Rather, there were somewhat ad hoc theories of the nineteenth century, designed to justify the conquest of lands in the interests of Empire. In taking over their countries, the British assumed that the inhabitants of these conquered lands could see that these superior white folk were in fact doing them a favor. "There is doubtless an instinctive reaching in nations and masses of people after alteration and readjustment, which has justice in it,' and which rises from real needs" (Mozley 1871). And so on and so forth. Good thinking when you are grabbing ever more parts of Africa but not a great deal of help in the trench warfare in which countries got mired in the Great War.

England has an established church, and its leaders, the bishops, are part of the upper level of government, the House of Lords. The country therefore expected the bishops to provide justification, which they did eagerly. No nonsense about a Just War. The Germans had to be defeated. Simple as that. All means, fair or foul. Virtuous violence. Britain was fighting a "Holy War." Such a form of warfare is distinguished from conflict governed by Just War criteria. For the latter, there are disinterested moral rules to be obeyed. For the former, anything goes so long as it is in the interests of the deity or religious position being endorsed. "Not just independently but repeatedly and centrally, official statements and propaganda declare the war is being fought for God's cause, or for his glory, and such claims pervade the media and organs of popular culture. Moreover, they identify the state and its armed forces as agents or implements of God" (Jenkins 2014, 6). This crucial distinction between Just War and Holy War starts us toward an understanding of the overheated rhetoric of the leaders of the Church of England. "We could not stand by inactive while treaties were trampled underfoot, and namely outrages wreaked on an innocent people. We could not suffer that noble heritage of Liberty and Empire, which we have received from our forefathers, to be stolen from us by brutal aggression of the German autocracy" (quoted in Marrin 1974, 132). Thus, the Bishop of Durham, Hensley Henson. He had nothing on the "Bishop of the Battlefields," Bishop of London, Arthur Winnington-Ingram. "I think the Church can best help the nation first of all by making it realize that it is engaged in a Holy War, and not to be afraid of saying so. Christ died on Good Friday for Freedom, Honour, and Chivalry, and our boys are dying for the same things" (139). Grotius had been wasting his time.

> To save the freedom of the world, to save Liberty's own self, to save the honour of women and the innocence of children, everything that is noblest in Europe, everyone that loves freedom and honour, everyone that puts principle above ease, and life itself beyond mere living, are banded in a great crusade—we cannot deny it—to kill Germans. (175)

Not that the Germans were much better. "German Christianity represents the right relation between Christ and His disciples, and our nature the most perfect consummation of Christianity as a whole. We fight, then, not only for our land and our people; no, for humanity in its most mature form of development; in a word, for Christianity as against degeneration and barbarism" (Bang 1917, 69). And so on and so forth, at length. After it had joined the fray, America likewise did little to redeem itself. The Congregationalist minister Newell Dwight Hillis was all set to sterilize ten million German men and segregate off their women— "that when this generation of Germans goes, civilized cities, states and races may be rid of this awful cancer that must be cut clean out of the body of society" (Hillis 1918, 59). We just have to defeat the Germans first.

Note that with Holy War, as against Just War, everyone on the other side is rightfully an object of hate. "Kill Germans." With such an understanding, one virtually expects atrocities—failure of *jus in bellum*—and one is not disappointed, if that is quite the right word. Best known are the deadly acts against civilians, as Germany invaded Belgium, at the end of August 1914. "The hardest-hit places were Aarschot on 19 August and Andenne on 20 August; the small industrial town of Tamines on the Meuse, where 383 inhabitants were killed on 22 August; the city of Dinant, where, on 23 August, the worst massacre of the invasion left 674 people, one out of every 10 inhabitants, dead; and the university town of Louvain (Leuven), where the treasured university library was burned and 248 civilians killed" (Schaepdrijver 2014). That is just a start: "hundreds of people were executed in the Belgian Ardennes; on one occasion 122 alleged *francs-tireurs* were killed in groups of 10; the last ones had to climb on the mound of corpses to be shot"; and "the invaders made a point of stressing their superiority. One makeshift triumphal arch in the small town of Werchter, north of Louvain, built close to where the victims of a group execution lay buried, bore the inscription 'To the Victorious Warriors.'" (Turn back to Chapter 1, Figure 1.2. The destroyed cathedral in the background is in Louvain.)

There were many other instances of such atrocities, regretfully not confined to one side only. Obviously Just War Theory was being broken: "There are certain Duties to be observed even toward those that have wronged us, for there is a Moderation required in Revenge and Punishment" (Grotius 1625, 3, XI, 1). Even more obviously no one cared that much. Or if they did, they overran their objections—more accurately, working within a Holy War framework, there were no objections. Tear gas, chlo-rine, phosgene, mustard gas. "It is a cowardly form of warfare which does not commend itself to me or other English soldiers." Nevertheless, since winning "can only be done by our copying the enemy in his choice of weapons, we must not refuse to do so" (Cook 1999, 37). Cicero and Kant are ignored.

The Second World War

The Second War is best seen as an extension of the First War. The First War—unlike its successor—did not wipe out Germany, invaded, with no control over its internal running. Alsace-Lorraine was returned to France and other bits and pieces in the East were given up, but otherwise the state was left intact, subject to the demands made in the Versailles Treaty, the result of the victors' meeting in 1919 and deciding on limitations and retributions that should be placed on Germany (MacMillan 2002). After the glory of the prewar state, the Weimar Republic was, unsurprisingly, despised by many Germans; although, to its credit, there were very positive aspects, such as the flowering of the arts. Unfortunately, the Great Depression brought to the end even remote hopes of success—Germany was badly affected, in major part thanks to the heavy debts it had incurred in the United States, as it rebuilt. In the 1920s, the National Socialist (Nazi) party was one of several organizations created to return Germany to greatness, but it was not until the Depression upended everything that its time had come (Evans 2003). In 1933, it came to power—The Third Reich, with Adolf Hitler as its leader, or Führer. In respects, particularly with respect to foreign policy, the Nazis inherited much of pre-First World War thinking, namely that Germany is threatened by its neighbors, and needed room to expand, most obviously eastward since that was where the most open land existed. Particularly with respect to internal policy and linking to external policy, the aim was to rearm and build up the military, so that, in five years or so, war could be launched, with the intent of gaining what was not achieved in the earlier war (Evans 2005; Tooze 2007).

At first, Hitler was strikingly successful in fulfilling his aims. Limitations on the armed forces imposed by the Versailles Treaty were ignored; the demilitarized Rhine was reoccupied; employment was hugely increased, building the army (Wehrmacht), navy (Kriegsmarine), and increasingly air force (Luftwaffe), not to mention civilian projects like the Autobahnen, built with an eye to their military utility. At age twenty-two, in 1936, the future American TV anchorman Howard K. Smith visited Germany for the first time.

> On trains, all day long, one passed long railway caravans of camouflaged tanks, cannon and war trucks lashed to railway flat cars, and freight depots were lined with more of these monsters hooded in brown canvas. In large towns, traffic had to be interrupted at intervals on some days to let cavalcades of unearthly machines, manned by dust-covered, steel helmeted Men-from-Mars roar through the main streets in manœuvres. (Smith 1942, 10)

Then, in 1938, with the Anschluss, Austria (the truncated country that was left at the end of the First War) was incorporated into the general Reich. The Weimar Republic became a bad memory (Gellately 2001). After that, things became more difficult. Hitler reached down into Czechoslovakia and occupied the Sudetenland, the western part of the land, with mainly German speakers. Horrified, but unwilling to start another war, the leaders of Britain and France met with Hitler in Germany and as a result the Munich Agreement was signed, September 30, 1938, giving Germany all it had grabbed in return for no more aggression. "Peace in our time," said the British prime minister—the Appeaser—Neville Chamberlain on his return to England. Unfortunately, it was not to last. In March 1939, Hitler seized the rest of the Czech side of the country, and Chamberlain, realizing that he had been foxed, started rearmament in earnest. War with Germany was coming, soon. He was right. In August 1939, Germany and Russia signed a nonaggression pact, and, on September 1, Germany invaded Poland. On September 3, 1939, in response, Britain and France declared war on Germany (Evans 2009).

Was there more systematic moral thinking in that second worldwide conflict? One would expect so. People were appalled at what had happened in the First War. One among many, the American biologist and peace advocate Vernon Kellogg wrote a devastating account of the Belgium atrocities—*Headquarters Nights* (1917)—and of the indifference of the German leadership. There was serious thinking about moral conduct in war. This was the central theme of the most influential work of them all, Reinhold Niebuhr's *Moral Man and Immoral Society* (1932). He makes a distinction between personal morality and public morality. "The thesis to be elaborated in these pages is that a sharp distinction must be drawn between the moral and social behavior of individuals and of social groups, national, racial, and economic; and that this distinction justifies and necessitates political policies which a purely individualistic ethic must always find embarrassing" (139). At the private level, for the Christian, the Sermon on the Mount is binding. At the public level, however, the individual may have to go against this. Reality intrudes. Moral "achievements are more difficult, if not impossible, for human societies and social groups."

This is not a classical Augustinian position. The saint is quite clear that in a just war, we are behaving morally. "What is the evil in war?" Augustine is not against war as such. He is against "love of violence, revengeful cruelty, fierce and implacable enmity, wild resistance, and the lust for power." This said, Niebuhr, a Lutheran, was obviously going to be much in tune with Augustine. When it came to the Second World War, Niebuhr's position was traditional. All agreed, as would we, that the march into Poland was a violation of the moral rules governing war. This applied even more so to Hitler's unannounced, unprovoked invasion of Russia on June 24, 1941. "Barbarossa." Emboldened by his successes in 1940 in the West, notably the conquest of France, Hitler aimed his forces—3.6 million soldiers, 3,600 tanks, and over 2,700 aircraft—at Moscow. At first, it seemed they were going to be successful, in a short time. However, increasingly the Soviets fought back, and this resistance, combined with the coming of the Russian winter, for which the Wehrmacht was inadequately prepared—shades of Napoleon—meant that the onslaught was halted before it reached Moscow, and the two sides settled into what was to be a four-year bloody struggle.

In a sense, the onslaught was without warning. No prior announcement and, indeed, thanks to the 1939 pact between Germany and the USSR, relations were better than they had been for a long time, if ever. However, if one turns to Hitler's 1925 manifesto, *Mein Kampf,* it is all there. "The foreign policy of a racial state has a duty to protect the existence of the race which forms the state on this planet by creating a natural, strong, and healthy relationship between the number and growth of the people and the quality of the soil and the size of the territory occupied. A healthy relationship only exists when the nutritional needs of a nation are met through its own territory and soil" (Hitler 1925). Apparently, this is a position backed by God—"we are placed on this world to eternally struggle for our daily bread." Adding: "The German people are crowded on an impossibly small territory today and facing a pitiful future, however, this situation has not been decreed by Fate, and to revolt against it is not an insult to Fate." But where to expand? "When we say territory and soil today in Europe, we can only think about Russia and the border-states under her control." And why is this? "The gigantic empire in the east is ripe for collapse. The end of Jewish domination in Russia will also be the end of the Russian state." If ever there was a case for condemnation for manifesting a "love of violence, revengeful cruelty, fierce and implacable enmity, wild resistance, and the lust for power," Hitler's thought and actions fit the bill. Cicero had it right. "All wars are unjust which are undertaken without provocation." You may question whether this applied to William the Conqueror. No questions about Hitler. Although note, significantly, Hitler himself took the invasion out of the Just War domain and pushed it into the Holy War domain. Hence, no need to treat the enemy as full human beings. Almost paradoxically, Hitler confirms fully the thesis about virtuous violence.

Equally, the Allies' response was a paradigmatic example of a justified defensive war. "For only a war waged for revenge or defense can actually be just." I am not sure you would speak of France and Britain as seeking revenge, but they are certainly reacting to Hitler's acts and wanting to knock him down because of them. Even the demand for unconditional surrender was not revenge. It was just terror that we might revert to the unsatisfactory ending of the First War. And revulsion at the totally immoral Nazi state. "A just war is wont to be described as one that avenges wrongs, when a nation or state has to be punished, for refusing to make amends for the wrongs inflicted by its subjects, or to restore what it has seized unjustly" (Aquinas 1981, II, q. 40). Aquinas quoting Augustine.

This said, there was dissent. Pacifists would not agree. They are not playing with Just War rules. One who was playing with such rules and who disagreed was Elizabeth Anscombe, later known as a disciple of Wittgenstein and a powerful analytic philosopher in her own right. As an undergraduate at Oxford, she converted to Catholicism, and then, with the vigor one rather expects from converts—think St Paul—with a coauthor (Norman Daniel), she brought her formidable intellect to bear on the justification for Britain, on the invasion of Poland, declaring war on Germany. She listed the conditions for a just war. "Just occasion (violation of rights); declaration by lawful authority; upright intention; right means of conduct; war the only possible means to right wrong; reasonable hope of victory; and probable good outweighs probable evil" (Anscombe and Daniel 1939, 72). She and her coauthor agreed that some of the conditions were met. The invasion of Poland violated its rights. War was declared by the lawful leaders. There was a reasonable hope of victory. And, if things were to be put right, war was necessary. Their objections started with intention. They didn't think France and Britain really cared a fig for Poland. They just wanted to push Germany down to size, a size less than theirs, as it was at the end of the last war. They also objected strenuously to the belief that this war was going to be constrained by right means of conduct. Modern warfare kills civilians and that is never justified. "The civilian population behind an army does not fulfill the conditions which make it right to kill a man in war. Civilians are not committing wrong acts against those who are defending or restoring rights." And, above all, they denied that the probable good outweighs the probable evil. "Where will it all end?" Answering themselves, "after the war, what prospects have we but of greater poverty, greater difficulties, greater misery than ever, for a space; until just another such war will break out" (81).

With hindsight, this does all rather come across as clever undergraduates trying to get attention. Anscombe's bishop was not pleased. The reasons for the Allies declaring war simply do not seem like people wanting merely to serve their own somewhat shady self-interests. Self-interest certainly, but not to grab things. More to prevent things that were wrong. In 1938, Prime Minister Neville Chamberlain had done all he could to prevent war, for all that he and others saw that Hitler was destroying the European balance of power so central to British foreign policy. Then, "in September 1939, faced with the German invasion of Poland and a tide of national anger, he was forced to commit a country which was by no means fully prepared to a war in defence of France," and to democracy itself (Gooch 1995, 1130). Not that there was much joy about any of this.

> At 1100 on Sunday 3 September 1939, the UK's ultimatum to Germany expired and, for the second time in 21 years, the two countries were at war. The mood of sombre determination with which the UK entered the Second World War—in marked contrast to the rapturous enthusiasm people had displayed in 1914—reflected not only apprehension about the future but also a recognition of the failure of British policies and British politicians over the previous decade. (Gooch 1995, 1129)

This contrasts with the gung-ho attitude, at this time, of Hitler and his fellow Nazis.

Add to this critique of Anscombe and Daniel the fact that, already, there was much evidence of the horrific nature of the Third Reich—*Kristallnacht* for a start—and, over the next years, the Nazis worked flat out to increase this evidence. That was the beginning of the war. After the war, having learned their lesson from the first war, the Allies—led by America—worked hard and gave generously to alleviate "greater poverty, greater difficulties, greater misery than ever." For all that the Soviet Union refused aid and would not let their satellite states like Poland and Hungary benefit, and while one can certainly argue that the Marshall Plan—American aid to Europe—was self-interested, in that it provided somewhat of a buffer as the Cold War began, it was nevertheless incredibly generous. The Nazi leaders were put on trial and executed—proper objects of hate—but this did not generally extend to the populations as a whole. My earliest, very happy memories are of being spoiled by Italian prisoners of war, who were working in the fields of rural England. Many of these prisoners stayed on in Britain after Italy changed sides in 1943. Toward the end of the war, there were many German prisoners. After the War, 25,000 stayed on. The Ruse family was not alone in inviting former enemies into their homes at Christmas.

The one place where Anscombe and Daniel had an important point was over civilians. There is a Catholic doctrine of "double effect" that says things that happen as unintended side-effects should not be judged as things done by intention. It is one thing to bomb a weapons factory, even though there may be civilians nearby who get hurt. It is another thing to bomb a city to kill the inhabitants, as Russia in the Ukraine. The authors had little time for this as an excuse, pretending you are doing the former when really you are doing the latter. Some acts of war are impermissible, and if they are going to be committed, going to war is wrong. If the authors had a point at the beginning of the war, it only intensified as the war continued. Obliteration bombing, trying to destroy cities, without regard to whether one is killing civilians or the military, became official policy by 1943. This left Niebuhr without an adequate response. All war is in some sense immoral, so obliteration bombing is simply more of the same. "Once bombing has been developed as an instrument of warfare, it is not possible to disavow its use without capitulating to the foe who refuses to disavow it" (Niebuhr 2015, 655). As an Augustinian, Niebuhr was committed to us all being tainted by original sin, so no good reason to pick out the bomber for special treatment.

Not everyone was willing to give such a practice an easy pass. Apart from anything else, Niebuhr's position is a bit of an evasion. His general philosophy—that individuals are moral and societies are not—rather lets individuals off the hook when bad things are done. But now, when individuals are doing bad things, Niebuhr scrambles somewhat to fit everything into place. It turns out we are not quite such a "moral man" after all. Some Catholic thinkers, working from a more traditional base, avoided this trap. The American Jesuit John C. Ford had much to say. Obliteration bombing violates Just War Theory and is deeply immoral. Take Hamburg: "The total weight of the bombs dropped on Hamburg in seven days equaled the tonnage dropped on London during the whole of the 1940–1941 blitz" (Ford 1944, 293). Continuing: "An RAF commentator said: To all intents and purposes a city of 1,800,000 inhabitants lies in absolute ruins. . . . It is probably the most complete blotting-out of a city that ever happened. No one can justify this. Ford argued that the problem of obliteration bombing boils down to two questions:

1. Do the majority of civilians in a modern nation at war enjoy a natural-law right of immunity from violent repression?
2. Does obliteration bombing necessarily involve a violation of the rights of innocent civilians? (271)

At once, Ford has his answer: "It is fundamental in the Catholic view that to take the life of an innocent person is always intrinsically wrong, that is, forbidden absolutely by natural law. Neither the state nor any private individual can thus dispose of the lives of the innocent" (272). The young and the old, women, doctors, clergy, teachers, and many others. "If you can believe that these classes of persons deserve to be described as combatants, or deserve to be treated as legitimate objects of violent repression, then I shall not argue further. If, when their governments declare war, these persons are so guilty that they deserve death, or almost any violence to person and property short of death, then let us forget the law of Christian charity, the natural law, and go back to barbarism, admitting that total war has won out and we must submit to it" (283).

One suspects that not everyone will at once concede all Ford's points. He includes women in the category of noncombatants, but apart from female members of the armed forces and the large numbers working in munitions factories, it is a little naïve to suggest that no women are aiding the war effort through the support of soldiers. Overall, though, the case is powerful, and is surely valid today (Grayling 2006). Few would now argue that it was morally right to bomb Dresden, virtually at the end of the war, destroying one of the gems of Europe and killing many people. Just War Theory did not stop the actions, but clearly and unequivocally it judged them wrong. Bishop George Bell of Chichester was one who, during the war, stood up and publicly criticized the bombing, regretfully showing that his fellow Anglican bishops had learned nothing from the previous war (Jasper 1967). The Archbishop of York declared that "it is a lesser evil to bomb the war-loving Germans than to sacrifice the lives of our fellow countrymen" (Maynard 1996, 198). It is thought that Bell's stance so alienated Prime Minister Churchill that, two years later, Bell was denied the Archbishopric of Canterbury. The irony of this whole discussion is that postwar analyses almost universally agreed that, in Europe, obliteration bombing was a failure. It failed to break the spirit of the Germans, and industrial production went on increasing during the war.

Did Just War Theory have any bite? Take up the issue of prisoners. If you look at the bare statistics, in both world wars many Germans were taken prisoner. The raw statistics, however, are a little misleading. The vast bulk of German prisoners of war in the First World War came right at the end, as the whole military operation collapsed (Ferguson 2004, 156). In the Second World War, the figures are even more distorting, because most of the prisoners came after the war was finished (164)! If you go back to the earlier phases of the wars, there are differences. The First World War was a Holy War. Kill all Germans. These were the explicit directions.

> A brigadier was heard by a soldier in the Suffolks to say on the eve of the battle of the Somme: "You may take prisoners, but I don't want to see them." Another soldier, in the 17th Highland Light Infantry, recalled the order "that no quarter was to be shown to the enemy and no prisoners taken." Private Arthur Hubbard of the London Scottish also received strict orders not to take prisoners, "no matter if wounded." His "first job," he recalled, "was when I had finished cutting some of the wire away, to empty my magazine on 3 Germans that came out of their deep dugouts, bleeding badly, and put them out of their misery, they cried for mercy, but I had my orders, they had no feelings whatever for us poor chaps." (Ferguson 2004, 158)

It wasn't until it was almost all over and Germany could no longer fight that huge numbers surrendered and there was no longer felt need or drive to kill them all.

No one could say that the Second World War was squeaky clean. When, late in 1944, Russian troops entered East Prussia, encouraged and egged-on by their superiors, their behavior was truly dreadful. Up to two million German women were raped, some of them sixty or seventy times. This was but one episode of unbelievable behavior on the Eastern Front. "Germans may have summarily executed as many as 600,000 Soviet prisoners; by the end of the first winter of the campaign some 2 million were dead" (Bartov 1996, 117). Later, we shall get details of the German killing squads, following Barbarossa. In the Pacific, neither side was much into the practice of taking prisoners. Apart from anything else, Japanese honor demanded they fight to the end, and, if taken prisoner, they tried to commit suicide. Understandably, Americans were not overly keen on looking to the welfare of their opponents. "It is clear from many accounts that American and Australian forces often shot Japanese surrenderers during the Pacific War. It happened at Guadalcanal, especially after 20 Marines fell victim to a fake Japanese surrender that turned out to be an ambush" (Ferguson 2004, 180). Quasi-amusingly, "a secret intelligence report noted that only the promise of ice cream and three days' leave would suffice to induce American troops not to kill surrendering Japanese" (182).

Back in Europe, to the West, there were many cases of maltreatment of prisoners. Perhaps best known is the German shooting of fifty Allied prisoners after the "Great Escape." The Allies too were not always willing to treat prisoners as fellow human beings. "Yet the scale of prisoner killing—the extent to which soldiers fought to the death—was far less in Western Europe than in Eastern Europe" (184). Indeed: "Massacres of POWs were the exception, not the rule, in the West." One should realize that behavior was not always driven primarily by moral motives but rather by the psychological realization that enemies are more likely to surrender if they expect fair treatment. This said, "only a minority of American soldiers regarded prisoner killing as legitimate." Instructive is the case of Major John Cochran, in March 1945, faced with a sixteen-year-old German boy—a Hitler Youth officer candidate—who first killed one of his men and then surrendered. "I was very emotional over the loss of a good soldier and I grabbed the kid and took off my cartridge belt. I asked him if there were any more like him in the town. He gave me a stare and said, 'I'd rather die than tell you anything.'" Cochran started to beat him up, when: "I was grabbed behind by Chaplain Kerns. He said, 'Don't!' Then he took the crying child away. The chaplain had intervened not only to save a life but to prevent me from committing a murder. Had it not been for the chaplain, I would have" (Ambrose 2002, 548). "Prevent me from committing a murder." People were not saints, but Cicero would have understood and approved.

One should add that, after the War, intertwined with the relief and sense of success, was significant guilt. The bombing and its effects still strike chords today. Not just the Germans. There was sickened realization of the huge sacrifices made by the bomber crews. In Britain, out of 125,000 aircrew, 50,000 were killed (46%), 8,500 wounded in action, and 10,000 became prisoners of war—those, that is, who were not killed by angry civilians as their parachutes floated down on German soil (Chorley 2007, 484). These young men were hardly innocent victims, but they were certainly being used by those in authority, indifferent to the loss of life. Significantly, after the War, "Bomber Harris"—Sir Arthur Harris, head of Bomber Command, and often known as "Butcher Harris"—did not get the customary peerage. He refused it when it was decided not to create a separate campaign medal to the bombers. A memorial to Bomber Command was dedicated only in 2012, and there was and still is lasting guilt and controversy.

Desert Storm

After the Second World War, increasingly people were becoming aware that war demanded serious moral thinking. In America particularly, this awareness intensified. The seemingly endless, seemingly pointless, conflict in Vietnam—My Lai above all— intensified this feeling. No explanation can exonerate Calley, but he should have been taught that this is morally grotesque. It was wrong and should not have been done. It is murder when soldiers "take aim at noncombatants, innocent bystanders (civilians), wounded or disarmed soldiers. If they shoot men trying to surrender or join in the massacre of the inhabitants of a captured town, we have (or ought to have) no hesitation in condemning them" (Walzer 1977, 128). In the light of incidents like these, thinking gathered steam, so much so that when later conflicts arose, people were a lot more ready to offer principles and follow up with detailed analyses.

In August 1990, Iraqis under Saddam Hussein invaded Kuwait. In January 1991, the United States under President George H. W. Bush responded by pushing them out. "Desert Storm." An offensive war by Iraq. In response, a defensive war by the United States. The Americans were led by General Norman Schwarzkopf, with troops on the ground and with advanced military technology like "smart" bombs, guided missiles using laser-guidance systems. The military theorist William V. O'Brien (professor of government at Georgetown University) analyzed the operation in detail from a traditional Just War perspective: "a military action may be legally permissible but not morally permissible if it conflicts substantially with the overall purposes of the just war" (O'Brien 1992, 799).

Rather running our two questions together, mainly because he thought the answers to both were affirmative, O'Brien ticks off the pertinent demands made by Just War Theory, starting with *jus ad bellum*.

1. Competent *authority*: "In the case of Desert Storm, President George Bush had competent authority from two sources: the Constitution of the United States and the Charter of the United Nations as implemented by the Security Council." ["First, the *authority* of the sovereign by whose command the war is to be waged." Aquinas]

2. The cause must be *just*: "These objectives clearly constituted several just causes: recovery of Kuwait, the victim of unjust and unlawful aggression; defense of Saudi Arabia and the Gulf States against the clear and present danger of further Iraqi aggression; restoration of security and stability to the Gulf area, vital for the world's economy and to peace in the

region; and protection of American nationals denied fundamental human rights by the Iraqi regime." ["War is waged in
order that peace may be obtained." Augustine]

3. One must have *comparative justice* against the opponent: "In
the months between the August 1990 invasion and occupation of Kuwait and the beginning of the U.S./U.N. coalition resort to force, there had been abundant evidence that
Saddam Hussein's forces were destroying Kuwait as a social,
political, and economic entity. Comparative justice required
that Kuwait be freed from this kind of occupation and that
Saudi Arabia and the Gulf States be freed from the specter
of suffering Kuwait's fate." ["Refusing to make amends for
the wrongs inflicted by its subjects, or to restore what it has
seized unjustly." Aquinas]

4. The *means employed* must be reasonable in the light of the
desired end: "The air war, launched on January 16–17, 1991,
completely eliminated the Iraqi air force and wrecked the
infrastructure of Iraq's armed forces and military-industrial
complex." "In the event, the timing of the air and ground
wars proved to be incredibly good, and the cost to the U.S./
U.N. coalition forces far less than anticipated. Whether the
cost to the Iraqis was proportionate is another question to
be addressed in the discussion of war-conduct." ["If not for
Justice, yet for Pity, we must not attempt any Thing which
may prove the Destruction of Innocents, unless for some
extraordinary Reasons, and for the Safety of many." Grotius]

5. Reasonable *peaceful alternatives* have been exhausted: "[T]wo
last-minute efforts to discover even a hint that the just objectives of the United States and the United Nations might be

achieved by peaceful means should be viewed in the light of the underlying fact of Iraqi intransigence from August 2, 1990 to January 15, 1991." ["Peace should be the object of your desire; war should be waged only as a necessity." Augustine]

6. *Right intention*: "[T]he right intention objective of establishing a just and lasting peace was promoted by the removal of the Iraqi security threat to the region while permitting Iraq to remain sufficiently united and strong to balance to some extent the power of Iran, another major source of regional instability." ["A just war is wont to be described as one that avenges wrongs." Aquinas]

Then *jus in bello*

7. *Proportion*: "Iraq was a nation mobilized for war. Civilian rights and needs had been and continued to be completely subordinated to the requirements of Saddam Hussein's government and armed forces. The U.S./U.N. coalition forces aimed at a quick, massive destruction of everything that made it possible for Saddam Hussein to wage war, without targeting civilians and civilian targets as such. This war-conduct strategy was proportionate to the political-military goal of defeating Iraq decisively and quickly." ["Tender Age must excuse the Child, and her Sex the Woman." Grotius]

8. *Discrimination* between legitimate and illegitimate targets. "Just war doctrine prohibits direct intentional attacks on noncombatants and civilian targets." "[M]ost U.S./

U.N. coalition actions were discriminatory. This was partly the result of the fact that most of the ground war fighting took place in the desert without the complication of civilians in the combat areas. Adherence to discrimination was also enhanced by complete air superiority and the capabilities of modern air-craft and ordinance." ["Those who apply themselves to the Study of Sciences and Arts beneficial to Mankind." Grotius]

The conclusion:

U.S./U.N. coalition observance of the positive laws of war was outstanding. Treatment of prisoners of war and humanitarian assistance to civilians fully met the requirements of the law. Of particular note is the fact that even before the start of hostilities, the United States renounced the use of chemical and biological and nuclear "weapons of mass destruction," even in retaliation for their use by Iraq. (O'Brien 1992, 822)

One might suspect self-serving, given that O'Brien not only served in the Second World War in the Pacific but also stayed in the Reserves, becoming a lieutenant-colonel. This is as it may. He was also a sometime president of the Catholic Association of International Peace. In the context of his discussion—and remember we are looking at the use of Just War Theory rather than making judgments about such uses—he rightly feels able to conclude: "The laws of war and the injunctions of humanitarian law were observed. Desert Storm was a just war" (823).

Conclusion

Much said already applies directly to other issues. Nuclear war for instance. Elizabeth Anscombe, in a 1957 self-published pamphlet on Hiroshima and Nagasaki—printed to protest the awarding of an honorary degree from Oxford to he who ordered the bombing, former president Harry S. Truman—placed her thinking in the context of Just War Theory. Anscombe agreed that, without using the bomb, the invasion of Japan was going to cause a lot of hurt on both sides, combatants and noncombatants. That was a function of the demand for unconditional surrender. Anscombe was not one who thought such a demand obvious and moral. Even if you agree that the bomb did alleviate the need for conventional fighting, it was wrong. The very use of the bomb entailed that innocent people would be killed, and not as a byproduct but thanks to conscious decision entailing that they would be killed. It is hard, however, to imagine that Anscombe would think that using the bomb was ever morally justified.

Others would agree. In old age, Robert McNamara, one of the architects of the American strategy in Vietnam, had much remorse about the life he had led. I once had an absolutely harrowing breakfast with him. Even more than Vietnam, he regretted the role he played in the Second World War in supplying commanders (especially General Curtis LeMay) risk analyses of the efficiency and costs of obliteration bombing. "Killing some 50 to 90 percent of the people in 67 Japanese cities and then bombing them with two nuclear bombs is not proportional, in the minds of some people, to the objectives we were trying to achieve" (Blight and Lang

2005, 114). Conversely, others would deny that Anscombe had made her case. "In World War II, President Truman was advised that exploding atomic bombs over Hiroshima and Nagasaki was morally necessary in the cost-benefit calculus of winning the war with the fewest American casualties" (Fiske and Rai 2014, 21). He simply was not prepared to sacrifice at least half a million lives in an invasion. One of those potentially lost lives, the literary theorist Paul Fussell (1970), who fought through the Battle of the Bulge, wrote thirty years later of the huge relief he felt to learn that, rather than being shipped out to Asia, he was going home. These emotions apart, even more certainly, many—most—would argue that the demands of unconditional surrender were not wrong. They were morally obligatory. It was not as if the Allies were going to put all the Germans and all the Japanese to the sword.

Revolutionary war is another category not discussed. Just War Theory might be thought to forbid any kind of revolutionary war, be it a more conventional war as the American War of Independence, or a guerilla war, as in Uganda. Remember, we need "the *authority* of the sovereign by whose command the war is to be waged. For it is not the business of a private individual to declare war" (Aquinas). In such cases, as I suggested at the beginning of this chapter, one suspects that there would be denial that the sovereign or equivalent has the standing demanded to exercise authority. If it is without moral underpinning—the English imposing their will on the Americans in the eighteenth century and on the Ugandans in the twentieth—revolutionary war is permissible. But it cannot just happen: "no aggressive behavior will happen unless people doubt the moral worth of the political regime as a whole—in other words, unless they come to view the entire system, as opposed to specific policies, leaders, or outputs, as illegitimate" (Rule 1988, 220). No less than other forms of war, revolutionary war shows there are criteria applicable to those who wage it.

Returning to the main discussion of the chapter, one can hardly pretend that Desert Storm was a conflict of the magnitude of either of the world wars. It does show that, to use a favorite phrase of Karl Popper, we can learn from our mistakes. We can be guided by Just War Theory. The Great War alone shows that the critic, the ex-marine captain, quoted earlier, is making a serious point with huge historical backing. The Second World War and Desert Storm shows the full answer must be more nuanced. That must be conclusion enough for now.

4 | THE CULTURE OF PREJUDICE

What did we learn from our science about prejudice? Most importantly, it is a two-part process, positive and negative. Ingroup and outgroup. First, "as a species we have evolved to rely on cooperation rather than strength, and on social learning rather than instinct as basic adaptations. The result is that, as a species, human beings are characterized by obligatory interdependence" (Brewer 1999, 433). Continuing: "By limiting aid to mutually acknowledged ingroup members, total costs and risks of nonreciprocation can be contained" (433). What does this mean? It means we must stick together with our tribe, however defined. We must promote and cherish, helping others within the tribe and expecting and getting help in return. "Unity is directed towards caring for and supporting the integrity of ingroups through a sense of collective responsibility and common fate. If someone is in need, we must protect and provide for that person; if someone is harmed, the entire group feels violated and must collectively respond" (Fiske and Rai 2014, 18).

Then, second, outgroup. These are people who threaten the internal harmony and stability of your tribe. "Ultimately, many

Why We Hate. Michael Ruse, Oxford University Press. © Oxford University Press 2022.
DOI: 10.1093/oso/9780197621288.003.0005

forms of discrimination and bias may develop not because out-groups are hated, but because positive emotions such as admiration, sympathy, and trust are reserved for the ingroup and withheld from outgroups." But obviously, lack of sympathy and so forth leads easily to dislike and even hatred. We expect a scale, from nonthreatening outsiders whom we tolerate, possibly even like, through those who are dangerous and of whom we should be wary, to those who really are enemies and from whom we must defend ourselves, with force and violence if necessary. "Discrimination between ingroup and outgroups is a matter of relative favoritism toward the ingroup and the absence of equivalent favoritism toward outgroups." In other words, "outgroups can be viewed with indifference, sympathy, even admiration, as long as intergroup distinctiveness is maintained" (Brewer 1999, 434).

Foreigners

What do those on the humanities side of campus have to say about prejudice? Start with Shakespeare. From the Second Act of *Richard II*.

> This royal throne of kings, this sceptred isle,
> This earth of majesty, this seat of Mars,
> This other Eden, demi-paradise,
> This fortress built by Nature for herself
> Against infection and the hand of war,
> This happy breed of men, this little world,

> This precious stone set in the silver sea,
> Which serves it in the office of a wall
> Or as a moat defensive to a house,
> Against the envy of less happier lands,—
> This blessed plot, this earth, this realm, this England.

When I was at primary school in England, there was not a child in the whole country unacquainted with those words. Those of us with Tiger Mothers could recite them.

Ingroup harmony! Don't let's have any guff about the Jews being the Chosen Race. God, who speaks with a King James Version accent, truly has chosen the English. Here we are, on this island, protected from outside forces, and able to live happily together: "This blessed plot, this earth, this realm, this England." Not too much about the outside, because God and nature are protecting us. Although if you want something about outgroup hostility, turn to *Henry V.*

> Once more unto the breach, dear friends, once more;
> Or close the wall up with our English dead.
> In peace there's nothing so becomes a man
> As modest stillness and humility:
> But when the blast of war blows in our ears,
> Then imitate the action of the tiger.

English tigers:

> On, on, you noblest English.
> Whose blood is fet from fathers of war-proof!

You archers—who wreaked such destruction on the French mounted Knights—may be yokels and peasants, but you are Englishmen. (Actually, quite a few were Welsh.)

> Be copy now to men of grosser blood,
> And teach them how to war. And you, good yeoman,
> Whose limbs were made in England, show us here
> The mettle of your pasture; let us swear
> That you are worth your breeding; which I doubt not;
> For there is none of you so mean and base,
> That hath not noble lustre in your eyes.
> I see you stand like greyhounds in the slips,
> Straining upon the start. The game's afoot:
> Follow your spirit, and upon this charge
> Cry "God for Harry, England, and Saint George!"

The emphasis now is on outsiders, seen as a threat, to be stopped by war. "Xenophobia and ethnocentrism are not just essential ingredients of war . . . they instinctively tell men whom to bond with versus whom to fight against" (Ghiglieri 1999, 211). These French are not your friends, they care about themselves and their well-being, not you and your well-being. You know this and you should teach this to your fellow tribe members and especially to the children. Which, of course, is precisely what Shakespeare was doing, nearly two hundred years later. "Wogs begin at Calais," indeed. (Technically, not quite true at the time of Henry V, reigned 1413–1422. The English had ruled Calais since 1347, so it was more a case of "wogs begin after Calais." They lost it in 1558, at end of the reign of Mary.)

Return to the present and Enoch Powell and immigrants. "We must be mad, literally mad, as a nation to be permitting the annual inflow of some 50,000 dependents, . . . It is like watching a nation busily engaged in heaping up its own funeral pyre." If ever there was an appeal to ingroup solidarity, this is it. Those foreigners are threatening us. "What's wrong with racism? Racism is the basis of a nationality. Nations are, upon the whole, united by identity with one another, the self-identification of our citizens, and that's normally due to similarities which are regarded as racial differences" (Powell 1969, 101). Adding: "it's not impossible but it's difficult, for a non-white person to be British" (106).

Remember, although there is prejudice against outsiders, there is not necessarily hatred. You just don't want them around us! Like our American allies in the Second World War. Overpaid! Oversexed! Over here! Seemingly paradoxically—at least to many people—Powell always denied that, because someone was outgroup, he thereby regarded them as inferior. "I have and always will set my face like flint against making any difference between one citizen of this country and another on grounds of his origins." Saying also: "It depends on how you define the word 'racialist.' If you mean being conscious of the differences between men and nations, and from that, races, then we are all racialists. However, if you mean a man who despises a human being because he belongs to another race, or a man who believes that one race is inherently superior to another, then the answer is emphatically 'No' " (Heffer 1998, 504). The threat of immigrants is not their skin color as such, but because they are foreigners. They do not belong. He suggested that the arrival of huge numbers of Germans or Russians into Britain "would be as serious—and in some respects more serious—than could follow from the introduction of a similar number of West Indies or Pakistanis" (Shepherd 1994, 65).

Cross the Atlantic to the New World. Immigrants, immigrants, immigrants. There were a lot. "Though less than 10 percent of the total population, immigration kept rising from 143,439 in 1821–1830 to 599,125 in 1831–1840, then to 1,713,251 in 1841–1850, and to 3,598,214 in 1851–1860." They were not evenly distributed. "Many settled in the big cities, and by 1860, the populations of Milwaukee, Chicago, and St. Louis were more than 50% foreign-born; New York, Cincinnati, Buffalo, and Detroit, more than 45%; Boston, Brooklyn, Pittsburgh, Louisville, New Orleans, and Newark, more than 35%; and Philadelphia and Baltimore, more than 24%" (Perlmutter 1992, 136). As the ingroup became threatened, the reactions and hostility grew in tandem. A striking, albeit somewhat unfortunate, symbol of ingroup threat was concern that the numbers, mainly in the North, were diminishing the powers of the Southern (still slave-owning) states. In reaction, there was the founding and growth of large numbers of nativist clubs—the Order of the American Star, Black Snakes, Tigers, Rough Skins, Red Necks, Thunderbolts, Gladiators, Screw Boats, Hard Times, and more. Best known was the American Party, called the "Know-Nothing" Party, which for a while had considerable electoral success, for instance electing the mayor of Chicago (Levi Boone), who promptly barred immigrants from city jobs.

Asians too came in for their fair—unfair?—share of hostility. In 1871, a mob in Los Angeles's Chinatown murdered nineteen residents. This represented a sentiment confirmed by the passage in 1875 of an act barring the entry of Chinese women—breeding had to be prevented—followed by a more general act in

1882 barring Chinese laborers. Very well known is that, in the Second World War, 120,000 Japanese were interned. 62% of them were American citizens. More recently anti-Asian sentiment was heated up by the Vietnam War, and now of course we have the pandemic, which started in China. All-too-predictably, President Trump referred to the cause as the "Chinese virus." Somewhat more imaginatively he called it the "Kung Flu."

To be open-minded, Trump is ecumenical in his hostility, tinged one suspects with fear—an emotion shared by many of his fellow citizens. He was elected president in 2016 in large part because he was anti-immigrant. "When Mexico sends its people, they're not sending their best. They're sending people that have lots of problems, and they're bringing those problems with them. They're bringing drugs. They're bringing crime. They're rapists" (Scott 2019). Comments a political journalist: "A lot of Americans are susceptible to the kinds of rhetoric that won Trump the presidency: especially his appeals to people's innate xenophobia and fears of threats both internal and external." Continuing: "Trump's campaign rhetoric in 2016 succeeded in attracting the voters most opposed to immigration during the primary. And in the general election, the strong contrast between Trump and Clinton ensured that voters' views of immigration played a larger role at the ballot box than it had in other recent elections" (Edsall 2019). The most obvious symbol of Trump's stance against immigrants is the demand that a huge wall be built between America and Mexico; but, there are many other things that he has enacted to cut the number of immigrants and to return many of them to their own countries. Fears that ingroup identity is being diluted if not lost, leads—as so often—to people shooting themselves in the foot.

Americans, including unemployed Americans, are not rushing to do the backbreaking work involved in picking the fruit and vegetables from the farms of Florida. At the very least, supplies are reduced and prices rise.

Explanations in terms of economics are important. All the evidence we have points to American cultural conflict starting to increase rapidly during the 1970s, exactly the time when major companies were moving in a big way to outsourcing abroad and automation at home. With consequences that neoliberals like Ronald Reagan and Margaret Thatcher, pushing the changes, conveniently failed to mention. Instead of everyone rising together, secure good-paying jobs for the working class were fading, leaving nothing but the smile on the Cheshire Cat, aka fat profits for investors. Literary allusions aside, the key point is that economic factors morph into cultural factors, especially those of the less educated and fortunate in society, who are nevertheless concerned about falling even further down the social scale. It is not just jobs that are lost but also well-established cultural verities. The political scientists Noam Gidron and Peter A. Hall (2019) argue: "Our key contention is that populist politics reflects problems of social integration. That is to say, support for radical parties is likely to be especially high among people who feel they have been socially marginalized, i.e. deprived of the roles and respect normally accorded members of mainstream society." Continuing that "changes in cultural frameworks" are "leading people who hold traditional social attitudes to feel socially marginalized as a result of incongruence between their values and the discourse of mainstream elites. The growing prominence of cultural frameworks promoting gender equality, multiculturalism, secular values and

LGBTQ rights is the most notable of such changes." Not to mention the widely held view that Asians have higher IQs than the rest of us, and hence will push us out of jobs and deny status. Unfortunately: "Steps toward inclusion are double-sided: they can lead people who hold more traditional values to feel marginalized vis-à-vis the main-currents of society." So, such people often "erect social boundaries separating 'respectable' people like themselves from others seen as lower down on that social ladder. Thus, the anti-immigrant and anti-ethnic appeals of populist right parties may be especially attractive to them, because they emphasize such boundaries." "Respectable people like themselves." That about says it all.

Class

A significant feature of a successful class system is that the lines can be crossed. Sometimes, expectedly, the toffs are willing—eager even—to reach out from their class to their advantage. Think of the not-unknown practice of American heiresses—backed by commercial success of their fathers—marrying impecunious members of the British upper classes. Also, one should not assume that rise on the social scale is absolutely impossible. Near the end of the Second World War, the British parliament passed what was known as the "Butler Act," so named after the sponsor, the conservative politician "Rab" Butler. It made it possible for the bright and industrious of all classes to obtain both secondary and tertiary education at the state's expense. One had to show one was qualified by passing the dreaded 11+, a combination of intelligence test and knowledge of the 3 Rs. In many families, said this author with feeling and experience, learning by heart large chunks of Shakespeare was considered a prerequisite for success. Knowledge of the Bard or not—and I say openly that, after Mozart, no one has brought greater joy to my life—it all had the desired effect, with a much-increased flow up from the lower classes to the middle classes. All part of a general trend. In England and elsewhere there was a knock-on, much-increased need of places of higher education—community colleges, technical institutions, universities, and the like. I was one of the first cohort of faculty at a new university founded in 1965 in Ontario, Canada. In that decade, that province alone started six new universities to add to those already there. Similar stories can be told across Anglophone Canada, not to mention eight new universities in Francophone Quebec.

It all paid off. Britain, to take one example, has moved "from a society of school leavers to a society of university graduates" (Sobolewska and Ford 2020, 24; see Figure 4.1). Unfortunately, not only are the elite now larger in number, more comfortable with their place and worth in society—in America, "while non-college households were treading water in terms of wealth, college households have increased their net worth by a factor of three compared to 1971" (Edsall 2020)—but also they are often more visible in their disdain for the uneducated. After the election of Donald Trump as president in 2016, the popular website *Daily Kos* blared forth the headlines "Be Happy for Coal Miners Losing Their Health Insurance," adding, "They're Getting Exactly What They Voted For." ("Racialisation"?) Perceptively, a recent commentator has written: "Sympathy for the working

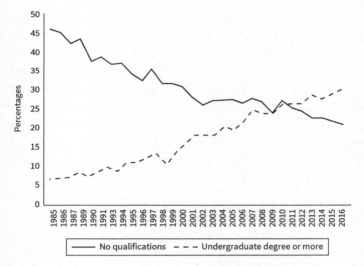

FIGURE 4.1 The change over thirty years, 1985–2015, between those with degrees and those with no such qualifications. (British Social Aptitude Surveys, 1985–2016.)

class has, for many, curdled into contempt" (Lears 2021, 8). The Harvard political philosopher Michael Sandel (2020a) writes: "It is important to remember that most Americans—nearly two-thirds—do not have a four-year college degree. By telling workers that their inadequate education is the reason for their troubles, meritocrats moralize success and failure and unwittingly promote credentialism—an insidious prejudice against those who do not have college degrees." He adds: "Survey research bears out what many working-class voters intuit: At a time when racism and sexism are out of favor (discredited though not eliminated), credentialism is the last acceptable prejudice." Continuing by noting a recent survey: "Beyond revealing the disparaging views that college-educated elites have of less-educated people, the study also found that elites are unembarrassed by this prejudice. They may denounce racism and sexism, but they are unapologetic about their negative attitudes toward the less educated."

In society, as in physics, to every action there is an equal and opposite reaction. Life can be terrifying for those left behind. Frighteningly informative is the following from an opinion piece in the *New York Times*.

In 2016, shortly after Mr. Trump's victory, Katherine J. Cramer, a political scientist at the University of Wisconsin-Madison, summed up the attitudes she observed after years of studying rural Americans: "The way these folks described the world to me, their basic concern was that people like them, in places like theirs, were overlooked and disrespected," she wrote in *Vox*, explaining that her subjects considered "racial minorities on welfare" as well as "lazy urban professionals" working desk jobs to be undeserving of state and federal dollars. People like my neighbors hate that the government is spending money on those who don't look like them and don't live like them—but what I've learned since I came home is that they remain opposed even when they themselves stand to benefit. (Potts 2019, quoting Cramer 2016)

" 'Lazy urban professionals' working at desk jobs." That tells everything. Especially the contempt for education. Remember Arkansas and the question of paying a living wage to librarians.

Really, though, it is a question of respect. "People would talk about opposing social programs because the recipients were lazy and not hardworking like themselves; those were often dog-whistle racist claims. But, at times, they were also talking about the laziness of desk-job white professionals like me." It all adds up. "The way these folks described the world to me, their basic concern was that people like them, in places like theirs, were overlooked and disrespected. They were doing what they perceived good Americans ought to do to have the good life. And the good life seemed to be passing them by."

The philosopher Berit Brogaard points out that this is an emotion—given the name "ressentiment"—discussed by Kierkegaard and more fully by Nietzsche. It "is an unpleasant reaction to a perceived lowly or declining social status that prompts a retaliatory reaction to those perceived as more powerful" (Brogaard 2020, 16). "They are all men of resentment, these physiologically impaired and worm-eaten men, a totally quivering earthly kingdom of subterranean revenge, inexhaustible, insatiable in its outbursts against the fortunate, and equally in its masquerades of revenge, its pretexts for revenge." And to what end? To bring the librarians down to our level. "When would they attain their ultimate, most refined, most sublime triumph of revenge? Undoubtedly, if they could succeed in pushing their own wretchedness, all misery in general, into the consciences of the fortunate, so that the latter one day might begin to be ashamed of their good fortune and perhaps would say to themselves, 'It's shameful to be fortunate. There's too much misery!'" (Nietzsche 1887).

It does not take Nobel Prize ability in economics to grasp the underlying issues. It was hinted at earlier when talking of the support of the English dockers (longshoremen) for the anti-immigrant policies of Enoch Powell. The upper and middle classes may be better off. The lower classes are in a far more precarious position than they were as late as the 1970s. There were good jobs, strong unions, sick and holiday pay, medical insurance, and a pension at the end of it all. That was expected, and given, by an organization like General Motors. No longer. The jobs are gone. Outsourced abroad or replaced by automation. "Treading water" at best. And the prospect is not that things will get better. Force the jobs back to the mainland and all that will happen is that the pace of automation will pick up and the few jobs offered will increasingly demand more education. And even then, the playing field will not be even.

> You are patiently standing in the middle of a long line stretching toward the horizon, where the American Dream awaits. But as you wait, you see people cutting in line ahead of you. Many of these line-cutters are black beneficiaries of affirmative action or welfare. Some are career-driven women pushing into jobs they never had before. Then you see immigrants, Mexicans, Somalis, the Syrian refugees yet to come. . . . Then you see President Barack Hussein Obama waving the line-cutters forward. He's on their side. In fact, isn't he a line-cutter too? (Jackson and Grusky 2018, 1114)

Go back to Arkansas. "This part of Arkansas sits on the Fayetteville Shale, which brought in natural gas exploration in the early 2000s. For about a decade, the gas companies paid local taxes on their property, equipment and the money they made from extracting natural gas, and landowners paid property taxes on the royalties they earned" (Potts 2019). People thought they had died and gone to heaven. All too soon, the vision faded. The price of natural gas plummeted in 2009 and profits declined. Production slowed. One of the biggest natural gas companies in the area, Houston-based Southwestern Energy, stopped paying taxes to the counties here, arguing that the rates were unfair. That about says it all.

> Status has always been part of American politics, but right now a variety of social changes have threatened the status of working class and rural whites who used to feel they had a secure, middle status position in American society—not the glitzy top, but respectable, "Main Street" core of America. The reduction of working-class wages and job security, growing demographic diversity, and increasing urbanization of the population have greatly undercut that sense and fueled political reaction. (Edsall 2020, quoting the sociologist Cecelia L. Ridgeway)

The prospects for change are not good. Even if—to continue with the example we have just been highlighting—gas does revive for a while, it is not going to last. Alternative, carbon-free sources of energy are on the way. In my politically conservative State of Florida—the "Sunshine State"—entrepreneurs have finally realized that there is gold in them thar hills. All over the state, fields of corn or cotton are giving way to huge solar farms. In my first fifteen years in Florida, all my electricity was generated by coal from West Virginia. A railway line runs along the edge of the little park where I walk my dogs every morning. At least twice a week, a train would rumble by carrying scores of open-top hopper cars piled high with coal. No longer. All my electricity is now home-grown solar.

Leave the discussion now. Things are never going to return to where they were. However, while Florida shows that things do change, the crucial question is whether that change can benefit all? As things went wrong for so many, could they also go well for so many? Hold that question. We shall return to it.

Race

In his four-year term of office, President Trump confirmed fifty-three appeals court judges. Not one was African American, or (for brevity) black. No comment. Or, rather, lots of comment. The appalling treatment of and attitudes to black people, from the first, in what is now the United States of America, has always been the gash of original sin, scarring from top to bottom what is, in so many respects, a body to be admired and emulated (Franklin and Higginbotham 2010). In 1619, the first Africans arrived. As we saw earlier, by the time of the Civil War, there were over four million slaves (Figure 4.2). "Let he who is without sin cast the first stone." Tempting though it is to conclude at once that the American slave owners were, to a person, evil people, it is at least worth pausing for a moment and ask what was going on. How could they practice and accept the exploitation of their fellow human beings like this? Prejudice—unlike war—is always wrong. How could people—in many respects surely decent, caring people—for hundreds of years engage in something so very wrong? Obviously, the answer is that

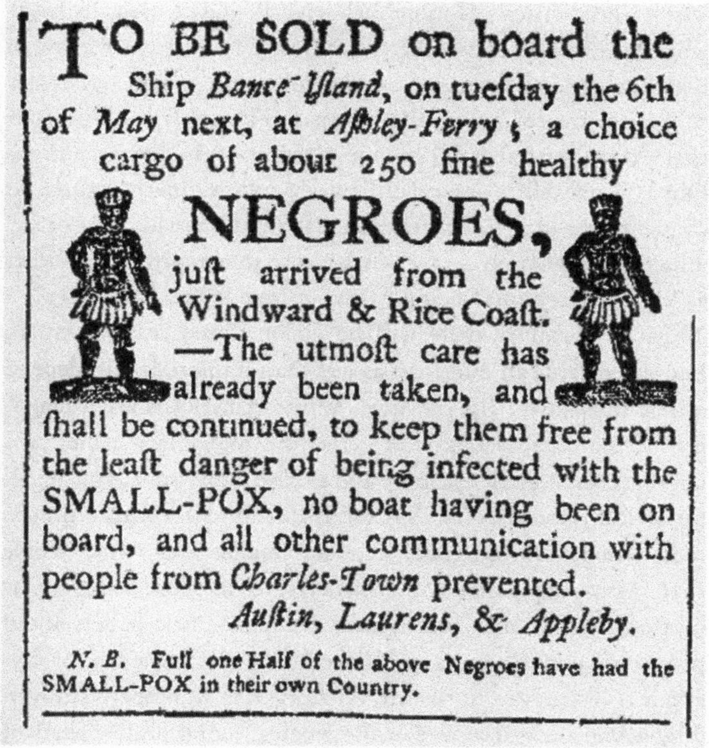

TO BE SOLD on board the Ship *Bance-Island*, on tuesday the 6th of *May* next, at *Ashley-Ferry*; a choice cargo of about 250 fine healthy

NEGROES,

just arrived from the Windward & Rice Coast.
—The utmost care has already been taken, and shall be continued, to keep them free from the least danger of being infected with the SMALL-POX, no boat having been on board, and all other communication with people from *Charles-Town* prevented.

Austin, Laurens, & Appleby.

N. B. Full one Half of the above Negroes have had the SMALL-POX in their own Country.

FIGURE 4.2 Poster for the sale of slaves.

they did not think of themselves as engaging in something so very wrong. It is not prejudice to judge pedophiles lesser people. It is not prejudice to judge black slaves lesser people. This brings out the tension between war and prejudice. Just War Theory presupposes, as we have seen, that the enemy are fully human. That is precisely why we need criteria of moral behavior. Prejudice basically starts when we deny humans their full status. Of course, as we saw in the last chapter, war does not always follow the moral course, and enemy are treated as less than human. Hume (1739–1740) saw that: "If the general of our enemies be successful [Hume mentions Oliver Cromwell!], 'tis with difficulty we allow him the figure and character of a man" (225). The Germans and Russians did not feel ashamed of themselves precisely because they regarded the other as "counterfeit human beings" (Livingstone Smith 2011, 101).

Fairly obviously there will be no one fixed reason why an ingroup regards an outgroup as less than human. It will depend on circumstances. "In the U.S., White Americans are a majority (77%), whereas Latinx Americans (18%), Black Americans (13%), Asian Americans (6%), and Native Americans (1%) are all numerical minorities" (U.S. Census Bureau, 2011). Accordingly, most Americans have more frequent contact with white people than with people of color, which results in more narrow perceptions, unfavorable preferences, and pessimistic beliefs about people of color" (Roberts and Rizzo 2020, 12). In the case of slavery, it is instructive to turn to Aristotle. He is, properly, universally acknowledged as one of the greatest moral philosophers of Western culture. He is also one who, in his *Politics*, argued strenuously for the legitimacy of slavery. It was no hypothetical discussion for, in Aristotle's lifetime, slavery was an accepted practice in Greece. Most slaves were not of Greek origin—in fact, there were questions about whether a Greek could be a slave—so they were "barbarians," meaning (we will not at all be surprised to learn) foreigners. Mrs. Plornish and her neighbors have a distinguished pedigree. The lower classes—peasants, farmers, and so forth—tended not to have slaves, but, as one entered the middle classes, reliance on slavery was the practice. Accepted as the norm and expectation. Now, from our perspective, the question is about how the slaves were regarded. Were they just the conquered who were there, willy-nilly, whether they liked it or not—in other words, slaves by custom rather than nature? Or were they what we might call "natural slaves," people who could properly be put in a slave role, because that was the nature they had. They were simply not up to being leisured philosophers? Aristotle is unambiguous. Slaves are slaves by nature. They are not as high up the ladder of life as are philosophers.

> But is there any one thus intended by nature to be a slave, and for whom such a condition is expedient and right, or rather is not all slavery a violation of nature?
>
> There is no difficulty of answering this question, on grounds both of reason and of fact. For that some should rule and others be ruled is a thing not only necessary, but expedient; from the hour of their birth some are marked out for subjection, others for rule. (Barnes 1984 1989–90; *Politics* 1254^{a}17–23)

"On grounds of reason"? Basically, Aristotle claims that slaves simply don't have the reasoning power of free men. "Where then there is such a difference as that between soul and body, or between men and animals (as in the case of those whose business it is to use their body and can do nothing better), the lower sort are by nature slaves, and it is better for them as for all inferiors that they should be under the rule of a master" (1254^{b}15–21). It is not that slaves don't have reason. Indeed, there were slaves with significant intellectual skills—doctors, teachers, stewards, artists—but, in some respects, they were lacking that crucial ingredient. It is rather as though they are technicians or mechanics, rather like your electrician or plumber, as opposed to the architect who designed the building. "For that which can foresee by the exercise of mind is by nature lord and master, and that which can with its body give effect to such foresight is a subject, and by nature a slave" (1252ᵃ31–33). "The slave has no deliberative faculty at all" (1260ᵃ12–13). Cultivating the virtues is a step up from teaching the ignorant or curing the sick.

"On grounds of fact"? Here, one suspects, is the real force behind Aristotle's claims. He lived in a slave society, and he saw that, day in and day out, slaves had servile roles that they performed. They were not like their masters with the freedom to follow their more theoretical interests. And they accepted this servile role! In his *Social Contract*, Rousseau took the point. Aristotle "had said that men are by no means equal naturally, but that some are born for slavery, and others for dominion."

> Aristotle was right; but he took the effect for the cause. Nothing can be more certain than that every man born in slavery is born for slavery. Slaves lose everything in their chains, even the desire of escaping from them: they love their servitude, as the comrades of Ulysses their brutish condition. If then there are slaves by nature, it is because there have been slaves against nature. Force made the first slaves, and their cowardice perpetuated the condition. (Rousseau 1762, 4)

It is a little misleading to talk of "cowardice." Cowardice means you know the right answer and don't dare take it. Here, the whole point is that you don't know the right answer, because you don't know the right question. You treat someone like a slave, they are your slave, subservient but at the same time taking comfort in the advantages—for instance, that it is in the interests of your master to see you are well fed and healthy. He doesn't want his property to go to ruin. More than one person has noted that, had the Irish been the slaves of the British, the famine would have passed them by because it would have been in the interests of their owners to see that they did not starve. There was food, enough. It was a question of to whom it was going to be given.

What is the moral of all of this? Most obviously, that slavery—race generally—is essentially a cultural phenomenon, which the oppressors think they have a right to keep up and the oppressed frequently accepting this fact. This is so, whether or not there is any underlying objective—biological?—basis to the beliefs. One suspects that many—most?—cases of prejudice have something similar going on. The Aristotle/Rousseau interaction is not entirely different from the working class accepting the superiority of the upper class. Or that the forces leading to hatred and fear of foreigners and immigrants might be at work here. "One factor that may be contributing to the escalation of hostility against non-whites and immigrants is that upward mobility is increasingly more difficult. Deprived of the opportunity of moving up the socio-economic ladder, lower classes among whites are left increasingly searching for scapegoats to blame for their situation, making them easy targets of the manipulation and misinformation of the far right" (Brogaard 2020, 311). Paradoxically, groups suffering from prejudice might themselves show hostility to other groups, that they might thereby affirm their membership of privileged groups. In Texas, at the beginning of the twentieth century, those lynching were often immigrants: "For each of the immigrant groups caught up in the violence—Italians, Irish, and Bohemians—the deaths of black men helped resolve the immigrants' ambiguous racial identity and to bestow the privileges of whiteness" (Nevels 2007, 7).

This all said, notoriously, relationships between whites and blacks were (and still are) complex. Hegel (1807) knew this. The master rules the slave. Increasingly, the master needs the slave. We see ourselves in the other and, at some level, transcend the relationship—thesis, antithesis, synthesis. Overall, whites were oppressing and enslaving the blacks. Thesis. But with people living in close quarters, there was bound to be social intimacy, and very often sexual intimacy. Antithesis. The question becomes about the possibility and nature of Synthesis. Prejudice against foreigners; prejudice against those of different classes; racial prejudice. Do they in some sense contain the seeds of their own termination? Can this be extended to other forms of prejudice?

Sexual Orientation

Poet's Corner, in Westminster Abbey, Britain's most celebrated cathedral, is a small area dedicated to the memories of the country's greatest literary and artistic figures—novelists, playwrights, poets, actors, composers, and others. The first thus commemorated was Geoffrey Chaucer, who wrote the *Canterbury Tales* (late fourteenth century). More recently, the nineteenth-century novelists Jane Austen, Charles Dickens, and George Eliot are honored there. A sacred place is a memorial to the poets of the Great War. On February 14, 1995, just above the monument to Chaucer, a small stained-glass memorial was unveiled to the memory of Oscar Fingal O'Flahertie Wilde. Dame Judi Dench and the noted light actor Michael Denison read an extract from *The Importance of Being Earnest*. Some change is progress. (See Figure 4.3.)

Surprisingly, Charles Darwin—perhaps *malgré lui*—had a hand in this change. From the mid-1830s, when he became an evolutionist, Darwin worried about why males have nonfunctioning female organs. Nipples on the chest, most obviously. Females the other way, too. The clitoris for a start. To explain such phenomena, he accepted the theory, promoted by the Scottish anatomist Robert Knox, of "primordial hermaphroditism" (Brooks 2021). The primeval ancestor of all animals was both male and female. To this day, as Darwin wrote in a private notebook, all human beings show the traces of both sexes—"every man and woman is hermaphrodite" (Darwin 1987, D 162). Came the late 1840s and the massive study of barnacles. Darwin was in clover, or perhaps one should say kelp (Browne 1995, 475–88). He discovered that there are hermaphrodite barnacles, there are hermaphrodite barnacles that nevertheless have males—very small males that Darwin called "complemental males"—that attach themselves for life to the much-larger hermaphrodites, there are females with complemental males, and there are regular two-sexed barnacles. What better proof could one have, thought Darwin, of the hypothesis of primordial hermaphroditism?

FIGURE 4.3 Memorial window to Oscar Wilde in Westminster Abbey.

Continuing, in his post-*Origin* book *The Variation of Plants and Animals under Domestication* (1868), Darwin acknowledged cross-sex behavior and extended it to humans—after discussing birds and mammals, he allowed "we see something of an analogous behaviour in the human species" (2, 51). And he made clear that he extended this observation to sexual behavior. By the time of the *Descent*, Darwin simply had to accept that homosexual behavior was something that would occur in the human species. But he didn't want to say so overtly and he certainly didn't want to allow that such behavior, presumably natural in some sense, was going on among civilized folk today and that it was acceptable. He came up with a good Victorian solution. It's all the fault of the savages!

"The greatest intemperance with savages is no reproach. Their utter licentiousness, not to mention unnatural crimes, is something astounding" (Darwin 1871, 1, 96). Adding: "The hatred of indecency, which appears to us so natural as to be thought innate, and which is so valuable an aid to chastity, is a modern virtue, appertaining exclusively, as Sir G. Staunton [an employee of the East India Company] remarks, to civilised life. This is shewn by the ancient religious rites of various nations, by the drawings on the walls of Pompeii, and by the practices of many savages."

Darwin's reticence fooled no one. One of his correspondents noted that it is more than savages who indulge in homosexual activities. It was to be found in Ancient Greece. "I know no more instructive fact—disagreeable as it is, it is of high scientific interest—than that one practice (to denote it by the general term I have been using), *paiderastia*, in many countries became systematised. Thus in Greece the relation between a man and his youthful lover was constituted by a form of marriage after contract between the relatives on both sides" (Darwin 1985–, 22, 56; letter from John McLennan, February 3, 1874). Then, publicly, the Catholic zoologist and Darwin critic St. George Mivart went after a short piece on human sexuality penned by Darwin's son George. He wrote, in the widely read *Quarterly Review*: "There is no hideous sexual criminality of Pagan days that might not be defended on the principles advocated by the school to which this writer [George Darwin] belongs. This repulsive phenomenon affords a fresh demonstration of what France of the Regency and Pagan Rome long ago demonstrated; namely, how easily the most profound moral corruption can co-exist with the most varied appliances of a complex civilisation" (Mivart, 1874, 70).

The fat was in the fire. Darwin's theory suggests that homosexual behavior is natural. A conclusion quite unacceptable to Mivart; but, manna from heaven to others. Darwin enthusiast, the English naturalist Edmund Selous, noted same-sex activity in birds, writing:

> If we say it is vitiated or perverted instinct, still there must be a natural cause for what we regard as the perversion. As is well known, hermaphroditism preceded, in the march of life, the separation of the sexes, and all of the higher vertebrate animals, including man, retain in their organisms the traces of this early state. If the structure has been partly retained, it does not seem unlikely that the feelings connected with it have, through a long succession of generations, been retained also, and that, though more or less latent, they are still more or less liable to become occasionally active. This view would not only explain such actions as I have here recorded, but many others scattered throughout the whole animal kingdom, and might even help to guide us in the wide domain of human ethics. (Selous, 1902, 182)

"Human ethics"! If homosexuality is natural, then should we condemn it as immoral? Our prejudice should be against people who condemn homosexuality, not those who practice it. They are not so outgroup after all. A conclusion to be explored further, later.

Religion

In the Popery Act of 1698, the British parliament passed onerous laws on Catholics, forbidding them certain positions and the like.

They were not, for instance, allowed to join the army. In 1778, the British parliament passed the Papists Act, which lifted some of these laws. Led by Lord George Gordon, this sparked a fierce reaction by fanatical Protestants, and in 1780 horrendous riots broke out in London (Haywood and Seed 2015). The government sent in the army to contain the troubles, which they did at the cost of probably five hundred lives or more. Charles Dickens wrote a novel, *Barnaby Rudge* (1841), which uses these "Gordon Riots" as background. He writes of the way in which people were pumped up to a frenzy. In the normal course of things, most people would have been quite indifferent to Catholic emancipation. If people want to give up sex to become priests, go through silly ceremonies with even sillier beliefs about bread and wine turning into flesh and blood, and above all letting a foreigner be head of your organization, then there really is no accounting for taste. "If a man had stood on London Bridge, calling till he was hoarse, upon the passers-by, to join with Lord George Gordon, although for an object which no man understood, and which in that very incident had a charm of its own,—the probability is, that he might have influenced a score of people in a month" (Dickens 1841, 277). However, when you start to heat things up, so you feel directly threatened, then action is necessary.

[W]hen the air was filled with whispers of a confederacy among the Popish powers to degrade and enslave England, establish an inquisition in London, and turn the pens of Smithfield market into stakes and cauldrons; when terrors and alarms which no man understood were perpetually broached, both in and out of Parliament, by one enthusiast

who did not understand himself, and bygone bugbears
which had lain quietly in their graves for centuries, were
raised again to haunt the ignorant and credulous; . . . then
the mania spread indeed, and the body, still increasing every
day, grew forty thousand strong. (277–78)

Notice what the prescient Dickens is telling us. As with homosexuals, the mere fact that there were Catholics around was not going
to worry the average Protestant. Live and let live. The Catholics
could even get up to a few tricks and no one was going to be too
much bothered. But when it appeared that the Catholics were
really going to threaten people—"degrade and enslave," "inquisition," "stakes and cauldrons"—then this was really threatening
and terrifying, getting people's dander up. The point is that being
outgroup does not in itself engender hatred and prejudice. There
must be something more. The threat to the ingroup from the outgroup, or from outgroup behavior by members of the ingroup.
Just like sexual orientation. No one cares too much what nature's
gentlemen do in the privacy of their own homes; but, when they
become corrupting schoolteachers, that is another matter. The
outgroup is threatening the ingroup. This is all a manifestation
of the sliding scale of reactions to outgroup individuals. As with
sex, religion is in the heart of things. Dickens knew whereof he
wrote: "A direct relationship between intense ingroup favoritism and outgroup antagonism might also be expected in highly
segmented societies that are differentiated along a single primary
categorization, such as ethnicity or religion" (Brewer 1999, 439).

Atheism does not much alter these conclusions. However, a
recent provocative analysis by the Canadian sociologist Stephen

LeDrew (2016) argues that much of the recent debate sparked by the New Atheists—Richard Dawkins of the *God Delusion* (2006), Sam Harris of *The End of Faith* (2004), and others—is better understood as a manifestation of the class issues that we discussed earlier in this chapter than of something directly involving religious prejudice, for or against. This is clearly the case with the religious. Today, in America especially, those losing out in the class wars are those who often are drawn to a simplistic evangelical Christianity. They identify with Donald Trump because (with reason) they see him equally despised by the educated, the successful, the culturally sophisticated. This is bound up with religion: "Trump's evangelical base does not care who he is or what he does so long as he delivers on Jerusalem, abortion, the trans ban in the military, prayer in school, and the rights of Christian businesses and individuals to discriminate" (Brown 2019, 172–73). LeDrew points out that this goes the other way too. The New Atheists are anything but a representative group of citizens. They are very well-educated, with jobs of high social status—professorships at leading universities and the like—who are in respects appallingly Eurocentric, especially when this is construed in terms of rejection of gross superstition and promotion of science as the solution to all problems, and more. Of this New Atheist movement, LeDrew claims: "The key idea within this ideology is the evolution of society from the premodern phase of religious superstition to the modern phase characterized by scientism and its application to social and political questions and problems. This involves a teleological vision of human progress, with 'premodern' giving way to 'modern' ways of thinking and living" (59). This is from a letter Richard Dawkins penned to an imaginary Muslim woman.

Stop whining, will you. Yes, yes, I know you had your geni-
tals mutilated with a razor blade, and . . . yawn . . . don't tell
me yet again, I know you aren't allowed to drive a car, and
you can't leave the house without a male relative, and your
husband is allowed to beat you, and you'll be stoned to death
if you commit adultery. But stop whining, will you. Think of
the suffering your poor American sisters have to put up with.
(LeDrew 2016, 199, quoting from a blog entry of 2011)

Remember the Harvard philosopher Michael Sandel (2020a):
"Beyond revealing the disparaging views that college-educated
elites have of less-educated people, the study also found that elites
are unembarrassed by this prejudice. They may denounce racism
and sexism, but they are unapologetic about their negative attitudes toward the less educated."

With reason, one might feel that it is Christians who show
prejudice against atheists. In major respects, this is obviously
true and holds today. However, what we have now is a group of
atheists—the New Atheists—who consider themselves superior
to nonatheists, particularly to those like less-sophisticated Muslim
groups and American Evangelicals, the religious groups who set
themselves against science. As one might put it ironically, we have
"a kind of providentialism without God" (Sandel 2020b, 42). As
part of their affirmation of ingroup identity, the New Atheists
belittle and pour scorn upon those to whom they feel superior.
And one of the ways in which they feel superior is in contempt
for those without the intellect and courage to see that God-talk is
almost entirely a function of a fear of death and of the unknown.
It is the same as educated mid-Westerners looking down on the

ignorant yobos who don't now have secure jobs, watch altogether too much television, oppose abortion, and whose kids play football rather than soccer.

Disability

Another Shakespeare play, *Richard III*. Edward, of the House of York, is king of England. The opening soliloquy is by his brother, Richard, Duke of Gloucester.

> Now is the winter of our discontent
> Made glorious summer by this sun of York;
> And all the clouds that lour'd upon our house
> In the deep bosom of the ocean buried.

All seems fair and set to remain so. Richard, however, has other ideas. Things do not bode well for the head of the House of York.

> I, that am rudely stamp'd, and want love's majesty
> To strut before a wanton ambling nymph;
> I, that am curtail'd of this fair proportion,
> Cheated of feature by dissembling nature,
> Deformed, unfinish'd, sent before my time
> Into this breathing world, scarce half made up,
> And that so lamely and unfashionable
> That dogs bark at me as I halt by them;
> Why, I, in this weak piping time of peace,
> Have no delight to pass away the time,

Unless to spy my shadow in the sun
And descant on mine own deformity:
And therefore, since I cannot prove a lover,
To entertain these fair well-spoken days,
I am determined to prove a villain
And hate the idle pleasures of these days.

Tradition has it that Richard was a hunchback; although, the recent discovery of his skeleton suggests that this is an exaggeration (Figure 4.4). Indeed, the whole play is semifictionalized to burnish the House of Tudor (on the throne when the play was written) over the House of York. But, stay with the play and portrait of Richard. Two things stand out. First, he is physically grotesque. The kind of person who repels on sight. "Deformed, unfinish'd." "Lamely and unfashionably." "Mine own deformity." Second, he is a truly evil person: "I am determined to prove a villain." Goals he scores, with some considerable success. These include ordering the murder of his two nephews, the "Princes in the Tower." However, at least from Richard's perspective, to parody the title of another Shakespeare play, all does not end well. He loses his mount at the Battle of Bosworth Field (1485)—"A horse, a horse, my kingdom for a horse"—and is killed by the Earl of Richmond, who promptly crowns himself Henry VII.

Here, as so often, Shakespeare captures so much of the nature and force of prejudice against the disabled. On the one hand, we are repelled (or at least made uncomfortable) by them. They are not the ideal of a human being. Of course, most of us are not, but that makes us especially insecure about our status. What will others think of us? Will they judge us as we judge the deformed? Will

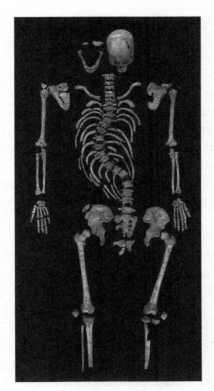

FIGURE 4.4 Richard III skeleton.

they include us in with the deformed? What kicks in is something we shall encounter so strongly when we turn to prejudice against Jews. We define ourselves—we reassure ourselves—against them as the "other." Even if they start in our ingroup, we work to cast them out, make them part of outgroup. And this brings in, on the other hand, the fact that we must justify our feelings and actions to ourselves and others. What better than to argue that those deformed, disabled, are in some way responsible for their fate? It is not their looks or their health, things over which they have no control, that are at stake. It is that morally they are bad, evil. It is right and proper to be against them. Virtuous violence.

Shakespeare was a paradigm, not an exception. From the sublime to the ridiculous, take Captain Hook in J. M. Barrie's play (1904) and subsequent novel (1911) about the boy who never grew up, Peter Pan. The same pattern. A handicapped person—he has lost a hand—who frightens and at the same time who threatens.

> He lay at his ease in a rough chariot drawn and propelled by his men, and instead of a right hand he had the iron hook with which ever and anon he encouraged them to increase their pace. As dogs this terrible man treated and addressed them, and as dogs they obeyed him. In person he was cadaverous and blackavized, and his hair was dressed in long curls, which at a little distance looked like black candles, and gave a singularly threatening expression to his handsome countenance. His eyes were of the blue of the forget-me-not, and of a profound melancholy, save when he was plunging his hook into you, at which time two red spots appeared in them and lit them up horribly.

You are prejudiced against such people but at the same time they give you reason for prejudice. They are threatening to your ingroup. You might think that some forms of disability are nonthreatening.

A person with limited intelligence perhaps? One suspects that while this might be true, at the same time there might be resentment at the burden they represent and, rational or not, a feeling they might do more to help themselves. This apart from the fact that some mental afflictions can be deeply threatening. Renfield the madman in *Dracula* is a case in point. "For half an hour or more Renfield kept getting excited in greater and greater degree. I did not pretend to be watching him, but I kept strict observation all the same. All at once that shifty look came into his eyes which we always see when a madman has seized an idea, and with it the shifty movement of the head and back which asylum attendants come to know so well." At once we know we are in the presence of evil, and so it transpires, as we learn that Dracula has been coaching him to consume, vampire-fashion, various insects and spiders, working up to birds. As vile and dangerous as Richard III and Captain Hook.

Not all the mentally handicapped are like this. Many—most—are rather pathetic. This can bring out the worst in the normal, the healthy. Smike, in Dickens's *Nicholas Nickleby* is a lad who is, in the language of the time, "simple." Employed at a school, Dootheboys Hall run by Wackford Squeers, where the hero Nicholas teaches for a while, his status is made all too clear. A spoon is missing.

A vast deal of searching and rummaging ensued, and it proving fruitless, Smike was called in, and pushed by Mrs. Squeers, and boxed by Mr. Squeers; which course of treatment brightening his intellects, enabled him to suggest that possibly Mrs. Squeers might have the spoon in her pocket, as indeed turned out to be the case.

Mrs. Squeers is now embarrassed: "Smike received another box on the ear for presuming to contradict his mistress, together with a promise of a sound thrashing if he were not more respectful in future." Inadequate, insecure, handicapped—the perfect mark for bullies. In line with what we have seen earlier in this section, Squeers has only one eye, which as cause or effect makes him yet more vile.

"Cause or effect"? Does (or, rather, can) disability make one bad-tempered and dangerous, or is it the case that the bad disposition makes one play up the disability, which need not raise any comment, or prejudice? The great children's novel *The Secret Garden*, by Frances Hodgson Burnett, deals directly with this issue. Mary Lennox is an unattractive, sour child, orphaned in India, sent to Yorkshire to live in the large house of her (absent) uncle. She finds that outside the house, hidden away, is a "secret garden." Gaining access, under the influence of the bracing Yorkshire climate and through the friendship of a local lad, Dickon, she starts to improve in health and to take a more positive attitude to life. She discovers she is not the only child in the house. The uncle has left, in secret, his handicapped son, Colin—the boy's back is twisted, making for pain and inability to function properly. Mary has little time for his self-pity and forces him to realize that his disability is all in his mind. " 'I felt the lump—I felt it,' choked out Colin. 'I knew I should. I shall have a hunch on my back and then I shall die,' and he began to writhe again and turned on his face and sobbed and wailed but he didn't scream." Bad mistake. " 'You didn't feel a lump!' contradicted Mary fiercely. 'If you did it was only a hysterical lump. Hysterics makes lumps. There's nothing the matter with your horrid back—nothing but hysterics! Turn over and let

me look at it!'" Continuing: "'There's not a single lump there!'
she said at last. 'There's not a lump as big as a pin—except backbone lumps, and you can only feel them because you're thin. I've
got backbone lumps myself, and they used to stick out as much as
yours do, until I began to get fatter, and I am not fat enough yet
to hide them. There's not a lump as big as a pin! If you ever say
there is again, I shall laugh!'" Colin is dragged out to the secret
garden, where he too improves, in body and mind. To the great
joy of his returning father. "Across the lawn came the Master of
Misselthwaite and he looked as many of them had never seen him.
And by his side with his head up in the air and his eyes full of
laughter walked as strongly and steadily as any boy in Yorkshire—
Master Colin!"

The point is not to trivialize disability. Rather, to show how
complex an issue it is. The attitudes taken do not have one simple
cause. None of this denies that, morally, we all have an obligation
to love and care for the disabled. Jesus makes that very clear. In
action—"Jesus went throughout Galilee, teaching in their syna-
gogues, proclaiming the good news of the kingdom, and healing
every disease and sickness among the people" (Matthew 4: 23)—
and in words—"For I was hungry and you gave me food, I was
thirsty and you gave me drink, I was a stranger and you welcomed
me, I was naked and you clothed me, I was sick and you visited
me, I was in prison and you came to me" (Matthew 5:35–36).
Quakers, with their belief of God in every person, are fully committed to care and concern for the disabled. My sister trained at
the "Retreat": founded in York in 1796 by the Quaker William
Tuke, it focused on caring for the mentally afflicted within a
family-style environment. Very different from those institutions

and approaches encountered in chapter 2. Secular thinkers also. Kant's moral dictum, the "Categorical Imperative," demands, in its most readily graspable form, that we should treat people as ends, rather than means. Mr. and Mrs. Squeers are hardly treating poor Smike as an end in himself.

The important point is to try to understand why we do not at once spring into action and sometimes, often, do so very much what we ought not to do. Take, to conclude this section, our attitudes and treatment of those injured in war, left with permanent disabilities, perhaps loss of limbs, perhaps mental—shell shock, or, today, PTSD. If any group deserves love and respect, it is theirs. Not so. Often unkindness comes from indifference, resentment, a wish to get on with one's own life. In *Lady Chatterley's Lover*, the baronet, Sir Clifford Chatterley, comes home (from the Great War) badly injured and sterile. Totally dependent on his wife Connie. "Big and strong as he was, he was helpless. He could wheel himself about in a wheeled chair, and he had a sort of bath-chair with a motor attachment, in which he could puff slowly round the park. But alone he was like a lost thing. He needed Connie to be there, to assure him he existed at all." As is well known, things do not go well, or perhaps one might say only too well. Before long, Connie is gallivanting around in the woods with the gamekeeper Mellors, and "John Thomas" and "Lady Jane" are having the time of their lives. By the end of the novel, Clifford and Connie are separated, she hoping to marry Mellors. She is now pregnant; although, it seems that if the child is a boy, he will inherit the baronetage. All does end well.

Connie is not repulsed by Clifford's state. Just unsympathetic. Feeling that, if life has played him a bad trick, life has done no less

for her. Often, as is made clear in the powerful poem, "Disabled,"
by Wilfred Owen, there is more.

> He sat in a wheeled chair, waiting for dark,
> And shivered in his ghastly suit of grey,
> Legless, sewn short at elbow. Through the park
> Voices of boys rang saddening like a hymn,
> Voices of play and pleasure after day,
> Till gathering sleep had mothered them from him.

The lad had been full of life, one of the chaps, until his dreadful
injuries. Life is no longer his; he is at the orders of others. Some
show pity, if manifested in a rather harsh and judgmental way.

> Some cheered him home, but not as crowds cheer Goal.
> Only a solemn man who brought him fruits
> Thanked him; and then inquired about his soul.

Others are simply repelled.

> Now he will never feel again how slim
> Girls' waists are, or how warm their subtle hands,
> All of them touch him like some queer disease.

Wilfred Owen wrote in a tradition. "Sophocles's Philoctetes, a
warrior who fights alongside Odysseus, . . . was bitten by a snake
while on a mission. A hideous wound results that cannot be healed
and frequently becomes painful, infected, bloody, and malodor-
ous. Though he possesses a moral claim as a comrade in need, his

fellow warriors cannot stand to be with him. They can do nothing to heal the wound, which frightens and offends them" (Gerber 1994, 548). Say it again: natural selection is not our friend. The legacy of ingroup thinking persists. Of course, Jesus is right; of course, Quakers are right; of course, Kant is right. We ought to love and cherish young men who gave so much to us all. Why then, as social animals, do we not go right ahead and do this? Because of our evolutionary history. Those of the group who, for whatever reason, could not pull their weight were going to be despised, feared, excluded. They had to be, if the group were to survive. That is, if we the healthy members of the group were to survive. In the next chapter, it will be our task to see if this is the end of the story.

Jews

A huge appeal of the National Socialists was their determination to give Germany that sense of ingroup, of belonging to a unity. *Ein Reich, ein Volk, ein Führer.* As the philosopher Martin Heidegger put it: "The Führer himself and only he is Reality in Germany today and in the future" (Koonz 2003, 194). That tells it all. We in the Third Reich are a living body, a whole, with each one of us a part of that vibrant organism: "the *state* is an enemy; it is to be replaced by the nation, which consists of self-sufficient individuals who collectively choose to sacrifice for a common goal of ethnic or religious glorification" (Stanley 2018, 152). Hitler inherited this way of thinking and it was the foundation of everything he thought and did.

All in all, the National Socialistic conception of state and culture is that of an organic whole. As an organic whole, the Volkish state is more than the sum of its parts, and indeed because of these parts, called individuals, are fitted together to make a higher unity, within which they in turn become capable of a higher level of life achievement, while also enjoying an enhanced sense of security. The individual is bound to this sort of freedom through the fulfillment of his duty in the service of the whole. (Harrington 1996, 176; quoting the party member Karl Zimmerman in 1933)

In old age, my stepmother admitted freely that the happiest years of her life were under the Third Reich. She was forced to join the girl's equivalent of the Hitler Youth—*Bund Deutscher Mädel*. Hiking in the Taunus mountains, nights out sleeping under canvas, singsongs around the campfire. A wonderful sense of belonging and joy at being part of the German family. Above all, indoctrination into the duty of self-sacrifice to the Reich. No wonder these were such memorable times in the life of a lonely only child of rather precious, elderly parents, devotees of the polymath and mystical guru Rudolf Steiner, who would never let her play with other children because they were "not good enough." As the war entered its third year and my stepmother her fourteenth: "It, alone of the civilian population is not demoralized; it is enthusiastic and keeps crying for more of the same. It remains, due to the many favours shown it, the most enthusiastic supporter of Adolf Hitler. I mean the German Youth; the little boys and girls" (Smith 1942, 172). Dr. Goebbels, the propaganda minister, knew his job. (See Figure 4.5.)

My Führer

I know you well and love you like my father and mother.

I will always obey you like my father and mother.

And when I grow up, I will help you like father and mother.

And you should be proud of me, like my father and mother.

FIGURE 4.5 Hitler and children. (Otto Zimmermann, *Hand in Hand fürs Vaterland*, 1936.)

A holistic ingroup. But what then of outsiders? Our theory tells us that because someone is an outsider they are not necessarily considered a danger or an enemy. Hitler's attitude toward Asians illustrates this perfectly. He did not consider them a threat, far from it, and during the war grew ever closer to the Japanese.

Pride in one's own race, and that does not imply contempt for other races, is also a normal and healthy sentiment. I have never regarded the Chinese or the Japanese as being inferior to ourselves. They belong to ancient civilizations, and I admit freely that their past history is superior to our own. They have the right to be proud of their past, just as we have the right to be proud of the civilization to which we belong. Indeed, I believe the more steadfast the Chinese and the Japanese remain in their pride of race, the easier I shall find it to get on with them. (Adolf Hitler, *The Political Testament of Adolf Hitler*, Note #5, February 1945–April 1945)

The Jews were different. They were on the spot, and already there was a history of anti-Semitism. They were a perfect target. There was work to do. Germany in the nineteenth century was notable for its enlightened treatment of its Jewish population, removing all sorts of barriers and allowing them to enter in full societal roles and acceptance. This continued into the twentieth century and beyond the Great War. Until Hitler came to power, 20% of Jews were marrying Gentiles (Lowenstein 2005). The needs of the ingroup necessitated identifying an outgroup and pumping up its unacceptable nature. This may not have convinced all Germans. Hitler's rhetoric certainly convinced Hitler himself. After Pearl Harbor, the immediate assumption was that the main driving factor behind America's reaction was the influence of Jews on the president, Franklin Roosevelt. Five days later, Hitler declared war on the United States. The day after, December 13, 1941, Goebbels wrote in his diary: "Regarding the Jewish question, the Führer is determined to settle the matter once and for all. He prophesied that if the Jews once again brought about a world war, they would experience their extermination. This was not an empty phrase. The world war is here. The extermination of the Jews must be its necessary consequence" (Herf 2006, 132). The Wannsee conference was less than two months later. Like all vermin, the Jews were dangerous and had to be eliminated. The outgroup was a threat to the ingroup and had to be dealt with accordingly. "The Final Solution did not develop as evil incarnate but rather as the dark side of ethnic righteousness" (Koonz 2003, 273).

Women

Women are very obviously not "others." For men, they are your mothers, your sisters, your wives, your daughters. And, likewise, men are fathers, brothers, husbands, sons for women. If you are thinking in terms of hunter-gatherer groups, the whole point is that the group must be integrated, with men and women both playing their roles, be it hunting or gathering, raising children, settling intragroup disputes. That said, men are not women and women are not men. And as guided by Aristotle and St. Paul, together with many, many others, men have traditionally been inclined to assert their authority, under the guise of superiority. And, once again, showing how the prejudiced-against internalize their secondary status, women have often, if not always, accepted it. One is amazed for instance to find how many intelligent, educated women opposed female suffrage. And while we may not accept their arguments, they were not obviously stupid. A major line was that the proper and most fruitful relationship between men and women is cooperation rather than competition.

This said, there are two points worth making. First, if one takes seriously the claim that hunter-gathers did not have the gender divisions of postagricultural societies, one should surely expect that even today there are going to be notable exceptions to the male dominance role. Culture may have had a major role in today's inequalities. No argument has been given that culture is directly backed by biology. And indeed, there are many examples where women did seize (or were given) the reins of power, using them effectively. No English monarch is as venerated as "Good Queen Bess," Elizabeth the First. In her long reign, England became firmly Protestant and was defended from outside threats, Spain particularly. She knew to cover her options. She was good at using her supposedly inferior nature to assert her superior wielding of power. From her speech at Tilbury (July 1588), to her troops gathered to repel the Spanish Armada.

> I know I have the body of a weak, feeble woman; but I have the heart and stomach of a king, and of a king of England too, and think foul scorn that Parma or Spain, or any prince of Europe, should dare to invade the borders of my realm; to which rather than any dishonor shall grow by me, I myself will take up arms, I myself will be your general, judge, and rewarder of every one of your virtues in the field. (Marcus, Mueller, and Rose 2002, 325)

From his grave, Plato was letting out a large hurrah!

The second point is that if women are freed from culturally imposed tasks, there is absolutely no reason at all to think they will prove less intelligent or able to control and direct things. Plotting the expected path of an antelope demands the ability to think and then to put these thoughts to full use. Designing and making traps for smaller mammals seem to demand no less ability to think and then to put the thoughts into action. For what it is worth, today the top-flight mathematicians tend to be male; but, against that, very talented mathematical females tend to be better at verbal skills than talented males. As the latter might say, six of one and half a dozen of the other. Certainly, anyone who has been in universities in the past half century can and will tell you that, when they are given the chance, young women are as good at if not better than young men.

> Roughly half the [American] population is female, and by most measures they are faring well academically. Consider that by age 25, over one-third of women have completed college (versus 29% of males); women outperform men in nearly all high school and college courses, including mathematics; women now comprise 48% of all college math majors; and women enter graduate and professional schools in numbers equal to most, but not all fields (currently women comprise 50% of MDs, 75% of veterinary medicine doctorates, 48% of life science PhDs, and 68% of psychology PhDs). (Ceci and Williams 2009, 5)

How has this all happened? Two obvious reasons. First, machines have transformed women's lives, at least in the West. No longer is the week dominated by washing by hand in the tub, hanging the clothes out to dry whenever there is a trace of sunshine, and then ironing—and more ironing—followed by folding and putting in the airing cupboard. Thanks to enterprises like the Bendix washing machine company—it first started making washers in 1938—lives filled with drudgery were no more. Hours spent over soapsuds could be replaced by hours over calculus textbooks. Another discovery freeing women and making them much more equal and ready to compete with men was the coming of the birth control pill in the 1960s. David Lodge's novel, *How Far Can You Go* (1980), about young Catholics at university in the late 1950s, and then the changes that came in the succeeding years, is a satirical but revealing account of how the status of young women changed from vulnerable creatures needing protection from savage predators—young men!—to equals socially and sexually. Humans, more than ready to take the forward, dominant role.

Humans are intelligent, social beings. There is nothing in Darwinian theory that says, for the optimal functioning of a group, males must be dominant over females. Perhaps in a postagricultural society, as with war, there will be factors that bring this on. A much-increased number of children on whom women are by necessity obliged to focus. But as and when these factors change or are reduced or eliminated—machines and contraceptives—so the necessity of male dominance will change or be reduced or eliminated. Women can regain their earlier status.

Time now to move on, changing direction somewhat. We need to see how what we have learned thus far can help us in our thinking about hatred, its reasons and possible ways of, if not eliminating it, bringing it under much greater control than has been the case in the past and is, alas, in major respects still the case today. Increasingly, there have been heavy-handed hints about how we might go about our task. Let us see if these hints lead to sound strategy.

5 | MOVING FORWARD

Human Nature

War and prejudice are moral issues. Philosophers divide questions about morality into two layers. First, there is "substantive" or "normative" ethics. What should I do? We know the answer to this. We are social beings. That is our nature. Darwinian selection has made us that way. Ethics—substantive ethics—is the tool by which we express and regulate our sociality. To be colloquial, it is what keeps us on the straight and narrow. It distinguishes good from bad, right from wrong. This is not to say that we always do or want to do what is good, what is right; but, generally, it keeps us in line. If it didn't work, we wouldn't be here. Claims like that of Thomas Henry Huxley, that morality, substantive ethics, goes against and hopefully controls our animal nature, are simply wrong. Empirically wrong. The same is true of the claims of people like Friedrich von Bernhardi, that war is natural and a good. War is a distortion, something forcing us away from our nature, something brought on by the advent of civilization.

Why We Hate. Michael Ruse, Oxford University Press. © Oxford University Press 2022.
DOI: 10.1093/oso/9780197621288.003.0006

In arguing that doing good is doing what is natural for us, there is no call for radical revision of over two thousand years of philosophers writing on this topic: "it is easy to forget that the major ethical theories of the philosophical tradition, and the major world religions, have more in common on the question of what is good, than otherwise" (Grayling 2006, 182). Aristotle, in his *Nicomachean Ethics*, argues that we should be virtuous; when Kant (1785) posits his earlier-mentioned "Categorical Imperative," the most readily graspable form is that we should treat people as ends, rather than means; and John Stuart Mill (1863), a "utilitarian," insists we should promote happiness and reduce unhappiness. Of course, we should take their advice and commands. What unites them all is the directive to do what is natural, to go with our human nature. It is natural to help a child who is lost and crying. It is what we ought to do. We are being virtuous; we are caring about the child because the child is a person and worthy of care in their own right; and we are maximizing happiness and minimizing unhappiness. It is unnatural to push a stranger under a train. It is not what we ought to do. It is not virtuous; we are not treating the stranger as an end but rather as a means to satisfy our perverted lust; and we are certainly not maximizing happiness. When our philosophers would differ, over the morality of slavery for example, the difference is not over the need to be natural, but over what constitutes "natural." Aristotle thought that by nature slaves are not the equals of Greeks. Kant (1785), typically, had a convoluted argument that one cannot ever sell oneself into slavery! Mill (1848), equally typically, was blunt. Involvement in the slave trade, "will be a lasting blot in English history" (312).

The second layer of moral understanding is "metaethics." Why should I do what I should do? For the Christian, as we have seen, doing what is natural is doing what God wants of us. "Every act of reason and will in us is based on that which is according to nature, . . . Accordingly the first direction of our acts to their end must needs be in virtue of the natural law." And God stands behind this, for the "light of natural reason, whereby we discern what is good and what is evil, which is the function of the natural law, is nothing else than an imprint on us of the Divine light. It is therefore evident that the natural law is nothing else than the rational creature's participation in the eternal law" (Aquinas 1981, *Summa Theologica*, IaIIae 91, 2). End of argument; although, note that, as with slavery, there are often disagreements about what is natural. These are based more on matters of fact that on issues strictly ethical. Is it right to practice artificial birth control? Pope Paul VI said it is unnatural, and hence wrong. It turns relationships between men and women into little more than opportunities for sexual gratification for pleasure. Others, good Christians, say it is not unnatural to use contraceptives, and hence can be a moral good. Their use can lead to responsible family planning and does not turn the users into immoral pleasure seekers, indifferent to human relationships. The very opposite.

For the nonbeliever, facts are also important, but what about the ultimate justification? The argument is that being natural in some sense gives an all-important feeling of self-worth: eudaimonia. That's how natural selection gets its results. Happiness? Mill's predecessor, Jeremy Bentham (1830), notoriously said that "pushpin is as good as poetry." In a sense, this is true. "All work and no play makes Jack a dull boy." There is nothing wrong with going out with your pals to the faculty club for a few beers. But happiness in the present context is somewhat more ethereal. A justifiable pride in having done the right thing. Aristotle tells us that "happiness is an activity of the soul in accordance with perfect virtue." Kant opines that "benevolence or goodwill is the pleasure we take in the prosperity and happiness of our neighbour." Mill talks of "dignity," of trying to avoid what one feels is "a lower grade of existence." He points out, something with which Aristotle and Kant agree entirely, that this is all bound up with humans being thinking beings, of being rational. That is what is truly natural. Himmler was evil in a way that a man-eating tiger is not. Himmler had the power of reason to know that what he was doing was wrong. The tiger does not. This leads to one of the most famous quotes in the whole of philosophy. "It is better to be a human being dissatisfied than a pig satisfied; better to be Socrates dissatisfied than a fool satisfied. And if the fool, or the pig, are of a different opinion, it is because they only know their own side of the question. The other party to the comparison knows both sides."

Human nature. We are social beings, and morality is a major factor behind our sociality. Mill again: "When people who are tolerably fortunate in their outward lot do not find in life sufficient enjoyment to make it valuable to them, the cause generally is, caring for nobody but themselves." We help each other because we think we should help each other. We cannot go it alone. "No man is an island." Darwinian thinking demands morality. Believer and nonbeliever can agree on this. Morality exists, and only exists, to keep us functioning efficiently as we have been fashioned by natural selection. The believer thinks there is something behind all of this; the nonbeliever is not so sure. But on the need to be natural, they come together. Immoral behavior like My Lai is not a predetermined result of our biological nature, but an unfortunate consequence of the distorting effects of the environment, including culture. To do the right thing is to reveal our true nature and to try to act as it dictates.

The Morality of War

Let's turn now to our interests, starting with war. The key is going to be that the force of change is individual selection, not group selection. This means that, if indeed individual selection is behind our morality, then, although we are social beings and would expect our moral understanding and domain to extend to all human beings, we are going to expect a gradient: Ingroup/outgroup kind of thinking. The Parable of the Good Samaritan rather suggests that we have equal obligations to all, and the Australian philosopher Peter Singer (1972) has argued along similar lines. "The fact that a person is physically near to us, so that we have personal contact with him, may make it more likely that we shall assist him, but this does not show that we ought to help him rather than another who happens to be further away" (232). Even without invoking Darwin, many—starting with David Hume—would disagree with this. "A man naturally loves his children better than his nephews, his nephews better than his cousins, his cousins better than strangers, where everything else is equal. Hence arise our common measures of duty, in preferring the one to the other. Our sense of duty always follows the common and natural course of our passions" (Hume 1739–1740, 483–484). The Bible, as so often, is ecumenical on the topic. "Anyone who does not provide for their relatives, and especially for their own household, has denied the faith and is worse than an unbeliever" (I Timothy 5:8). And generally, if one heard of someone buying their way into the Kingdom of Heaven by sending the bulk of their salary to feed the needy poor in Africa—Mrs. Jellyby in *Bleak House*—while their own kids are fed from a foodbank and clothed from Good Will, if that—Jo, the crossing sweeper in the same novel—one would recoil with horror. It's not natural!

One can see at once how all of this, backed by Darwinian causes, helps explain our preparedness to go to war. We have greater obligations to members of our own tribe than to members of other tribes. While we may not want to go to war, sometimes we feel we must. Morally must. It is not that we innately hate the outgroup, and it is certainly not that we want to plunge into war; but, if the circumstances bring these things on, then so be it. We can't be pals with and help everybody. "Our brains were not designed to care deeply about the happiness of strangers. Indeed our brains might indeed be designed for indifference or malevolence toward strangers" (Greene 2013, 257). In the language of Just War Theory, *jus ad bellum*. Note, in the light of much we have learned earlier, this does not mean that we must go to war, or that we are necessarily justified in building up the kind of military-influenced society that was pre–Great War Germany. Darwinism doesn't offer much justification for aggressive war. Simply going out and grabbing what others have because we want them finds no place in our ethics. It is defensive war that Darwinism allows. Encourages even.

This said, because we have greater obligations to our own tribe, it does not follow that what Peter Singer says is totally irrelevant. If only on grounds of reciprocal altruism, there is value in treating the enemy as human beings—we respect you, you respect us. Just War Theory—*jus in bello*. Darwinian moral thinking endorses the imperatives of someone like Aquinas or Grotius. If you set out to bomb women and children, with the aim of bringing an enemy to its knees, you are not doing the right thing. Again, if only on grounds of reciprocal altruism, one must treat prisoners with dignity. Although one is surely being urged to go beyond crude self-interest. The enemy are fellow humans. Starving prisoners or making them work to their literal death in the mines, as was the practice of the Nazis toward the Russians, is hardly inculcating a sense of self-worth. You are certainly not treating them as ends in themselves. Decent, virtuous people don't need help to see that what the Germans did to the Russian prisoners was wrong. People intent on promoting happiness do not treat Russian prisoners as did the Germans; nor do they behave to German women as the Russians did in East Prussia. Our values come from us, they are part of our nature, and we are proud that we have our duties and obligations. It is our abilities and responsibilities that give us reason to cherish our high status. The Germans and Russians should have been ashamed of themselves. The same is true of those who pushed for obliteration bombing.

Avoiding War

Let us recap briefly pertinent events of the two world wars of the last century, one that should not have been fought and one that had to be fought. With respect to the First World War, just like the character in *Rilla of Ingleside*, many people from many countries were convinced that war was coming. It was just a matter of time. But why was it "inevitable"? As a preliminary to asking about the possibility of change, start right in with the "killer ape" hypothesis. Is it plausible to think in terms of innate human violence and does this help in understanding the beginning of World War I? The answer is: "Not a great deal." Prussia had a dominant military caste and spoke for all the states (Clark 2009). It was sufficiently powerful that it had direct access to the Kaiser and acted independently of the civilian leaders. One result was the start of that already-mentioned naval arms race with Britain, building massive battle ships. The British—who already had by far the largest navy in the world—responded by building massive battle ships of their own. The enthusiasm for battle shown by members of the German General Staff is no great surprise. *Headquarters Nights* (1917) makes painfully clear the aggressive nature of their thinking. There was nothing particularly innate about any of this. A boy from the Junker class—Prussian landed nobility—was sent off to military academy at a very young age, and from then on it was nonstop training of the intensity that we usually associate with ballet dancers or—those who know *Oliver Twist* will recall how Fagin trained his young associates— pickpockets. If they had not come from a country that had had to fight nonstop for its place in the sun, if they had been packed off to Plato's Academy, where all the training would have been directed at serving the good of the state, they would have been very different. Say what you will about philosopher kings, they are not killer apes. Believe me.

At the individual level, there were certainly those as blood-thirsty as Robert Ardrey sketched out. Almost continuously from 1906 to 1917, Count Franz Conrad von Hötzendorf was the Austro-Hungarian chief of state. He wanted to declare preventa-tive war on Italy to counter its influence in the Balkans and the Adriatic. Serbia was another target of his hate. Again, the chances of a preventative war were missed. "The army . . . is an instrument to be used by goal-conscious, clever politicians as the ultimate defence of their interests" (MacMillan 2014, 236). And so on and so forth. However, what is remarkable is how many people were not bloodthirsty, stumbling into situations for the peaceful resolution of which they were totally incapable. Tsar Nicholas of Russia was a paradigm case—inclined "towards peace" he was nevertheless "weak and easily swayed" (584). The tragedy was that, unlike Britain, where the monarch has no political power, in Russia the Tsar was all powerful. As also in Germany. Would that someone had taken note of Immanuel Kant. He warned of the dangers of hereditary leaders having power. Being born to their position, they just don't care: "the plunging into war is the least serious thing in the world." Worse than that, for such a ruler "does not lose a whit by the war, while he goes on enjoying the delights of his table or sport, or of his pleasure palaces and gala days. He can therefore decide on war for the most trifling reasons, as if it were a kind of pleasure party" (Kant 1795, 123).

"Gala days"! One senses that, later in life, the Kaiser's happi-est memories involved parades of robot-like troops, in smart uni-forms, with horses and bands. Whatever. Wilhelm was a complete disaster as a leader. Constantly changing his mind, now asserting authority and now doing nothing, flattering and yelling, he was everything one does not need, starting with the appalling decision to drop Bismarck just as soon as he possibly could. Anyone further from a killer ape it would be hard to imagine—"he shrank from war as soon as he had actually to confront its reality" (MacMillan 2014, 590). Franz Ferdinand, heir to the throne of Austro-Hungary and whose assassination was the spark that lit the tinder, was by all accounts not a very nice man—"greedy, demanding, intolerant." Anti-Semitic too. But he didn't want war and was going to fire Conrad at the first opportunity.

England tells a similar story. Admiral "Jacky" Fisher was all set to launch a preventative strike against the German navy. "My God, Fisher, you must be mad!" was the reaction of his monarch, George V (130). The foreign secretary Sir Edward Grey was very unwilling to go to war—he would rather go birdwatching—and changed his mind only on the worry that Germany intended to invade Belgium, whether the Belgians liked that idea or not. This hesitancy was reflected in the nation as a whole, with the moral obligation to honor our treaties conflicting with the idea that really it isn't our fight. Apart from anything else, no one could stomach Belgium given the appalling exploitation of the inhabitants of the Congo, where small children had their hands and feet amputated if they failed to meet their daily rubber quota (Ewans 2002). So much for the cause of the First World War being original sin and its sidekick, the killer-ape hypothesis. Better bemoan the lack of wiser people, of more sensible political systems. The war need not and should not have happened. And it is no real counter to say that the ever-increasing and more dominant Germany made war inevitable. Herbert Spencer (1892) particularly stressed how trade neutralizes war enthusiasm. Since the Second World

War, Germany has again emerged as the dominant country. But now, thanks particularly to the EU, its fate is so bound up with the fates of others, that war would simply be stupid. To refer yet again to Kant, he stressed again and again the need to form organizations connecting different countries: "reason, from her throne of the supreme law-giving moral power, absolutely condemns war as a morally lawful proceeding, and makes a state of peace, on the other hand, an immediate duty. Without a compact between the nations, however, this state of peace cannot be established or assured" (Kant 1795, 133–34).

Going over material already introduced but stressing and highlighting issues pertinent to our interests here, about killer apes and the inevitability of conflict, move on to the second example, the origins of the Second World War in Europe. Remember, the Second War is best seen as an extension of the First War. The eleventh hour, of the eleventh day, of the eleventh month marks Armistice Day, not Unconditional Surrender Day. Germany defeated, but still left to run its own internal business. To say that no one behaved particularly sensibly during the postwar era is nigh tautological. In 1923, aggravated that Germany was not paying its retributions as demanded by the postwar Versailles Treaty, France invaded the Ruhr, causing massive inflation with the German middle-classes losing all and reduced to penury. It was to be expected that, in response to the troubled times, right-wing groups would begin to organize in Germany. The Munich Putsch of 1923, when the National Socialists tried to take over Bavaria—leading to Hitler being incarcerated (during which time he wrote *Mein Kampf*)—was but one episode. It was hardly foreordained, but with hindsight entirely understandable that Hitler and his Nazi Party were able to seize power in 1933, and the Third Reich was underway.

Hitler always intended conquest in the East. Remember, on September 1, Germany invaded Poland. On September 3, 1939, in response, Britain and France declared war on Germany. The rest, as they say, is history. Our tale takes us to its conclusion in the United States of America. Franklin Roosevelt, the president, was always favorably inclined toward Britain, but with reserve. There were strong isolationist sentiments in the United States, with the feeling that this is "not our war." Increasingly, however, Roosevelt did much to aid Britain—France was now conquered and Russia came only belatedly on the scene. Matters were taken out of American hands. We know already that, on December 7, 1941, the Japanese bombed the American fleet at anchor in Pearl Harbor, in the Hawaii archipelago. War was on, and a day or two later Germany declared war on the United States, so once again America was dragged into a European conflict, which was to last until the Allies were victorious in 1945.

Does any of this demand the killer ape hypothesis? Glossing over his looks, if anyone was a killer ape, it was Adolf Hitler. Whether this was innate or acquired is almost irrelevant; and, in a sense, unanswerable. Had Germany after 1918 not been the shattered, insecure country that it was, Hitler could hardly have been a success (Staub 1992, 24). One much doubts that a Hitler, in the Canada of today, would within a decade end up as all-powerful Führer. Canadians don't like pushy people. That said, one can point to factors in Hitler's early life that much influenced him, for example the anti-Semitism he encountered as a young man living in Vienna—the mayor, Karl Lueger, was notorious in this respect—as well as the feeling of despair at the loss of the war and the desolation in the early years thereafter (Kershaw 1999). But many had similar experiences and showed no sign of being Adolf Hitler manqué. Was Hitler a one-off? With relief, one can say that in many respects he was, but obviously he had supporters with similar mindsets.

Today, it seems almost indecent to ask if the allies had counterparts to Hitler. Joseph Stalin almost certainly qualifies. Winston Churchill? From his early autobiographical writings, it does seem as if he enjoyed a good fight. The horrors of the First World War—including the disaster at Gallipoli for which he was primarily responsible—seem to have sobered him significantly. Through the thirties, his warnings were about the need to respond to Hitler rather than an urging for more warfare, and, while in the Second World War he was prepared to take the battle to the enemy—obliteration bombing for instance—his strategy was mainly responding to the enemy. No doubt there were others who were bloodthirsty, General George Patton for example. But it is noteworthy how many of the Allied battle commanders were reserved and cautious, especially those who, like Field Marshall Bernard Montgomery, had gone through the horrors of the First War.

Balancing these people, German and otherwise, there were the outright appeasers—Chamberlain notably, and his fellow politician Lord Halifax, who was eager, after France had fallen, to see if an armistice could be forged between the battling sides. Although other aspects to Chamberlain's personality are surely relevant. Chamberlain could have given Enoch Powell a run for his money when it came to foreigners. A different person might have formulated a better approach to Hitler. And then there was the American president, Franklin Roosevelt. Whether for personal or for political reasons—with Roosevelt the two were usually identical—we just saw that he was unwilling to engage directly in war with Germany (or Japan for that matter), until his hand was forced by Pearl Harbor and then the declaration of war by Germany. In short, despite the examples of Hitler and Stalin, explanation solely in terms of innate violence and aggression is at best simplistic. Most people simply don't want to go to war unless they have to. And it is interesting to note that when they do go to war aggressively, as with Hitler, often it is because the ingroup feels threatened and wants to protect itself against the outgroups, including obviously such things as fighting for land that will benefit the ingroup at the expense of the outgroup. In other words, responding to circumstances that did not arise when we were still hunter-gatherers.

Claims about the all-pervasiveness of original sin, manifesting itself as an innate tendency to warfare and violence, need significant qualifying. We must cleanse our thinking of a religious remnant that seems not altogether helpful. Conversely, the claim that warfare is a latecomer, brought on by changes in circumstance, powered originally by the success and rise of agriculture seems, at a minimum, promising. The coming of warfare seems more contingent than preordained. "It is important to realize that well over 99 percent of our species' evolutionary history has involved living as foragers in small nomadic bands. In their lifelong camping trip, our Pleistocene ancestors faced some daunting adaptive problems" (Waller 2007, 153). Expectedly, what worked well then does not necessarily work well now. "Human behavior in the *present* is generated by universal reasoning circuits that exist because they solved adaptive problems in the *past*. As a result, these past-oriented circuits will not always necessarily generate adaptive behavior in the present." They can even backfire. "In some cases, what the circuits were designed to accomplish in the hunter-gatherer context even can lead to maladaptive behavior in response to contemporary environmental contexts" (154).

The point is not that war is avoidable and about to vanish. That is just naïve. "Buried in the midst of all of our progress in the twentieth century are well over a 100 million persons who met a violent death at the hands of their fellow human beings in wars and conflicts. That is more than five times the number from the nineteenth century and more than ten times the number from the eighteenth century" (Waller 2007, xiv). Despite this, what we have learned inspires me to get away from the view that we are helpless passengers on a fragile vessel in a turbulent ocean, and that, inevitably, our craft is going to turn over, drowning many of us. There are things we can do. Work to make sure that not just we but other nations have more reliable methods of government. Can you imagine if Edward the Eighth, he of Mrs. Simpson fame, and well-known Hitler admirer, had had the input and power that was possessed by Kaiser Wilhelm? The best solution to problems is not to have the problems in the first place. One much doubts the Versailles Treaty was responsible for all the ills for which it was blamed, but the allies of the Second World War had learned their lesson and did a much better job of dealing with and reintegrating their defeated foes. The United Nations has certainly not ended war, but it has made the world a much safer place than it might have been. One cannot, one should not, pretend that all is now roses. Desert Storm was but a part of ongoing conflicts in the Middle East. All too well known is the appalling behavior of young American soldiers in Iraq toward prisoners of war. They were punished, true, but the very fact that it could happen shows disregard, by those in command as much as any, for basic moral behavior in times of war. The critic quoted earlier argues that this alone shows the futility, not to say immorality, of relying on Just War Theory. "Professional officers consider part of the psychological training of their troops to be training in hatred, and this becomes more systematized and subtler as the war goes on" (Meagher 2014, 146, quoting Gray 1998, 161). True, but if this book has shown anything it is that hatred is not an unavoidable, irradicably given aspect of human life. As was said at the end of the Introduction: "The wonderful thing about our human nature is that, although it buckles under the course of history, it does not let that history be the sole determinant."

The eminent military historian John Keegan writes: "War, it seems to me, after a lifetime of reading about the subject, mingling with men of war, visiting the sites of war and observing its effects, may well be ceasing to commend itself to human beings as a desirable or productive, let alone rational, means of reconciling their discontents" (1993, 58). Michael Howard, no less distinguished, writes that it has become "quite possible that war in the sense of major, armed conflict between highly developed societies may not recur, and that a stable framework for international order will become firmly established" (1991, 176). Leave things at that. Pray that the Ukraine is a blip on the road to a better future.

Prejudice

What about prejudice? Our scientific background assumption is that ingroup/outgroup feelings and commitments are a legacy of our hunter-gatherer past, and that it is these that, for better or for worse, influence and guide our feelings and actions today. We are no longer going blind into the discussion. If we have made one big discovery, binding together virtually all instances of prejudice, it is that ignorance is a major factor. People are prejudiced against others because they think them objectively inferior and/or a threat, and that is rarely if ever true—or if true, not something impervious to cultural rectification.

Foreigners

Prejudice toward foreigners is obviously a legacy of our (prehistoric) past. Can attitudes be changed? We have today a case study that begs to be taken up: Brexit. Anticipating, we shall see an uncanny mirroring of much we have seen before. In the past fifty years, the devastation wrought on the working classes by increased efficiency in automation and by economics, especially outsourcing; the false promise of neoliberalism that removing restraints will lead to a plethora of new jobs, and that thanks to greater access to education and the like, through hard work and dedication, all will move up, gradually, together; the Potemkin Village allure of people like Donald Trump, offering ready solutions to all ills, at the same time satisfyingly putting the boot into the successful, primarily the meritocracy. One hardly need add that, like all such allures, we end with nothing: "the snark *was* a boojum you see."

On June 23, 2016, the United Kingdom voted to leave the European Union. The vote was 17.4 million in favor of leaving against 15.1 in favor of staying. If one were to isolate one factor that brought this on, as in earlier days the answer is simple: immigration. This time, not from the former British Empire—the West Indies and the Indian subcontinent—but from the poorer countries in the east of the EU. "Tens of thousands of Poles, Lithuanians, Hungarians and others flowed into British airports and coach stations, attracted by plentiful jobs at wages above those available back home. Within a decade, the Polish had overtaken more established first-wave communities from south Asia and the Caribbean to become the largest migrant origin group in Britain" (Sobolewska and Ford 2020, 145). These newcomers could not be ignored, because, unlike earlier immigrants, they spread across Britain, making their presence felt in conservative small towns hitherto unsullied by outsiders. Enoch Powell had warned that an influx of Europeans would, in some respects, be "more serious" than the immigration from the former empire, a point noted and promoted by the "Leave" campaigners. Antiforeigner sentiment led to pressure for a referendum on EU membership, and the rest, as they say, is history. This is from a television interview (on Fox News) of Nigel Farage, the leader of the Brexit movement, on the night (in June 2016) when the British voted to leave the Common Market (having joined in January 1973):

> I've seen the people gathering in party mood and yes flying the Union Jack. And you know why? Because that's our national flag. We don't want the European star-spangled banner. We don't want their anthem. We don't want their

president. We don't want their army. We, in six hours' time, are going to be free of this. And it is because of that that this is the greatest day in modern British history.

Most momentous day? Yes. Greatest day? Hardly. "Uncertainty over Brexit slowed the U.K.'s growth from 2.4% in 2015 to 1.5% in 2018. The U.K. government estimated that Brexit would lower the U.K.'s growth by 6.7% over 15 years" (Ball 2016). British banking, no longer with ready access to the EU, is on its way to being decimated. Trickle-down effects will affect most things with an international flavor—airfares, internet, even telephone charges. It is important to emphasize that the leavers and nonleavers were not a compound. They were an uneasy mixture. Most significantly, the educated wanted to stay. The uneducated wanted to leave. (See Figure 5.1.)

Seventy-eight per cent of people with no formal qualifications voted to leave the EU, as did 61% of people whose highest qualification was a GCSE or O-level.

By contrast, only 26% of people with a degree-level qualification voted Leave.

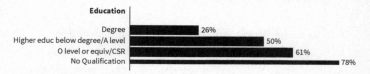

FIGURE 5.1 Brexit: Educated vs. uneducated. (NatCen Social Research.)

FIGURE 5.2 Brexit: Rich vs. poor. (NatCen Social Research.)

Relatedly, the rich wanted to stay. The poor wanted to leave. (See Figure 5.2.)

> The lowest-income group of voters in the survey, on an annual income of £14,400 (£1,200 a month) or less, were by far the most likely to back Brexit, with 66% support.
>
> The only group in the research who supported Remain were voters earning over £44,400—roughly speaking, higher-rate tax payers—of whom only 38% voted to leave the EU.

Those doing well in life and the economy wanted to stay. Those who were not wanted to leave. (See Figure 5.3.)

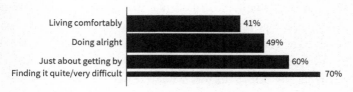

FIGURE 5.3 Brexit: Happy with lot vs. unhappy with lot. (NatCen Social Research.)

People who thought the country had got worse in the last decade overwhelmingly voted for Brexit, and this effect was even stronger for those who felt they had personally lost out.

The picture is clear. Other possible dividing factors, like sex, were practically irrelevant. (Male 54% leave; Female 49% leave.)

It is not always easy to feel sympathy for the British. Given the way in which they gained and ruled their empire—mention has been made of the by-no-means-atypical episode at Amritsar, not to mention a thousand years of self-interested trips to Europe—what were the British doing in France that they had to fight the battle of Agincourt? There is a (considerable) measure of Schadenfreude in seeing them turning in the wind in the face of immigrants. Smug satisfaction apart, it is understandable that there were reactions to the influx of people from the Caribbean and Indian subcontinent and then later from eastern Europe. Different customs, different languages, different religions. Understandable, but not thereby justifiable. One must do something to reduce the urge to prejudice. For a start, one needs to show that the immigrants bring benefits, especially for those on the losing side of society. Filling vital gaps, and not just as baristas. Around 1960, it seemed as though half of the nurses in the National Health System came from the West Indies. Actually, it was more like 20 percent, and a somewhat higher percentage of Asian general practitioners. The West Indian nurses were responding to desperate cries from the National Health Service, NHS, for help. Many of the doctors, particularly, were replacing British doctors, who were part of that cohort moving to the Europeanized parts of the Commonwealth seeking better opportunities. The exodus was just getting underway. Between

1961 and 1981, there were more than a million more emigrants out of Britain than immigrants into Britain (Winder 2004, 3). I have two schoolmates who, on graduating from medical school, caught the next boat to Australia. I can attest that there was no British opprobrium felt by any of this. No one ever said to them, or to me, that we were ungracious and disloyal in leaving as soon as we had finished our fancy education on the state's tab. Dominions of the Commonwealth—Canada, Australia, New Zealand especially— were still considered attached to the Mother Country, which in turn felt a huge debt to its children because of help in the World Wars. Gallipoli was part of our heritage, as was Dieppe.

At the same time, those who stayed home need to make efforts to integrate the immigrants. Stop feeling sorry for yourself and start being a bit more positive. A little more comparative religion in schools, trying to understand what it means to be a Muslim or a Hindu, might be a start. There are no proselytizing plots to circumcise your daughters. Trying to avoid creating ethnic ghettos, a recipe for prejudice. The Nazis showed us that. Efforts to intermix, especially through sports. It is hard to hate someone who is your wicket keeper. As a kid, I worshipped the West Indian Alf Valentine, in the 1950s the best left-arm, slow bowler in the world, and the professional at my local cricket club. This shows that relating need not just be work and no play. Affluent people do more traveling, more working across boundaries. Think of being a university teacher/researcher and how internationally based it has all become. People have to learn about other countries and the people who live in them. Subsidizing exchange trips abroad for schoolchildren might be a start. Hard to feel entirely negative about the French, if you have spent a couple of weeks with a family and the mother has shown you that there is more to food than toad in the hole and spotted dick. Adolescents mixing might then go on to learn that France has other attractions.

All this, apart from the most obvious of all. Immigration can be a very good thing. After all, the Brits are themselves Bell Beaker folk! The other side to the rise in status of women is that birth rates drop. There is a desperate need of immigrants to keep up the ratio of younger people, to support increasing numbers of pensioners and so forth. "The birth rate in England and Wales is now the lowest it has ever been since records began. Only 11 babies were born for every 1,000 people in 2018, with 657,076 born overall. To put this in perspective, 957,782 babies were born in 1920 despite the overall population being 22m fewer than it is today" (Leachman 2019). Conversely: "The UK is an increasingly aged nation and that is only set to become more so. There are 26.6m people in the UK aged between 40 and 79—these are the people who, in the next 20 years, will be needing care or approaching that point. In contrast, there are fewer than 14m young people under the age of 19—the people who in the next 20 years will be providing that care." The country needs immigrants. Today, the healthcare system is short a hundred thousand workers. and the same is true of adult social services. Moral or not, it is simply stupid not to have any controls on immigration. Brexit may be equally or more stupid, but one can understand how it happened. The answer is to realize, as so often, it is a question of balance. Prejudice will not help us to achieve it.

Class

Already, we have been talking about class. The affluent, educated, secure—the upper and middle classes—are far more foreigner friendly than the poor, uneducated, insecure—the working "lower" classes. We saw that this is as true in America, and no doubt elsewhere, as in Britain. Apart from anything else, the affluent tend not to be living cheek-by-jowl with foreign newcomers.

> Unfortunately, because of the overgenerous benefits offered to the rest of the world, the people swarming into our borough (into council housing ahead of local residents in need) feel they have a right to everything for nothing and they have absolutely no respect for us or where they live. (Letter from a woman in the East End of London to the then-Prime minister of England, David Cameron, February 10, 2012; Gest 2016, 59)

The tensions will not be solved in a day. There are however some obvious moves to make. There is clearly place for rethinking many aspects of higher education. Often the criticism is that university teachers are overwhelmingly liberal or socialist and spend much time and effort indoctrinating their students. Yet, while most teachers do tend to be toward the liberal end of the spectrum, it simply isn't true that professors are no more than Soviet propagandists. That is precisely what virtually all of us think we should not be. The aim is to give students the tools, and then they are on their own. This notwithstanding, more attention—at all levels of higher education—could be given to understanding social structures and their implications. Focusing less on bolstering one's *CV*, and more on the needs of society. Making the fruits of one's learning for all to benefit. Thinking, for instance, about what great political theorists of the past have had to say and their relevance today. Understanding religions in a comparative context. Trying to learn a bit more about human nature as psychologists have discovered. Reading Plato, not to mention Kant, on philosopher kings! Students would finish their training a little wiser and, one hopes, a little more modest. Less inclined to assume that, because they have a university degree, they are thereby superior to those whose education ended after high school.

Going to the other end of the spectrum, the hostility of the uneducated to those more successful in society, as with immigration it is not enough just to criticize those prejudiced. Keep always in mind the horrendous effects the loss of jobs has had on the lives of lower-class people. From a life of meaning and security to nothing. Nothing but inadequate food, inadequate lodging, inadequate everything. Coupled with, to return to the theme of the last section, resentment of others. Something must be done to speak to the worries. Something realistic. Famously, in 1867, during the debate on the Reform Bill, enfranchising the working class, echoing Disraeli, the English politician Robert Lowe said: "The moment that you entrust the masses with power, something must be done about their education." True, but mandating university education for everyone is not going to work. Start thinking about alternatives. Infrastructure is one thing that comes to mind. If nothing else, it will not be easy to outsource it. Another is thinking more seriously about service jobs. Not everyone needs to be a brain surgeon—or a professor of philosophy, for that matter.

If the pandemic has taught us anything, the conditions of nursing homes and residences for old people and similar institutions are in an appalling condition. Too few workers, with too little training, in conditions that one would never allow for one's pets. There are massive opportunities here for getting people, presently at the uneducated end of the spectrum, involved. One or two years of community-college-based, hands-on training, in dealing with (to take one group) old people—their hygiene, their dietary needs, their health, and their overall psychological well-being. Understanding that, even for those without dementia or other dreadful handicaps, growing old is not easy. No longer able to do simple tasks that would be easy for a twenty-year-old—lugging a heavy BBQ from one end of the garden to the other, for instance. Not only would training projects like these create jobs, as, or more, importantly, they would help people to develop a sense of self-worth and pride. In respects, this is the major problem: "the single-minded focus on education had a damaging side effect: eroding the social esteem accorded those who had not gone to college" (Sandel 2020b, 89).

Do not think that I am being condescending, suggesting that we should make people think they are better than they are. We have all encountered people, not of great standing or education, but to whom instinctively we turn if we want understanding and support—secretaries, janitors, custodians. People whose empathy makes us feel as humble as we are grateful. People of social sensitivity far greater than your average philosophy professor. (Not hard to find!) My point is that of Rousseau: if you are raised to think yourself less than stellar, you internalize it, even though you resent. My point also is that change can happen. These things are going to cost money. One does not have to be an extreme socialist to think that the successful and rich could make a bigger contribution—as was the norm fifty years ago. It is not a demand or prescription for total government control. One could well imagine that private nursing homes, properly regulated, would search out innovative methods and approaches more readily than those run by civil servants. For me, it is unthinkable to teach in other than a publicly funded university. One lifetime is too short to repay my debt to the Butler Act. But, oh, how often I find myself envying the dimensions of freedom of faculty at the Ivy League schools and top liberal arts colleges. I am simply saying that things, at the moment, are not good, our science tells us we are not locked into them, and so it is time to start rethinking and changing.

Race

The ornithologist Edmund Blyth, writing on the topic of the India Mutiny, to his frequent correspondent, who referred to him fifty (!) times in the second volume of the *Descent*: "How amazingly the force of character of our countrymen & countrywomen has been evinced in the course of this terrible struggle! The wonderful superiority of the European to the Asiatic, from the days of Xenophon and Alexander even unto now!" He is just warming to his theme. "Against such overwhelming odds, nobody here ever conceived the possibility of the insurrection proving successful,—this grand struggle of barbarism against a higher civilization ennobled by the application of all the sciences" (Darwin 1985–, 7, 3; letter to Darwin, January 8, 1858). The worst kind of Victorian jingoism. Still going strong into the twentieth century. Although, as so often, based on shaky premises. If there are differences, they are cultural and changeable, not written in stone—or, rather, in the DNA. Thanks to human-driven science, we now know that there simply is no reason to believe that black people—or people of any other group—have not the intelligence of white people.

Even before you get into psychological testing and the like, the biology is against it (Templeton 2013). "A race or subspecies requires a degree of genetic differentiation that is well above the level of genetic differences that exist among local populations. One commonly used threshold is that two populations with sharp boundaries are considered to be different races if 25% or more of the genetic variability that they collectively share is found as between population differences" (Smith, et al., 1997). The differences between chimpanzees and humans are truly striking. In the case of the former, the empirical evidence "confirms the reality of race in chimpanzees using the threshold definition, as 30.1% of the genetic variation is found in the among-race component.... In contrast to chimpanzees, the five major "races" of humans account for only 4.3% of human genetic variation—well below the 25% threshold. The genetic variation in our species is overwhelmingly variation among individuals (93.2%)." This is consistent with what we learned in the Introduction. *Homo sapiens* went through bottlenecks. There simply is not that much genetic variation in our species.

This does not mean that there is no link between genes and geographic groups. A much-discussed study found that there are some consistent correlations—Europeans come out as one cluster and Africans another. Sometimes the divisions are quite fine. According to lore and language similarity, the somewhat isolated Kalash in northern Pakistan have origins linking them to Europeans, and genetics backs this up. "Genetic clusters often corresponded closely to predefined regional or population groups or to collections of geographically and linguistically similar populations" (Rosenberg et al. 2002, 2384). The point is that these clusters are, overall, although detectable very slight, often inferred from gradation in the frequency of genes rather than from distinctive diagnostic genotypes." Nowhere like strong enough to justify the loaded use that is so often made of the concept of "race." As pointed out earlier, where the differences are in any way adaptively significant, they are related to such things as protection from the sun and have no implications at all about such things as intelligence.

Without being a Pollyanna, race does seem to be one area that shows that people of good will can and do make a difference. In the First World War, despite great bravery, US African Americans had to fight with the French, because white Americans would not fight alongside them. (See Figure 5.4.) By the mid-twentieth century, things did start to change. The African American contribution to the Second World War was no small factor. In 1948, the former segregationist, President Harry Truman, integrated the armed forces. In 1954, the Supreme Court, in *Brown v. Board of Education*, argued that "separate but equal" schools are inherently unequal, and so school segregation was declared unconstitutional and legally prohibited. No big rush—Emmett Till was murdered in 1955—but dripping away on the rocks. Few who lived through the 1960s will have clear and unsullied memories of Lyndon Johnson. The dreadful Vietnam War hangs like a gloomy, damp, disease-infected fog over all recollections. Yet, if ever there was an American president to whom society should be ever grateful, it is Lyndon Johnson. He—and surely only he was able—saw through the Civil Rights Act of 1964, banning discrimination in public places, ensuring that Black Americans could receive a proper education, helping promote access to voting, and much more.

FIGURE 5.4 A 1918 recruitment poster aimed at African Americans.

Johnson did not finish the job. We still have very far to go. The ongoing spate of killings of black people by police officers—most notably George Floyd on May 25, 2020, who died of asphyxiation after a white police officer knelt on his neck for nearly ten minutes—tells us this too vividly. "Black Lives Matter" is a plea for understanding and change, the widely promoted slogan of a social movement in large part spurred by happenings such as this. And this is but the tip of a very big iceberg (Wilkerson 2020). Think of the huge controversy sparked by the *New York Times* "1619 Project," claiming that the American Revolution was less about Enlightenment ideas of liberty and more about protecting a slave society (Hanna-Jones 2019). Many reputable historians thought this a gross exaggeration, but one would think that something like this should at least be a topic for in-class discussion. After all, George Washington had 124 slaves, and managed close to another 200. When his duties led to his living in Pennsylvania, because the state had a law freeing slaves after living there for six months, Washington would rotate his slaves so none of them were freed (Larson 2020). Many states, especially in the South, have now passed laws excluding discussion of this item, and all like ideas contained in the overall "Critical Race Theory," from the classroom.

Compared to Germany, and its efforts to recognize its ill deeds toward Jews (of which, more shortly), America lags badly (Wilkerson 2020, especially chapter 27). But change has happened and is going on happening. My children went to a high school and I taught at a university that, sixty years ago, were segregated. I sit down next to black people in restaurants. My daughter dated a young black man for a couple of years. Some of her pals were envious. My—and my wife's—first votes in a presidential election were for a black man. My last vote was for a (successful) black, female, vice-presidential candidate. And despite the opposition of former president Donald Trump, memorials celebrating the Confederacy—statues and the like—are being removed from prominent places on campus and tucked away in museums, as illustrations of what must never happen again. My daughter's local high school, the Robert E. Lee High School, named after the commander of the Confederate forces in the Civil War, in Jacksonville, Florida, with a majority (around 70%) of students black, has just voted to change its name. (See Figure 5.5.)

Change is possible. Black people are not innately inferior and we are starting to realize and act on this. As importantly, those so long under the burden of racial prejudice are realizing this and no longer prepared to stay in the lower echelons of society. From Rosa Parks and earlier, to Stacey Abrams and no doubt later, change is possible. Barack Obama captures it all:

> There is abolition, and the Civil War, and then there's backlash, and the rise of the K.K.K., and then Reconstruction ends, and Jim Crow arises, and then you have a civil rights movement, a modern civil rights movement, and desegregation. And that in turn leads to push back and ultimately Nixon's Southern strategy. What I take comfort from is that in the traditional two steps forward, one step back, as long as you're getting the two steps, then the one step back, you know, is the price of doing business. (Klein 2021)

FIGURE 5.5 Robert E. Lee High School.

Sexual Orientation

Most of us are deeply uncertain about Freud and his theories. But one can forgive a lot on reading his "Letter to an American Mother," written in 1935.

> Dear Mrs. . . . I gather from your letter that your son is a homosexual. I am most impressed by the fact that you do not mention this term yourself in your information about him. May I question you, why you avoid it? Homosexuality is assuredly no advantage, but it is nothing to be ashamed of, no vice, no degradation, it cannot be classified as an illness; we consider it to be a variation of the sexual function produced by a certain arrest of sexual development. Many highly respectable individuals of ancient and modern times have

been homosexuals, several of the greatest men among them (Plato, Michelangelo, Leonardo da Vinci, etc.). It is a great injustice to persecute homosexuality as a crime, and cruelty too. If you do not believe me, read the books of Havelock Ellis. By asking me if I can help, you mean, I suppose, if I can abolish homosexuality and make normal heterosexuality take its place. The answer is, in a general way, we cannot promise to achieve it. In a certain number of cases we succeed in developing the blighted germs of heterosexual tendencies which are present in every homosexual, in the majority of cases it is no more possible. It is a question of the quality and the age of the individual. The result of treatment cannot be predicted. What analysis can do for your son runs in a different line. If he is unhappy, neurotic, torn by conflicts, inhibited in his social life, analysis may bring him harmony, peace of mind, full efficiency whether he remains a homosexual or gets changed. . . . Sincerely yours with kind wishes, Freud

Today, a bit old-fashioned in some ways—before one starts to speak about "arrest of development," one would need a lot more argument to persuade one that Freud's framework was correct—but ahead of its time in arguing what we now believe is true. Homosexuality is not a matter of choice and, if homosexuals are unhappy, it is not because of their sexual orientation, but because society makes them unhappy. It is our fault as much as anyone's.

"Ahead of its time." But not entirely coming out of nowhere. Freud had his influences and sources, and one of the most important was Charles Darwin and the *Descent*. Freud counted it one of the ten most significant books he knew (Freud 1960, 269). The crucial point is that, as with foreigners, as with race, knowledge is all-important. The key to change is better understanding. Today, when thinking of proximate causes, most researchers think in terms of hormones, particularly as they affect fetal brain development. Comparative levels of testosterone during the third and sixth months of hypothalamus development seem to be the all-important factors (LeVay 2010). The possible causal role of natural selection is, as they say, highly contested. Repeated studies estimate the number of male homosexuals at around 3–4 percent; females are somewhat less. Of course, being homosexual does not mean that one will not have children, but the Kinsey studies show that orientation (especially of males) is a very significant (behavioral) factor in having fewer offspring (Bell and Weinberg 1978). Could the selective cause be kin selection, with gay or lesbian siblings helping other family members to reproduce? Could it be "parental manipulation," with the mother's biology kicking in to control the reproduction of her offspring? It might not be a good thing to have them all competing equally, if resources are limited. Could it be a case of heterozygote fitness, where the heterozygote (possessor of different genes, alleles, at the same place, locus, on the pared chromosomes) has more offspring, balancing the fact that the homozygotes (the same alleles at a locus) have fewer offspring? Whatever the case, it does seem that homosexuality is "natural," and there is no reason at all to think it a deviancy, like psychopathy.

Facts like these have led to change, if slowly. In the 1950s, as readers of the (English) Sunday newspaper *News of the World* knew well, the police were extremely active in enforcing the law against (male) homosexual activity. It was known as the "blackmailer's charter," because, when a wretched victim drew attention to his predicament, not only was the blackmailer prosecuted, but the victim too. For all that, as critics pointed out, sending a homosexual to prison was about as effective as sending a drunkard to a brewery, in 1954 over a thousand gay men were in jail because of their illegal activities. The law was not repealed until 1967. Even then there were restrictions not lifted until 2000. Gay sex was forbidden in a hotel or in a house where another person was present, even if that person were in another room! At the same time, slowly homosexuals of both sexes (as well as others under the category LGBT) were granted the rights of heterosexuals. Civil unions were allowed from 2005 and same sex marriage from 2014. (A similar tale can be told of the United States.)

The pope's recent pronouncements warn us that we still have a way to go. There is somewhat of a tendency to think that the prejudice against males is greater than that against females. This may be true. Lesbianism was not illegal in Britain. There is no cause for complacency. "Who is the better parent, a convicted killer or a lesbian? In 1996, Mary Ward found out the answer when she lost custody of her daughter Cassey, to her ex-husband, John Ward, because she was a lesbian." Cassey, now aged twelve, had lived all her life with her mother. "In his decision, the judge explained that he granted custody to the father because he believed "Cassey should be given the opportunity to live in a nonlesbian world" (Anderson 2010, 193). Thoughtfully, the judge cited as evidence of stability the fact that John Ward's fourth marriage had now lasted two full years. "Never mind that John Ward had served eight years in prison for a second-degree murder conviction for shooting and killing his first wife." One is reminded of Edward

Blythe on the subject of Indians. Change is possible. Change has occurred. We are not yet at journey's end.

Religion

Prejudice and religion is a two-way process. The prejudice of the religious toward others, homosexuals for instance. And the prejudice of the nonreligious toward the religious. Think of the jokes we have all made about earnest people in suits on one's doorstep, Jehovah's Witnesses, pushing the *Watch Tower*. No one can quite equal Richard Dawkins: "Odious as the physical abuse of children by priests undoubtedly is, I suspect that it may do them less lasting damage than the mental abuse of having been brought up Catholic in the first place" (2002, 9). Note that, generally, religious people play the game introduced earlier in this book, arguing that they are rightfully against certain groups. Hence, they would not regard their condemnations as prejudice. It is not prejudiced to be against pedophiles. It is not prejudiced to be against homosexuals. To which one can only say that, to the contrary, it starts to sound like prejudice more and more, as we discover more and more things like the causes of sexual orientation. Obviously, one is going to be against homosexuals if they are going to indulge in sexual behavior with children, not only causing pain then but perhaps significantly undermining future sexual happiness. But, if there is no good reason to think this, then judgments can and should change. My attitude to Jehovah's Witnesses changed from scorn to humility when I learned of their unbelievable bravery in standing up to Hitler during the Third Reich. Unflinching, even unto death at the hands of the executioner. They have earned their time on my doorstep.

I am not alone in not being static. Christians, since the time of Augustine, have been good at changing interpretations and injunctions. Think how they have wriggled out of pacifism. Leviticus may seem to ban same-sex activity. If one can argue that the prohibition is really against prostitution, especially religious homosexual prostitution, then one might be let off the hook with respect to noncommercial sexual behavior (Bailey 1955). Conversely, one might find religion less and less threatening and, so, less and less reason to be prejudiced against such behavior. A good start is the fact that religious commitment, including church attendance, is getting less and less, even in America, the traditional exception when it comes to discussions of Western societies getting less and less religious. Be this as it may, religious prejudice, either way, is less and there is no reason why things should not continue this way. This, of course, is talking of the West. Elsewhere the story might be different. One is not encouraged by new Indian laws against interreligious marriage.

Disability

Fanny Cleaver, in Charles Dickens's last completed novel, *Our Mutual Friend*, is better known by the name she chose for herself, "Jenny Wren." She is dreadfully handicapped: "my back's bad, and my legs are queer." She suffers much pain. She is a far deeper portrait of disability than the better-known, overly sentimental picture of a suffering child, Tiny Tim, in *A Christmas Carol*. Jenny yearns to be like others, healthy and whole. She dreams—for it can only be a dream—of a husband. "Jenny Wren had her personal vanities—happily for her—and no intentions were stronger in her breast than the various trials and torments that were, in the fulness of time, to be inflicted upon 'him.'" To her good friend, Lizzie Hexam, she asserts confidently: "when I am courted, I shall make Him do some of the things that you do for me." Adding: "I'll trot him about, I can tell him!" Such a sad, and understandable, fantasy. Apart from her physical disability, Jenny's life—she ekes out a living as a doll's dressmaker—is hard, not the least because she supports her pathetic, needy, alcoholic father—her "bad boy." Little wonder that, to the world about her, Jenny is sharp, wary, if not downright unfriendly. As with her imaginary husband, as with her all-too-real father, she infantilizes men. But, together with Lizzie, she does have a caring friend, an old Jew Mr. Riah, who works for a grasping moneylender. Riah shows compassion—love—trying where possible to make easier Jenny's sad journey through life. He has little to offer, but where he can, he gives. On the roof of his dwelling place, he has created a haven that Jenny could, for an hour or two, forget her burdens. A haven, where "perhaps with some old instinct of his race, the gentle Jew had spread a carpet."

Let us seize on this, taking up the theme of this book, that humans are such a contradictory mixture. Together with exclusion and hatred, there is love and friendship. In this spirit, while recognizing what evolution has wrought, let us ask about improving the lot of the disabled and of our attitudes toward them. Truly dreadful things happened in the twentieth century, but—perhaps, in part in reaction to these dreadful things—people did start to move forward. And this included attitudes and responses to disability. Country after country—from large ones like China and India to small ones like Monaco and Malta—has enacted laws to reduce prejudicial acts against the disabled. To take an example from the United Kingdom, the *Equality Act 2010* makes explicit mention of disability and prescribes actions that should be taken. For instance, in the matter of education, publicly financed schools must have "accessibility strategies" for disabled students.

An accessibility strategy is a strategy for, over a prescribed period—

(a) increasing the extent to which disabled pupils can participate in the schools' curriculums;

(b) improving the physical environment of the schools for the purpose of increasing the extent to which disabled pupils are able to take advantage of education and benefits, facilities or services provided or offered by the schools;

(c) improving the delivery to disabled pupils of information which is readily accessible to pupils who are not disabled.

Most disabled people are not children; but, putting much effort into the care of children pays the biggest dividends, preparing them for a full and worthwhile life and, at the same time—and we have seen much to agree that this is as or more important—teaching others about the disabled, seeing that they are human beings and not freaks, dangerous and demanding.

In America, the *Americans with Disabilities Act* of 1990 lays out bluntly the needs and challenges, working toward solutions. In the preamble, the Act states as a matter of fact: "physical or mental disabilities in no way diminish a person's right to fully participate in all aspects of society, yet many people with physical or mental disabilities have been precluded from doing so because of discrimination; others who have a record of a disability or are regarded as having a disability also have been subjected to discrimination." It goes on to acknowledge the ways in which there has been discrimination. It then makes the moral declaration: "the Nation's proper goals regarding individuals with disabilities are to assure equality of opportunity, full participation, independent living, and economic self-sufficiency for such individuals." It adds also pragmatic reasons for tackling discrimination against the disabled: "the continuing existence of unfair and unnecessary discrimination and prejudice denies people with disabilities the opportunity to compete on an equal basis and to pursue those opportunities for which our free society is justifiably famous, and costs the United States billions of dollars in unnecessary expenses resulting from dependency and nonproductivity." From there it plunges into the nuts and bolts of what this all implies. For instance: "The ameliorative effects of the mitigating measures of ordinary eyeglasses or contact lenses shall be considered in determining whether an impairment substantially limits a major life activity."

No one expects that passing laws prohibiting prejudice against the disabled is going to change things overnight, or perhaps even—more pessimistically—going to change things to such an extent that such prejudice is something of the past, like wearing a crinoline or smoking in class. It is true that disability is first and foremost a family problem, something that the philosopher Martha Nussbaum (2006) points out perceptively tends to fall disproportionately on women. Society can do much, more than it does now, but dealing with resentment and dislike—"why me?"— is, and will continue to be, something that must start at the personal level. But, to use a trite phrase, every journey begins with a single step. Knowing that the state is providing proper schooling for your handicapped child is a good start. The burden is shared.

Evolutionarily speaking, is such an attempt to reduce prejudice even plausible? There are grounds for optimism. Start with the fact that, essentially, we are social beings and that morality is an important tool in making this possible. Caring about the disabled is a moral obligation. Those most involved in care, family members, are (as we have seen) going to be precisely those biologically morally predisposed to help those in need. However, it is not just family members. "No man is an island." As my little story of the cub pack and the Down's syndrome children shows, we are all helped. Affirming the dignity of the disabled affirms the dignity of all of us. Continue with the fact that, as we have seen repeatedly in this book, cultural changes can put our biology out of context and proper functioning. End with the thought that, as cultural change can make things difficult for us—violence following on the move to agriculture—so cultural change can make things better for us. Accept that the problem with attitudes toward the disabled stems from our hunter-gatherer days, when groups simply could not carry those not pulling their weight. Realize that now culture has changed this. First, we can carry those not pulling their weight, and, if the acts we have seen above are close to the truth, as a group we might benefit materially from integrating the disabled. Second, we can now work to release our social nature from the barriers our biology sets up against ingroup threats. As stressed again and again in this chapter, knowledge and technology are vital here. We know now that the mentally handicapped are neither necessarily evil—Renfield—nor pathetic—Smike. We know that someone with a physical handicap is not thereby cruel and a threat. We know also now how to overcome disabilities. Preventing them in the first place. The vaccine against polio. Or through (for want of a better term) machinery. Greatly improved prostheses for one. Much-improved therapies, supplemented with newly discovered drugs, for a second. And more. This can backfire. One suspects that in America today, simply because of increased length of lifespan, there are more people with dementia than a hundred years ago. It is estimated that in Britain in 2025 there will be a million people with dementia. By 2040, it is calculated that this number will be closing in on a million and a half (Anonymous 2021). Predictions such as this are challenges, not roadblocks. Culture has dug many holes for us to fall into. Now let us use culture to build ladders so we can escape from them.

Jews

Countries other than Germany have histories of prejudice against Jews. In England, Edward I expelled all Jews on July 12, 1290. They were kept out for over 350 years, until Oliver Cromwell permitted their return in 1657. There was persecution, notably a massacre (in 1190) of about 150 Jews holed up in Clifford's Tower in York. But overall, no mass killings comparable to the Holocaust, and, for what it is worth, prominent citizens of York were fined for letting the killing (mainly suicide) occur. Why then was there such prejudice against Jews in Germany, that a huge, state-sanctioned murder could occur, especially when one learns that a lot of the killing was not done by exceptional mad fiends, sadists, but often by men who were truly ordinary? In all other respects, particularly those in the *Einsatzgruppen*—paramilitary death squads—they were good citizens. Daniel Goldhagen, in his famous (or notorious) *Hitler's Willing Executioners: Ordinary Germans and the Holocaust* (1996), picking up on what we have seen was the thinking of Martin Luther, has a relatively simple, unicausal explanation. From the Middle Ages, at least, anti-Semitism was, as it were, in Germans' blood. As so often, Christianity had a role in this prejudice. From this, all followed: "German antisemitic beliefs about Jews were the central causal agent of the Holocaust. They were the central causal agent not only of Hitler's decision to annihilate European Jewry (which is accepted by many) but also of the perpetrators' willingness to kill and to brutalize Jews" (9).

Obviously, even if this be true, there are major questions left dangling. Most particularly, why did it all explode in the 1930s? Hitler triggered it, no doubt, but why was Germany then ripe for the triggering? Christopher Browning, author of *Ordinary Men: Reserve Police Battalion 101 and the Final Solution in Poland* (1998), which covers much of the same material as Goldhagen, questions the supposedly deep anti-Semitism of Germans. Making points that we made earlier, Browning argues that, even under the Third Reich, while, obviously, people were prepared to let things happen, generally there was apathy and indifference, combined often with a distaste for what was happening but an inclination to look away. Distaste, but also an affirmation of the state. "Everywhere people tended to accept a definition of reality provided by 'experts,' their government or their culture" (Staub 1992, 88). And this ties in with the fact that, as we have insisted, a major factor behind the slaughter was the push—something that goes back into the nineteenth century and the unification of Germany—to see Germany as a united whole, with a distinctive character, a *Volk*. Prejudice against the Jews was more that of stressing the ingroup nature of "pure" Germans than of stressing the outgroup nature of the Jews. Putting things together, Browning sees the preparedness of ordinary people to do dreadful things as part of this desire to conform, to be part of the ingroup, and hence hostile to the outgroup.

> Crucial to understanding the behavior of ordinary Germans in uniform . . . were the "myths" of Kameradschaft and Volksgemeinschaft (comradeship and community). These powerful "myths" must be understood as the Germans knew them, for they were the lenses through which Germans saw the world, constructed their reality, and derived the moral framework that in turn shaped their behavior.
>
> The myth of the Volksgemeinschaft derived from Germany's euphoric sense and collective memory of unity transcending class, party, and confession, as proclaimed by the Kaiser in August 1914. With Germans traumatized by the defeat of 1918 and the Great Depression, the Nazis were able to appropriate the emotive power of the myth while transforming its essence from political, social, and religious inclusivity to racial exclusivity. (240)

The Nazis used the German sense of, and desire for, ingroup holistic membership to promote their version of outgroup hatred, namely prejudice toward the Jews. It was not so much a question of what the Jews were inherently, but of how their existence could be downgraded by insecurities about ingroup membership. Historian Robert Gellately (2001) records significant numbers of regular Germans who denounced Jews and, for that matter, others whom they felt were undermining the cohesion of the Reich. Listening to foreign radio was a common reason for informing the authorities, the Gestapo in particular. "Far from spending their every waking moment worrying about the Gestapo and being torn by anxieties over the surveillance and terror system, many people came to terms with it" (199).

Combine this with a strong urge to obedience to leaders. The classic experiments of Stanley Milgram (where he got people to give horrendous shocks to strangers if they didn't measure up to standard) show how engrained is this urge. It has nothing to do with killer apes or original sin and everything to do with groups—especially hunter-gatherer groups—functioning smoothly.

> Milgram recognized that humans must often function within organizations. He argued that an evolutionary bias favors the survival of people who can adapt favorably to hierarchical situations and organized social activity. As a result, according to Milgram, we have developed an evolutionary potential for obedience. It is not a simple instinct for obedience, he asserts, but a potential for obedience that interacts with the influence of society and situations. In short, the standard workings of selection pressures have left us with an inherent propensity, a deeply engrained behavior tendency, to obey those positioned hierarchically above us. (Waller 2007, 113)

"Many Germans went along, not because they were mindless robots, but because they convinced themselves of Hitler's advantages and of the 'positive' sides of the new dictatorships" (Gellately 2001, 257). Had Germany won the First World War, there would have been no need of the Nazis and their hatreds. Had it not been Germany, where the culture of obedience was virtually a religious command—for many, no "virtually" about it—one doubts the hatreds would have so readily led to awful consequences.

That is the overriding lesson for us here. Prejudice against the Jews is not an inevitable part of human nature or human society. Pessimistically, the thoughtful Jewish thinker Richard Rubenstein wrote: "I regarded Naziism and the camps as far more than the sport of history. They revealed the full potentiality of the demonic as a permanent attribute of human nature" (1966, 216). Is this true? Modern-day Germany gives reason for optimism about change. On the one hand, the country is facing up to the past. The American philosopher Susan Nieman (2019), long settled in Berlin, makes a point that resonates strongly with me. As the British have their comforting narratives, as the American South had its comforting narrative, so Germany had its comforting narrative. For a good twenty years after the end of the Second World War, Germans insulated themselves from guilt by making themselves victims. Whenever the War was raised, my German stepmother at once would refer to the suffering of the German people due to obliteration bombing, lack of food and heating toward the end of the War and the early years after, and the violence of the invading troops. It was only as this generation was succeeded by their children, who had no immediate experience of the War, that Germany started to wrestle with its guilt and recognize the wrongs and begin the task of genuine contrition. To a large extent, with respect to slavery, this has still not fully happened in the United States.

On the other hand: "Out of evolutionary dirt grows the flower of human goodness." Germany is showing how morally one can and should behave to outgroup people. Linking up with discussion earlier in this chapter, it was Germany who in 2015 took in 1.2 million refugees from the Middle East, about 1.5% of the total country's population (Rogers 2021, 29). In the past, Germany has had an uneasy relationship with its immigrants, many from Turkey, but this time the story has been one of much success. Jobs have been found, apprenticeships started, even ten thousand students in university. Not unbroken success. Often the new jobs are much less prestigious than the old jobs, and prejudice does exist. But, overall, the immigrants have been welcomed and integrated. Assuaging some of the worries that will have arisen in readers' minds on reading the earlier discussion: "rural regions have largely proven to be as adept at managing integration as large cities" (30). With careful thought and management: "recent experiences have shown that even small communities in Germany 'can handle immigration.'" It is not unjustified optimism by those without experience. Just as well. As is the case for Britain, Germany "desperately needs immigrants to maintain its tax base and social security net in the decades to come. Federal statistics predict that 27 percent of Germans will be above the age of sixty-seven by 2060" (31). Little wonder that "the country needs 260,000 additional workers every year to safeguard its economy and welfare benefits." One suspects that, in years to come, many dissertations, papers, books will be written on this topic, comparing Britain and Germany.

Women

A society that elects Donald Trump as its president, rather than Hillary Clinton, can hardly be said to be entirely free of sexual bias. However, things have changed and continue to change. Already, women have made significant gains in education and in society generally. Women have or are moving into high status jobs in medicine and elsewhere. Much remains to be done, but it can be done and will be done. At a point like this, it is worth stressing that, for both war and prejudice, the key to understanding is that, as the evolutionary psychologists Leda Cosmides and John Tooby stress: "Our modern skulls house a stone age mind." Expounding: "In many cases our brains are better at solving the kinds of problems our ancestors faced on the African savannahs than they are at solving the more familiar tasks we face in a college classroom or modern city" (1997, 11). And this, more than anything, is the concluding thesis of this book. We are first and foremost social beings. We have adaptations to make sociality work. Some are within the tribe, like morality and dominance and obedience and virtuous violence, to some extent. Some are without the tribe, treating others from friendly wariness to outright hostility. In the new world into which agriculture pitched our hunter-gatherer ancestors, the old-way adaptations proved inadequate and, because there has not been enough time for natural selection radically to recast human nature, hatred emerges—war and prejudice.

This is a grave conclusion, but, as changed circumstances have brought this on, so changed circumstances guided by us could move us forward. We do not have to do the work of natural selection. There is no call for massive plans of genetic reconstruction, finding and inserting genes that make us nicer people—unwilling to go to war, unwilling to hate people because they are not as us. Those genetic potentials are already in place. Agriculture has knocked them off balance. Now the task is to undo. And this is a cultural task. Gender differences are a paradigmatic example. If, as seems plausible, hunter-gatherer societies were significantly more egalitarian, then much male dominance is cultural, laid on societies by the move to new and unfamiliar conditions. The task ahead is not to change men and women biologically. It is to counter the new and unfamiliar conditions. Not by simplistic reversion to the past. We don't have to go back to being hunter-gatherers. We must reinstate those conditions that made true female equality a reality.

Expectedly, the luddites are striking back. In the United States, state government after state government—consisting almost entirely of (white) male members—is enacting antiabortion laws. If this is not designed to keep women in their place, it is hard to know what is. The usual appeal, apart from to pseudo-science, is to Christianity. This is somewhat shaky ground. Aristotle argued that initially the fetus has a vegetable soul, and "ensoulment" happens after forty days for males and ninety days for females. St. Augustine followed the philosopher in thinking that the human soul does not enter the fetus until some while after conception. This was the tradition until the mid-nineteenth century. Anticipating Linda Lovelace, Theodore of Tarsus, Archbishop of Canterbury (668–690), ruled that oral intercourse requires from 7 years to a lifetime of penance; an abortion requires only 120 days. Then, in 1854, the Catholic Church proclaimed the dogma of the "Immaculate Conception," namely that Mary was conceived without original sin. It was only a matter of time before all abortion was considered murder. This was the handiwork of Pope Pius IX in 1869, a position that today is embraced not just by Catholics but also by Protestant evangelicals. When an abortion is denied to a woman, carrying a deformed fetus, that may after birth suffer for years from excruciating pain, it is hard not to sympathize with Richard Dawkins's views on organized religion.

Drawing discussion of prejudice to an end, reemphasize a point made earlier. Just as it is wrong to think divisions of types of war absolutes—Was the Crimean War offensive or defensive?—so it is wrong to think that prejudices are always separate. In the 1970s, evangelical churches openly allowed (encouraged) abortion for a range of reasons. From a Southern Baptist Convention statement of 1971: "Be it further resolved, that we call upon Southern Baptists to work for legislation that will allow the possibility of abortion under such conditions as rape, incest, clear evidence of severe fetal deformity, and carefully ascertained evidence of the likelihood of damage to the emotional, mental, and physical health of the mother." Then, the Supreme Court lifted tax-free status of private schools designed to avoid integration. Consciously, the evangelical leaders, realizing they could hardly promote the virtues of white-only schools, started to promote abortion opposition as a rallying point (Edsall 2021). Writes professor of religion Randall Balmer:

At a time when open racism was becoming unfashionable, these politicians needed a more high-minded issue, one that would not compel them to surrender their fundamental political orientation. And of course the beauty of defending a fetus is that the fetus demands nothing in return—housing, health care, education—so it's a fairly low-risk advocacy.

Other prejudice-fertile issues were soon entangled in the tale. Disability. Religion. And class. Political scientist David Leege writes: "The people perceived to be pushing government's role in equal opportunity and racial integration were now the same as those pushing permissive abortion laws, namely, the highly educated from New England, banking, universities, the Northern cities, and elsewhere." No doubt, if one kept digging, other areas of opposition to these ideas and their promoters, prejudice from evangelicals and fellow travelers, would soon emerge.

Biology is not destiny. Or, perhaps, biology is destiny. It is all a question of understanding the biology, and then working with it through culture to get the results we desire. War and prejudice undoubtedly exist and cause great unhappiness and harm. Despite the efforts of conservative politicians, it is not necessarily the inevitable fate of humankind to be so burdened. Change has come and there is no theoretical or empirical reason why it should not continue.

| EPILOGUE

As I explained at the beginning of this book, the topic, hatred, is very personal. I grew up as a Quaker in the years after the worst conflict this planet has ever seen. Questions about how to understand war, how to prevent a recurrence, were as much part of my childhood heritage as Laurel and Hardy or *The Wind in the Willows* or Handel's *Messiah* at Christmas time. Prejudice was a worry—an obsession—of my teens. The horrendous hostility the English showed to foreigners. Not just Germans. You could always get a good laugh at the expense of the Americans, resented because they were now the world leaders not us. Then the internal British tensions between those with established pedigrees and those without. I give thanks to my nonexistent God that I emigrated to Canada at the age of twenty-two, away from it all. And, hovering above everything, was the problem—and it was a problem—of homosexuality. At school we were warned: "Stay away from public lavatories, especially on a Saturday afternoon." You could find yourself in magistrate's court on Monday morning. "There but for the grace of God go I." I personally never felt the

Why We Hate. Michael Ruse, Oxford University Press. © Oxford University Press 2022.
DOI: 10.1093/oso/9780197621288.003.0007

need of God's grace, but I simply could not understand how some-one whom nature had made different from me would need God's grace. If anyone were to blame, it was God Himself.

If I say this book has been a labor of love, that is true. Even more, it has been a labor of obligation. Obligation to my teachers—in my Quaker childhood, at my primary and secondary schools, at universities in England, Canada, and the United States—and then to my colleagues at the universities at which I have taught, and to the wider academic world, in philosophy and in other sub-jects like (obviously) biology, history, and religion. More recently, anthropology and archaeology. Above all, to my students, espe-cially those who are handicapped. When you teach others, it does not take long to realize how little you know and how much work lies ahead. I think of this book as a voyage of discovery. When I set out, I had little anticipation of the sights I would see and the lands I would visit. I had absolutely no idea of the importance of agriculture, for all that for thirty-five years I taught at a university extended out from the Ontario Agricultural College. I had even less idea of the importance, when we were hunter-gatherers, of group solidarity—ingroup—against strangers—outgroup. This, despite the fact that, all of my life, I have been a passionate sup-porter of the Wolverhampton Wanderers (the "Wolves") soccer team and loathe and detest all soccer teams from Lancashire.

The existentialist-novelist Albert Camus said that life is "absurd." If you can get even a whiff of the excitement I have had in writing this book, learning new things and making fresh con-nections, you will understand why he could not have been more wrong. Read it, learn from it, and now pick up the torch and do better.

REFERENCES

Adovasio, J. M., O. Soffer, and J. Page. 2007. *The Invisible Sex: Uncovering the True Roles of Women in Prehistory*. New York: Collins.

Allport, A. 2020. *Britain at Bay: The Epic Story of the Second World War, 1938–1941*. New York: Knopf.

Allport, G. [1954]1958. *The Nature of Prejudice*. Garden City, NY: Doubleday.

Ambrose, S. E. 2002. "The last barrier." *No End Save Victory: New Second World War Writing*. Editor R. Cowley, 527–51. London: Putnam Adult.

Anderson, D. 2005. *Histories of the Hanged*. New York: Norton.

Anderson, K. J. 2010. *Benign Bigotry*. Cambridge: Cambridge University Press.

Anonymous. 2021. How many people have dementia in the UK? *Alzheimer's Society Blog*. https://www.alzheimers.org.uk/blog/how-many-people-have-dementia-uk.

Anscombe, G. E. M. [1957]1981. Mr Truman's degree. *Ethics, Religion and Politics: Collected Philosophical Papers, Volume III*. Editor G. E. M. Anscombe, 62–71. Oxford: Blackwell.

Anscombe, G. E. M., and N. Daniel. [1939]1981. The justice of the present war examined. *Ethics, Religion and Politics: Collected Philosophical Papers, Volume III*. Editor G. E. M. Anscombe, 72–81. Oxford: Blackwell.

Apostolou, M. 2017. Is homosexuality more prevalent in agropastoral than in hunting and gathering societies? Evidence from the standard cross-cultural sample. *Adaptive Human Behavior and Physiology* 3, no. 2: 91–100.

Aquinas, St. T. 1981. *Summa Theologica*. Translators Fathers of the English Dominican Province. London: Christian Classics.

Ardrey, R. 1961. *African Genesis: A Personal Investigation into the Animal Origins and Nature of Man*. New York: Atheneum.

Arquilla, J. 2012. The Big Kill: Sorry, Steven Pinker, the world isn't getting less violent. *Foreign Policy.* https://foreignpolicy.com/2012-12/03/the-big-kill/.

Atran, S. 2004. *In Gods We Trust: The Evolutionary Landscape of Religion.* New York: Oxford University Press.

Bada, J. L., and A. Lazcana. 2009. The origin of life. *Evolution: The First Four Billion Years.* Editors M. Ruse and J. Travis, 49–79. Cambridge, Mass.: Harvard University Press.

Bailey, D. S. 1955. *Homosexuality and the Western Christian Tradition.* London: Longmans, Green.

Ball, J. 2016. Here's who voted for Brexit—and who didn't. *BuzzFeed News.* https://www.buzzfeed.com/jamesball/heres-who-voted-for-brexit-and-who-didnt.

Bang, J. P. 1917. *Hurrah and Hallelujah: The Teaching of Germany's Poets, Prophets, Professors and Preachers.* New York: George H. Doran.

Barnes, J., editor. 1984. *The Complete Works of Aristotle.* Princeton: Princeton University Press.

Barrie, J. M. 1911. *Peter and Wendy.* London: Hodder and Stoughton.

Bartov, O. 1996. Savage war. *Confronting the Nazi Past: New Debates on Modern German History.* Editor M. Burleigh, 125–39. London: Palgrave Macmillan.

Bell, A., and S. Weinberg. 1978. *Homosexualities: A Study of Diversity among Men and Women.* New York: Simon and Schuster.

Bellah, R. 2011. *Religion in Human Evolution: From the Paleolithic to the Axial Age.* Cambridge, Mass.: Harvard University Press.

Bentham, J. 1830. *The Rationale of Reward.* London: Robert Heward.

Bierman, J., and C. Smith. 2004. *War without Hate The Desert Campaign of 1940–43.* London: Penguin.

Blight, J. G., and J. M. Lang. 2005. *The Fog of War: Lessons from the Life of Robert S. McNamara.* Lanham, Md.: Rowman and Littlefield.

Boehm, C. 2013. The biocultural evolution of conflict resolution between groups. *War, Peace, and Human Nature: The Convergence of Evolutionary and Cultural Views*. Editor D. P. Fry, 315–40. Oxford: Oxford University Press.

Bowler, P. J. 1984. *Evolution: The History of an Idea*. Berkeley: University of California Press.

Bowler, P. J. 1989. *The Mendelian Revolution: The Emergence of Hereditarian Concepts in Modern Science and Society*. London: The Athlone Press.

Boyle, R. 1996. *A Free Enquiry into the Vulgarly Received Notion of Nature*. Editors E. B. Davis and M. Hunter. Cambridge: Cambridge University Press.

Brewer, M. B. 1999. The psychology of prejudice: Ingroup love or outgroup hate? *Journal of Social Issues* 55: 429–44.

Brigden, S. 2000. *New Worlds, Lost Worlds: The Rule of the Tudors, 1485–1603*. London: Penguin.

Brogaard, B. 2020. *Hatred*. New York: Oxford University Press.

Brooks, R. 2021. Darwin's closet: The queer sides of the *Descent of Man* (1871). *Zoological Journal of the Linnean Society* 191, no. 2: 323–46.

Brophy, A. L. 2003. *Reconstructing the Dreamland. The Tulsa Riot of 1921: Race, Reparations, and Reconciliation*. Oxford: Oxford University Press.

Brown, P. 1967. *Augustine of Hippo: A Biography*. London: Faber and Faber.

Brown, W. 2019. *In the Ruins of Neoliberalism: The Rise of Antidemocratic Politics in the West*. New York: Columbia University Press.

Browne, J. 1995. *Charles Darwin: Voyaging. Volume 1 of a Biography*. London: Jonathan Cape.

Browne, J. 2002. *Charles Darwin: The Power of Place. Volume 2 of a Biography*. London: Jonathan Cape.

Browning, C. 1998. *Ordinary Men: Reserve Police Battalion 101 and the Final Solution in Poland*. New York: Harper.

Butovskaya, M. L. 2013. Aggression and conflict resolution among the nomadic Hadza of Tanzania as compared with their pastoralist neighbors. *War, Peace, and Human Nature: The Convergence of Evolutionary and Cultural Views*. Editor D. P. Fry, 278–96. Oxford: Oxford University Press.

Calvin, J. [1536]1962. *Institutes of the Christian Religion*. Grand Rapids: Eerdmans.

Ceci, S. J., and W. M. Williams. 2009. *The Mathematics of Sex: How Biology and Society Conspire to Limit Talented Women and Girls*. New York: Oxford University Press.

Chagnon, N. 1988. Life histories, blood revenge, and warfare in a tribal population. *Science* 239: 985–92.

Chorley, W. R. 2007. *RAF Bomber Command Losses. Volume 7*. Hinkley: Midland Counties.

Churchill, S. E. 1998. Cold adaptation, heterochrony, and Neandertals. *Evolutionary Anthropology* 7: 46–61.

Cicero, M. T. 1829. *De Re Publica*. Translator G. W. Fetherstonhaugh. New York: G. and C. Carville.

Cicero, M. T. 1913. *De Officiis*. Translator W. Miller. Cambridge, Mass.: Harvard University Press.

Clark, C. 2009. *Iron Kingdom: The Rise and Downfall of Prussia, 1600–1947*. Cambridge, Mass.: Harvard University Press.

Cook, T. 1999. *No Place to Run: The Canadian Corps and Gas Warfare in the First World War*. Vancouver, B.C.: UBC Press.

Cooper, J. M., editor. 1997. *Plato: Complete Works*. Indianapolis: Hackett.

Cosmides, L., and J. Tooby. 1990. The past explains the present: Adaptation and the structure of ancestral environments. *Ethology and Sociobiology* 11: 375–424.

Cosmides, L., and J. Tooby. 1997. *Evolutionary Psychology: A Primer*. http/wwwpysch.ucsb.edu/research/cep/primer.html .

Craig, O. E., et al. 2013. Earliest evidence for the use of pottery. *Nature* 496: 351–54.

Cramer, K. J. 2016. For years, I've been watching anti-elite fury build in Wisconsin: Then came Trump. *Vox*. https://www.vox.com/the-big-idea/2016-11/16/13645116/rural-resentment-elites-trump.

Dart, R. 1953. The predatory transition from ape to man. *International Anthropological and Linguistic Review* 1, no. 4: 201–17.

Darwin, C. 1859. *On the Origin of Species by Means of Natural Selection, or the Preservation of Favoured Races in the Struggle for Life*. London: John Murray.

Darwin, C. 1868. *The Variation of Animals and Plants under Domestication*. London: Murray.

Darwin, C. 1871. *The Descent of Man, and Selection in Relation to Sex*. London: John Murray.

Darwin, C. 1958. *The Autobiography of Charles Darwin 1809–1882. With the Original Omissions Restored. Edited and with Appendix and Notes by His Grand-Daughter Nora Barlow*. London: Collins.

Darwin, C. 1985–. *The Correspondence of Charles Darwin*. Cambridge: Cambridge University Press.

Darwin, C. 1987. *Charles Darwin's Notebooks, 1836–1844*. Editors P. H. Barrett, P. J. Gautrey, S. Herbert, D. Kohn, and S. Smith. Ithaca, N.Y.: Cornell University Press.

Dawkins, R. 1976. *The Selfish Gene*. Oxford: Oxford University Press.

Dawkins, R. 2002. Religion's real child abuse. *Free Inquiry* 22, no. 4: 9.

Dawkins, R. 2006. *The God Delusion*. New York: Houghton, Mifflin, Harcourt.

Dettwyler, K. A. 1991. Can paleopathology provide evidence for "compassion"? *American Journal of Physical Anthropology* 84, no. 4: 375–84.

De Waal, F. 2007. *Chimpanzee Politics: Power and Sex among Apes: 25th Anniversary Edition*. Baltimore: Johns Hopkins University Press.

Dickens, C. [1837]1948. *Oliver Twist*. Oxford: Oxford University Press.

Dickens, C. [1839]1948. *Nicholas Nickleby*. Oxford: Oxford University Press.

Dickens, C. [1841]1948. *Barnaby Rudge*. Oxford: Oxford University Press.

Dickens, C. [1843]1948. *A Christmas Carol*. Oxford: Oxford University Press.

Dickens, C. [1853]1948. *Bleak House*. Oxford: Oxford University Press.

Dickens, C. [1857]1948. *Little Dorrit*. Oxford: Oxford University Press.

Dickens, C. [1865]1948. *Our Mutual Friend*. Oxford: Oxford University Press.

Dover, K. J. 1978. *Greek Homosexuality*. Cambridge, Mass.: Harvard University Press.

Durkheim, É. 1912[1915]. *The Elementary Forms of the Religious Life*. Translator J. W. Swain. New York: Macmillan.

Dyble, M., G. D. Salali, N. Chaudhary, A. Page, D. Smith, J. Thompson, L. Vinicius, R. Mace, and A. B Migliano. 2015. Sex equality can explain the unique social structure of hunter-gatherer bands. *Science* 348 (6236): 796–98.

Edsall, T. B. 2019. Trump has a gift for tearing us apart: There are a lot of different ways to build walls. *New York Times*, December 11.

Edsall, T. B. 2020. The resentment that never sleeps. *New York Times*. nytimes. com.

Edsall, T. B. 2021. Abortion has never been just about abortion. *New York Times*. nytimes.com.

Edsall, T. B. 2021. Joe Biden is about to find out what's left of America: Have Trump and trumpism made the United States ungovernable? *New York Times*. https://www.nytimes.com/2021-01/20/opinion/joe-biden-inauguration.html?action=click&module=Opinion&pgtype=Homepage.

Ellsworth, S. 1992. *Death in a Promised Land: The Tulsa Race Riot of 1921*. Baton Rouge: LSU Press.

Epstein, J. 2020. Is there a doctor in the White House? Not if you need an M.D. *Wall Street Journal*, December 12.

Evans, R. J. 2003. *The Coming of the Third Reich*. New York: Penguin.

Evans, R. J. 2005. *The Third Reich in Power*. New York: Penguin.

Evans, R. J. 2009. *The Third Reich at War*. New York: Penguin.

Ewans, M. 2002. *European Atrocity, African Catastrophe: Leopold II, the Congo Free State and Its Aftermath*. London: Routledge.

Faulkner, W. 1936 [1986]. *Absalom! Absalom!* New York: Vintage.

Ferguson, N. 2004. Prisoner taking and prisoner killing in the age of total war: Towards a political economy of military defeat. *War in History* 11, no. 2: 148–92.

Ferguson, R. B. 2013a. Pinker's list: Exaggerating prehistory war mortality. *War, Peace, Human Nature: The Convergence of Evolutionary and Cultural Views*. Editor D. P. Fry, 112–31. Oxford: Oxford University Press.

Ferguson, R. B. 2013b. The prehistory of war and peace in Europe and the Near East. *War, Peace, and Human Nature: The Convergence of Evolutionary and Cultural Views*. Editor D. P. Fry, 191–240. Oxford: Oxford University Press.

Ferguson, R. B. 2015. History, explanation, and war among the Yanomami: A response to Chagnon's *Noble Savages*. *Anthropological Theory* 15: 377–406.

Fiske, A. P., and T. S. Rai. 2014. *Virtuous Violence: Hurting and Killing to Create, Sustain, End, and Honor Social Relationships*. Cambridge: Cambridge University Press.

Ford, J. C. 1944. The morality of obliteration bombing. *Theological Studies* 5: 261–309.

Franklin, J. H., and E. Higginbotham. 2010. *From Slavery to Freedom: A History of African Americans, 9th Edition*. New York: McGraw-Hill.

Freud, S. 1935. Letter to an American mother. *Gay/Lesbian Resources*. http://psychpage.com/gay/library/freudsletter.html .

Freud, S. 1960. *Letters of Sigmund Freud, 1873–1939*. Translators and editors T. Stern and J. Stern. New York: Basic Books.

Friedlander, S. 1997. *Nazi Germany and the Jews: The Years of Persecution 1933–39*. London: Weidenfeld and Nicolson.

Friedlander, S. 2008. *Nazi Germany and the Jews: 1939–1945. The Years of Extermination*. New York: Harper Perennial.

Fry, D. P. 2013a. War, peace, and human nature: The challenge of achieving scientific objectivity. *War, Peace, and Human Nature: The Convergence of Evolutionary and Cultural Views*. Editor D. P. Fry, 1–21. Oxford: Oxford University Press.

Fry, D. P. 2013b. The evolution of cooperation: What's war got to do with it? *Reviews in Anthropology* 42: 102–21.

Fry, D. P. 2014. Group identity as an obstacle and catalyst of peace. *Pathways to Peace: The Transformative Power of Children and Families*. Editors J. F. Leckman, C. Panter-Brick, and R. Salah, 79–92. Cambridge, Mass.: MIT Press.

Fry, D. P., C. A. Keith, and P. Söderberg. 2020. Social complexity, inequality and war before farming: Congruence of comparative forager and archaeological data. *Social Inequality before Farming. Multidisciplinary Approaches to the Study of Social Organization in Prehistoric and Ethnographic Hunter Gatherer-Fisher Societies*. Editor L. Moreau, 303–20. Cambridge: McDonald Institute for Archaeological Research.

Fussell, P. [1970]2013. *The Great War and Modern Memory, New Edition.* Oxford: Oxford University Press.

Gellately, R. 2001. *Backing Hitler.* Oxford: Oxford University Press.

Gerber, D. A. 1994. Heroes and misfits: The troubled social reintegration of disabled veterans in "The Best Years of Our Lives." *American Quarterly* 46: 545–74.

Gest, J. 2016. *The New Minority: White Working Class Politics in an Age of Immigration and Inequality.* New York: Oxford University Press.

Ghiglieri, M. P. 1999. *The Dark Side of Man: Tracing the Origins of Male Violence.* Reading, Mass.: Perseus Books.

Gidron, N., and P. A. Hall. 2019. Populism as a problem of social integration. *Comparative Political Studies* 53, no. 7: 1027–59.

Gilmour, D. 2018. *The British in India: A Social History of the Raj.* New York: Farrar, Straus, and Giroux.

Goddard, H. H. 1912. *The Kallikak Family: A Study in the Heredity of Feeble-Mindedness.* New York: Macmillan.

Goldhagen, D. 1996. *Hitler's Willing Executioners: Ordinary Germans and the Holocaust.* New York: Knopf.

Gooch, J. 1995. UK (Introduction). *The Oxford Companion to the Second World War.* Editor I. C. B. Dear, 1129–30. Oxford: Oxford University Press.

Goodall, J. 1986. *The Chimpanzees of Gombe: Patterns of Behavior.* Cambridge, Mass.: Belknap.

Gordin, M. D. 2007. *Five Days in August: How World War II Became a Nuclear War.* Princeton, N.J.: Princeton University Press.

Gray, J. G. 1998. *The Warriors: Reflections on Men in Battle.* Lincoln, Neb.: Bison.

Grayling, A. C. 2006. *Among the Dead Cities: Is the Targeting of Civilians in War ever Justified?* London: Bloomsbury.

Grayling, A. C. 2017. *War: An Enquiry.* New Haven: Yale University Press.

Greene, J. 2013. *Moral Tribes: Emotion, Reason, and the Gap between Us and Them.* New York: Penguin.

Grossman, D. 2009. *On Killing: The Psychological Cost of Learning to Kill in War and Society.* New York: Back Bay Books.

Grotius, H. [1625]1901. *The Rights of War and Peace, including the Law of Nature and of Nations*. Editor A. M. Campbell. New York: M. Walter Dunne.

Haas, J., and M. Piscitelli. 2013. The prehistory of warfare: misled by ethnography. *War, Peace, and Human Nature: The Convergence of Evolutionary and Cultural Views*. Editor D. P. Fry, 168–90. Oxford: Oxford University Press.

Haeckel, E. 1866. *Generelle Morphologie der Organismen*. Berlin: Georg Reimer.

Haidt, J. 2012. *The Righteous Mind: Why Good People Are Divided by Politics and Religion*. New York: Vintage.

Hanna-Jones, N. 2019. The 1619 project. *The New York Times*. August 14. https://www.nytimes.com/interactive/2019-08/14/magazine/1619-america-slavery.html.

Harrington, A. 1996. *Reenchanted Science: Holism in German Culture from Wilhelm II to Hitler*. Princeton, N.J.: Princeton University Press.

Harris, S. 2004. *The End of Faith: Religion, Terror, and the Future of Reason*. New York: Free Press.

Hayden, B. 1987. Alliances and ritual ecstasy: Human responses to resource stress. *Journal for the Scientific Study of Religion* 26: 81–91.

Hayden, B. 2014. Social complexity. *The Oxford Handbook of the Archaeology and Anthropology of Hunter-Gatherers*. Editors V. Cummings, P. Jordan, and M. Zvelebil, 643–62. Oxford: Oxford University Press.

Hayden, B. 2019. Was Le Placard used by secret societies? *The Grotte du Placard at 150*. Editor C. Delage, 186–97. Oxford: Archeopress.

Hayden, B. 2020. Foragers or feasters? Inequalities in the Upper Paleolithic. Ms.

Haywood, I., and J. Seed. 2015. *The Gordon Riots: Politics, Culture and Insurrection in Late Eighteenth-Century Britain*. Cambridge: Cambridge University Press.

Heffer, S. 1998. *Like the Roman: The Life of Enoch Powell*. London: Weidenfeld and Nicholson.

Herf, J. 2006. *The Jewish Enemy: Nazi Propaganda during World War II and the Holocaust*. Cambridge, Mass.: Harvard University Press.

Hersch, S. M. 1972. *Cover-Up: The Army's Secret Investigation of the Massacre at My Lai 4*. New York: Random House.

Hegel, G. W. F. [1807] 1977. *Phenomenology of Spirit*. Translator A. V. Miller. Oxford: Oxford University Press.

Hetherington, M., and J. Weiler. 2018. *Prius or Pickup? How the Answers to Four Simple Questions Explain America's Great Divide*. Boston: Houghton Mifflin Harcourt.

Hillis, N. D. 1918. *The Blot on the Kaiser's 'Scutcheon*. New York: Fleming H. Revell.

Hitler, A. 1925[1939]. *Mein Kampf*. Translator J. V. Murphy. London: Hurst & Blackett.

Hobbes, T. [1651] 1982. *Leviathan*. Harmondsworth, Mddx.: Penguin.

Holmes, A. F., editor. 2005. *War and Christian Ethics, Second Edition*. Grand Rapids, Mich.: Baker Academic.

Howard, M. 1991. *The Lessons of History*. New Haven: Yale University Press.

Hrdy, S. B. 1999. *Mother Nature: A History of Mothers, Infants, and Natural Selection*. New York: Pantheon Books.

Hughes, T. 1861. *Tom Brown at Oxford*. London: Macmillan.

Hume, D. [1739–1740]1978. *A Treatise of Human Nature*. Oxford: Oxford University Press.

Hume, D. [1757]1963. A natural history of religion. *Hume on Religion*. Editor R. Wollheim, 31–98. London: Fontana.

Huxley, T. H. [1893]2009. *Evolution and Ethics with a New Introduction*. Editor M. Ruse. Princeton: Princeton University Press.

Jackson, M., and D. B. Grusky. 2018. A post-liberal theory of stratification. *The British Journal of Sociology* 69: 1096–133.

Jarvenpa, R., and H. J. Brumbach. 2014. Hunter-gatherer gender and identity. *The Oxford Handbook of the Archaeology and Anthropology of Hunter-Gatherers*. Editors V. Cummings, P. Jordan, and M. Zvelebil, 1243–65. Oxford: Oxford University Press.

Jasper, R. C. D. 1967. *George Bell, Bishop of Chichester*. Oxford: Oxford University Press.

Jenkins, P. 2014. *The Great and Holy War: How World War I Became a Religious Crusade*. New York: HarperOne.

Johanson, D., and K. Wong. 2009. *Lucy's Legacy: The Quest for Human Origins*. New York: Crown.

Johnson, G. R. 1986. Kin selection, socialization, and patriotism: An integrating theory. *Politics and the Life Sciences* 4: 127–40.

Jones, E. 1849. *The Land Monopoly: The Suffering and Demoralization Caused by It, and the Justice & Expediency of Its Abolition*. London: Charles Fox.

Jones, H. 2017. *My Lai, Vietnam, 1968, and the Descent into Darkness*. Oxford: Oxford University Press.

Kant, I. [1785]1959. *Foundations of the Metaphysics of Morals*. Indianapolis: Bobbs-Merrill.

Kant, I. [1795]1903. *Perpetual Peace: A Philosophical Sketch*. Translator M. Campbell Smith. London: Allen and Unwin.

Keegan, J. 1993. *A History of Warfare*. New York: Vintage.

Kellogg, V. L. 1917. *Headquarters Nights: A Record of Conversations and Experiences at the Headquarters of the German Army in France and Belgium*. Boston: Atlantic Monthly Press.

Kelly, R. 2000. *Warless Societies and the Origin of War*. Ann Arbor: University of Michigan.

Kelly, R. 2005. The evolution of lethal intergroup violence. *PNAS* 102: 24–29.

Kelsay, J. 2007. *Arguing the Just War in Islam*. Cambridge, Mass.: Harvard University Press.

Kershaw, I. 1999. *Hitler 1889–1936: Hubris*. New York: Norton.

King, W. 1864. The reputed fossil man of the Neanderthal. *Quarterly Journal of Science*: 88–97.

Kishlansky, M. 1997. *A Monarchy Transformed: Britain, 1603–1714, 6th Edition*. London: Penguin.

Kissel, M., and N. C. Kim. 2019. The emergence of human warfare: Current perspectives. *American Journal of Physical Anthropology* 168: 141–63.

Klein, E. 2021. Obama explains how America went from "Yes we can" to "MAGA." *New York Times.* https://www.nytimes.com/2021-06/01/opinion/ezra-klein-podcast-barack-obama.html?action=click&module=Opinion&pgtype=Homepage.

Koonz, C. 2003. *The Nazi Conscience.* Cambridge, Mass.: Belknap.

Lahr, M. M. et al. 2016a. Inter-group violence among early Holocene hunter-gatherers of West Turkana, Kenya. *Nature* 529: 394–8.

Lahr, M. M. et al. 2016b. Reply: Contesting the massacre at Nataruk. *Nature* 539: E10–E11.

Larson, E. J. 2020. *Franklin & Washington: The Founding Partnership.* New York: William Morrow.

Leachman, C.-E. 2019. "It's a national crisis": UK's birth rate is falling dramatically. *The Conversation.* https://theconversation.com/its-a-national-crisis-uks-birth-rate-is-falling-dramatically-121399.

Lears, J. 2021. Orthodoxy of the elites. *New York Review of Books* 68, no. 1: 8–11.

LeDrew, S. 2016. *The Evolution of Atheism: The Politics of a Modern Movement.* New York: Oxford University Press.

LeVay, S. 2010. *Gay, Straight, and the Reason Why: The Science of Sexual Orientation.* Oxford: Oxford University Press.

Lieberman, D. E. 2013. *The Story of the Human Body: Evolution, Health, and Disease.* New York: Vintage.

Livingstone Smith, D. 2007. *The Most Dangerous Animal: Human Nature and the Origins of War.* New York: St. Martin's Press.

Livingstone Smith, D. 2011. *Less Than Human: Why We Demean, Enslave, and Exterminate Others.* New York: St Martin's Griffin.

Lodge, D. 1980. *How Far Can You Go?* London: Secker and Warburg.

Lorenz, K. 1966. *On Aggression.* London: Methuen.

Lovejoy, A. O. 1923. The supposed primitivism of Rousseau's *Discourse on Inequality. Modern Philology* 21: 165–86.

Lowenstein, S. M. 2005. Jewish intermarriage and conversion in Germany and Austria. *Modern Judaism* 25: 23–61.

Luther, M. 1955-. *Luther's Works*. Editors J. Pelikan, H. T. Lehmann, C. Boyd-Brown, and B. T. G. Mayes. Saint Louis: Concordia Publishing House.

MacMillan, M. 2002. *Paris 1919: Six Months That Changed the World*. New York: Random House.

MacMillan, M. 2014. *The War That Ended Peace: The Road to 1914*. New York: Random House.

Malthus, T. R. [1826]1914. *An Essay on the Principle of Population, Sixth Edition*. London: Everyman.

Marcus, G. 2004. *The Birth of the Mind*. New York: Basic Books.

Marcus, L., J. Mueller, and M. Rose, editors. 2002. *Elizabeth I: Collected Works*. Chicago: University of Chicago Press.

Marlowe, F. 2010. *The Hadza Hunter-Gatherers of Tanzania*. Berkeley: University of California Press.

Marrin, A. 1974. *The Last Crusade: The Church of England in the First World War*. Durham, N.C.: Duke University Press.

Maynard, J. 1996. *Bennett and the Pathfinders*. Tintern: Arms and Armour.

Meagher, R. E. 2014. *Killing from the Inside Out: Moral Injury and Just War*. Eugene, Ore.: Cascade.

Mellen, R. 2021. Regarding same-sex unions, Pope Francis must navigate a divided church. *Washington Post*, March 16. https://www.washingtonpost.com/world/2021-03/16/catholic-opinion-gay-marriage-pope-francis/.

Middleton, R. 2011. *War of American Independence 1775–1783*. London: Routledge.

Milam, E. L. 2019. *Creatures of Cain: The Hunt for Human Nature in Cold War America*. Princeton, N.J.: Princeton University Press.

Mill, J. S. [1848]1871. *Principles of Political Economy*. London: Longmans, Green, Reader and Dyer.

Mivart, S. G. J. 1874. [Review] Researches into the early history of mankind [etc.]. *Quarterly Review* 137: 40–77.

Mill, J. S. [1863]2008. Utilitarianism. Editor J. Bennett. http://www.earlymoderntexts.com/assets/pdfs/mill1863.pdf.

Montgomery, L. M. 1921. *Rilla of Ingleside*. Toronto: McCelland and Stewart.

Morison, I. 2014. *A Journey through the Universe.* Cambridge: Cambridge University Press.

Mozley, J. B. 1871. *War: A Sermon Preached before the University of Oxford.* London: Longman's, Green.

Nevels, C. S. 2007. *Lynching to Belong: Claiming Whiteness through Racial Violence.* College Station: Texas A & M University Press.

Newborn, J. 2006. *Sophie Scholl and the White Rose.* Oxford: Oneworld Publications.

Newson, L., and P. J. Richerson. 2021. *The Story of Us: A New Look at Human Evolution.* Oxford: Oxford University Press.

Niebuhr, R. [1932]2015. Moral man and immoral society. *Major Works on Religion and Politics.* R. Niebuhr, 135–350. New York: Library of America.

Niebuhr, R. 2015. The bombing of Germany. *Major Works on Religion and Politics.* R. Niebuhr, 654–55. New York: The Library of America.

Nieman, S. 2019. *Learning from the Germans: Race and the Memory of Evil.* New York: Farrar, Straus and Giroux.

Nietzsche, F. [1887]2006. *On the Genealogy of Morality.* Editor K. Ansell-Pearson. Cambridge: Cambridge University Press.

Nussbaum, M. C. 2006. *Frontiers of Justice: Disability, Nationality, Species Membership (The Tanner Lectures on Human Values).* Cambridge, Mass.: Belknap Press.

O'Brien, W. V. 1992. Desert Storm: A just war analysis. *St. John's Law Review* 66: 797–823.

Pagano, A. S., S. Mirquez, and J. T. Laitman. 2019. Reconstructing the Neanderthal eustachian tube: New insights on disease susceptibility, fitness cost, and extinction. *The Anatomical Record* 32: 2109–25.

Peoples, H. C., P. Duda, and F. W. Marlowe. 2016. Hunter-gatherers and the origins of religion. *Human Nature* 27: 261–82.

Perlmutter, P. 1992. *Divided We Fall: A History of Ethnic, Religious, and Racial Prejudice in America.* Ames: Iowa State Press.

Pinker, S. 2011. *The Better Angels of Our Nature: Why Violence Has Declined.* New York: Viking.

Potts, M. 2019. In the land of self-defeat. *New York Times*, October 4. https://www.nytimes.com/2019-10/04/opinion/sunday/trump-arkansas.html.

Powell, E. 1969. *Freedom and Reality*. Kingswood: Elliot Right Way Books.

Rawls, J. 1971. *A Theory of Justice*. Cambridge, MA: Harvard University Press.

Reich, D. 2018. *Who We Are and How We Got Here Ancient DNA and the New Science of the Human Race*. New York: Pantheon.

Robbins, J. 2020. Black killings reveal unwelcome racial truth about America. *Boston Herald*, August 31.

Roberts, S., and M. Rizzo. 2020. The psychology of American racism. *OSF Preprints*. https://doi.org/10.31219/osf.io/w2h73 .

Rogers, T. 2021. Welcome to Germany. *New York Review of Books* 68, 7: 29–31.

Rosenberg, N. A., J. K. Pritchard, J. L. Weber, H. M. Cann, K. K. Kidd, L. A. Zhivotovsky, and M. Feldman. 2002. Genetic structure of human populations. *Science* 298: 2381–85.

Rousseau, J.-J. [1762]2020. The social contract. *Selected Political Writings*. Translator G. D. H. Cole, 3–83. Las Vegas: Independently Published.

Rousseau, J.-J. 1755. Discourse on Inequality. https://www.aub.edu.lb/fas/cvsp/Documents/DiscourseonInequality.pdf879500092.pdf.

Rule, J. B. 1988. *Theories of Civil Violence*. Berkeley: University of California Press.

Ruse, M. 2015. *Atheism: What Everyone Needs to Know*. Oxford: Oxford University Press.

Ruse, M. 2019. *A Meaning to Life*. Oxford: Oxford University Press.

Sandel, M. 2020a. Disdain for the less educated is the last acceptable prejudice: It's having a corrosive effect on American life—and hurting the Democratic Party. *New York Times*, September 2. https://www.nytimes.com/2020-09/02/opinion/education-prejudice.html.

Sandel, M. 2020b. *The Tyranny of Merit: What's Become of the Common Good?* New York: Farrar, Straus and Giroux.

Saussure, C. de. 1902. *A Foreign View of England in the Reigns of George I & II: The Letters of Monsieur César de Saussure to his Family*. Translator M. Van Muyden. London: John Murray.

Schaepdrijver, S. de. 2014. The German atrocities of 1914. *British Library: World War One*. https://www.bl.uk/world-war-one/articles/civilian-atrocities-german-1914.

Scott, E. 2019. Trump's most insulting—and violent—language is often reserved for immigrants. *Washington Post*, October 2. https://www.washingtonpost.com/politics/2019-10/02/trumps-most-insulting-violent-language-is-often-reserved-immigrants/.

Selous, E. 1901–02. An observational diary of the habits—mostly domestic—of the great crested grebe (*Podicipes cristatus*). Continued as: An observational diary of the habits—mostly domestic—of the great crested grebe (*Podicipes cristatus*), and of the peewit (*Vanellus vulgaris*), with some general remarks. *Zoologist* 5: 161–83; 5: 339–50; 5: 454–62; 6: 133–44.

Singer, P. 1972. Famine, affluence and morality. *Philosophy and Public Affairs* 1: 229–43.

Shepherd, R. 1994. *Ian Macleod*. London: Hutchinson.

Smith, A. [1776]1937. *The Wealth of Nations*. New York: Modern Library.

Smith, H. K. 1942. *Last Train from Berlin*. New York: Alfred A. Knopf.

Smith H. M., D. Chiszar, and R. R. Montanucci. 1997. Subspecies and classification. *Herpetological Review* 28: 13–16.

Sobolewska, M., and R. Ford. 2020. *Brexitland*. Cambridge: Cambridge University Press.

Sosis, R., and C. Alcorta. 2003. Signaling, solidarity, and the sacred: The evolution of religious behavior. *Evolutionary Anthropology* 12: 264–74.

Sosis, R., and E. Bressler. 2003. Cooperation and commune longevity: A test of the costly signaling theory of religion. *Cross-Cultural Research* 37: 211–39.

Spencer, H. 1870. On ancestor worship and other peculiar beliefs. *Fortnightly Review* 13: 535–50.

Spencer, H. 1892. *The Principles of Ethics*. London: Williams and Norgate.

Stanley, J. 2018. *How Fascism Works: The Politics of Us and Them*. New York: Random House.

Staub, E. 1992. *The Roots of Evil: The Origins of Genocide and Other Group Violence*. Cambridge: Cambridge University Press.

Stojanowski, C. M., A. C. Seidel, L. C. Fulginiti, K. M. Johnson, and J. E. Buikstra. 2016. Contesting the massacre at Nataruk. *Nature* 539: E8–E11.

Strafford, J. 2009. *Our Fight for Democracy: The United Kingdom and the European Union*. London: The Bruges Group.

Syal, R. 2021. UK inquiry blames "pervasive racism" for unequal commemoration of troops. *The Guardian*.

Templeton, A. R. 2013. Biological races in humans. *Studies in the History and Philosophy of Biology and the Biomedical Sciences*. 44: 262–71.

Testart, A. 1982. *Les chasseurs-cueilleurs ou l'Origine des inégalités*. Paris: Société d'Ethnographie.

Thatcher, M. 1993. *Downing Street Years*. New York: HarperCollins.

Tooby, J., and L. Cosmides. 2010. Groups in mind: The conditional roots of war and morality. *Human Morality and Sociality: Evolutionary and Comparative Perspectives*. Editor H. Hogh-Oleson, 191–234. New York: Palgrave-Macmillan.

Tooze, A. 2007. *The Wages of Destruction: The Making and Breaking of the Nazi Economy*. New York: Viking.

Trump, D. J. 2016. Transcript: Donald Trump's taped comments about women. *New York Times*, October 8. https://www.nytimes.com/2016-10/08/us/donald-trump-tape-transcript.html.

Tuttle, R. H. 2014. *Apes and Human Evolution*. Cambridge, Mass.: Harvard University Press.

United Kingdom Government. 2010. *Equality Act*. National Archives; legislation.gov.uk.

United States Congress. 1990. *The Americans with Disabilities Act*. 42 U.S.C. § 12101.

von Bernhardi, F. 1912. *Germany and the Next War*. London: Edward Arnold.

Waller, J. 2007. *Becoming Evil: How Ordinary People Commit Genocide and Mass Killing*. Oxford: Oxford University Press.

Walzer, M. 1977. *Just and Unjust Wars*. New York: Basic Books.

Whewell, W. 1840. *The Philosophy of the Inductive Sciences*. London: Parker.

White, F. J., M. T. Waller, and K. J. Boose. 2013. Evolution of primate peace. *War, Peace, and Human Nature: The Convergence of Evolutionary and Cultural Views.* Editor D. P. Fry, 389–405. Oxford: Oxford University Press.

Wilkerson, I. 2020. *Caste: The Origins of Our Discontents.* New York: Random House.

Wilson, M. L. 2013. Chimpanzees, warfare, and the invention of peace. *War, Peace, and Human Nature: The Convergence of Evolutionary and Cultural Views.* Editor D. P. Fry, 361–88. Oxford: Oxford University Press.

Winder, R. 2004. *Bloody Foreigners: The Story of Immigration to Britain.* London: Little Brown.

Zilhão, J. 2014. The Neanderthals: Evolution, paleoecology, and extinction. *The Oxford Handbook of the Archaeology and Anthropology of Hunter-Gatherers.* Editors V. Cummings, P. Jordan, and M. Zvelebil, 191–213. Oxford: Oxford University Press.

INDEX

For the benefit of digital users, indexed terms that span two pages (e.g., 52–53) may, on occasion, appear on only one of those pages.

Abelard, Pierre, 89
abortion, 257–58
Absalom, Absalom!
    (Faulkner), 80–81
adaptations (Darwin), 5–6
African Americans, demographics
    of, 176–78
African Genesis (Ardrey), 31–32
agriculture, 20–21, 37–38, 46–47.
    See also hunter-gatherer
    emerging hatred and, 256
    homosexuality and, 89–90
    inequality and, 114–15
    population movement
        and, 70–72
    war and, 48–49, 56–57
Alexander I, Tsar, 23–24, 25–26
allegiance. *See* ingroup
Allport, Gordon, 60–61, 112–13
alternatives, peaceful, 155
altruism
    contingent, 63
    individual versus group, 15

reciprocal (Darwin), 15, 63–64, 214
American ("Know Nothing")
    Party, 166
Americans with Disabilities
    Act, 247–48
animism, 95–97
Anne of Green Gables
    (Montgomery), 135
Anschluss, 140
Anscombe, Elizabeth, 144–45, 146–
    47, 158–59
anti-Semitism. *See* prejudice: against
    Jewish people
aquaculture, 48–49
Aquinas, St. Thomas, 121–28, 130,
    144, 214
archaeology, 34–40
Ardrey, Robert, 31–32, 33, 58–
    59, 163
Aristotle, 5–6, 112–13, 178–82, 204,
    209, 210–11, 257–58,
asylums, 104–5
atheism, 94, 188–89

atrocities. *See also* casualties
Aarschot, Tamines on the Meuse,
Dinant, Louvain (Leuven),
Ardennes, 138
My Lai, 118, 120–21, 153, 211–12
Russian, in East Prussia, 151
Augustine, St., 125–28, 130–31, 142
Austin, Jane, 182–83
Australopithecus afarensis, 3–4
Australopithecus africanus, 29–30
authority, sovereign, for a just war,
127–28, 154, 159–60
automation, 168–69, 173–74, 224

Balmer, Randall, 258–59
Barnaby Rudge (Dickens), 186–88
barnacles, 4–5, 183
Barrie, J. M., 194
Baxter, Richard, 57–58
"Bedlam" (New Order of our Lady of
Bethlehem), 102–4
behavior
cooperative, 13–14, 45–46, 62–63,
96–97 (*see also* ingroup: ver-
sus outgroup)
moral and immoral, 118–19, 176–
78, 212–13, 222–23
Bell, Bishop George, 149–50
"Bell Beaker culture," 70–72, 229–30
Bellah, Robert, 47–48, 96–97
Bentham, Jeremy, 210
Big Bang theory, 1
bin Laden, Osama, 26–27, 127–28
bipedalism, 3–4
Bismarck, Otto von, 134–35, 163
"Black Lives Matter," 238

"blackmailer's charter," 242–43
Bleak House (Dickens), 213
Blyth, Edmund, 234–39, 243–44
Boehm, Christopher, 32–33
Boleyn, Ann, 24–25
bombing, obliteration, 147–50, 158–59
Bonaparte, Napoleon, 23–24, 50–51
bonobos, 44–45
Borodino, Battle of, 23–24
Bosworth Field, Battle of, 192
brain
bipedalism and the, 35
cooperative, 28–29
development, 3–4, 14, 241–42
happiness of others and the, 213
modern "stone age," 256
size, 3–4, 45–46, 82–83, 114–15
breeding, selective, 4–5
Brexit, 224–28, 230
Brogaard, Berit, 173
Brown, John, 28
Brown v. Board of Education, 236
Browning, Christopher, 250–52
Bund Deutscher Mädel, 201
Burnett, Frances Hodgson, 196–97
Bush, Billy, 109–13
Bush, President George H. W., 154
Butler, "Rab," 169–70
Butler Act, 169–70, 233–34

Calley, Lieutenant William, Jr., 118–
19, 153
Calvin, Jean, 97, 130–31
Cambrian Explosion, 1–3
Camus, Albert, 261
cannibalism, 29–31

Canterbury Tales (Chaucer), 182–83
captive taking (slave raiding), 43. *See also* slavery
casualties, 17–19, 28–29. *See also* atrocities
    after the "Great Escape," 151–52
    among World War II bomber crews, 152–53
    Belgian, 138
    Chinatown (L.A.), 166–67
    Clifford's Tower, 250–51
    of Dresden obliteration bombing, 149–50
    Eastern Front, 151
    of the *Einsatzgruppen*, 108
    "Gordon Riots," 186–87
    of Hamburg obliteration bombing, 148–49
    Holocaust, 250–51
    Jebel Sahaba, 48–49
    Kenyan, 48–49
    through mass killings, 19–20
    twentieth century, 222–23
Catherine of Aragon, 24–25
cause, just, 127–28, 154–55
Cavaliers, 24–26
Chagnon, Napoleon, 40, 43–44
Chamberlain, Prime Minister Neville, 140–41, 145–46, 220–21
change, 5–6. *See also* agriculture
    attitudinal, 224
    conservatism and, 78
    cultural, 68–69, 168–69, 234–35, 249–50
    individual selection and, 212–13
    right reason and, 122

    societal, 37–38, 43, 175, 206–7, 236–39, 256
    understanding and, 241–42, 244
Charles I, King, 24–26
Charles II, King, 24–26
Chatterley, Connie, and Sir Clifford, 198–99
Chaucer, Geoffrey, 182–83
chimpanzees, 44
Christian Ethics (Baxter), 57–58
Christmas Carol, A (Dickens), 245–46
Christmas truce of 1914, 138
Churchill, Prime Minister Winston, 149–50
Cicero, 121, 129–30
Civil Rights Act of 1964, 236
Cleaver, Fanny ("Jenny Wren"), 245–46
Clinton, Hillary, 112–13
Cochran, Major John, 151–52
Colin, 196–97
competition, 13–14, 32–33
complexity, 46–49
conduct, moral, 121–22, 141–42. *See also* morality
conflict. *See also* war
    Armenian-Turkish, 17–18, 39–40
    competition and, 32–33
    Greenwoods District (Tulsa, Oklahoma), 18–19
    Indian-British, 18–19
    Irish-British, 18–19
    Jewish-German, 17–18, 39–40
    Kulak-Russian, 17–18, 39–40
    as a natural state (Hobbes), 54–55
    pogroms, 17–18
    Rwandan, 17–18

conflicts. *See also* atrocities
"consilience of inductions"
    (Whewell), 6
cooperation. *See* behavior: cooperative
Cornwallis, General Charles, 26–27
Cosmides, Leda, 32–33, 256
cowardice, 180–81
Cramer, Katherine J., 172
"Critical Race Theory," 238
Cromwell, Oliver, 24–26, 250–51
Cronos, 93
"Categorical Imperative" (Kant), 209

Daniel, Norman, 144–45, 146–47
Dart, Raymond, 29–30, 58–59
Darwin, Charles, 4–9, 11–12, 63–64,
    120, 183–86, 234–35
Darwin, George, 185–86
Darwinism, 34–49
Dawkins, Richard, 9–11, 94, 188–
    90, 244
de Rochambeau, Count (Jean-Baptiste
    Donatien de Vimeur), 26–27
de Waal, Franz, 113
dementia, 249–50
Dench, Dame Judi, 182–83
Denison, Michael, 182–83
Denisovans (*H. s. denisova*), 3–4,
    81–82, 85
Descent of Man, The (Darwin), 13–14,
    183, 234–35, 241–42
Dickens, Charles, 65–72, 182–83,
    186–88, 195–96, 245–46
"Disabled" (Owen), 198–200
discrimination, 64, 65, 161–62
    target, 156–57

Disraeli, Benjamin, 77
dissent, 144–45
domestication, 37–38
Donne, John, xii
"double effect" doctrine, 147
Douglas, Lord Alfred, 89
Dracula (Stoker), 194–95
duty, 212
Dyer, Acting Brigadier-General
    Reginald, 18–19

Edsall, Thomas B. 167–68, 170–72,
    175, 258
education
    contempt for/hostility to, 76–77,
        172–73, 232
    higher, 231–32
Edward I, King, 250–51
Edward IV, King, 191
Edward the Confessor, 22–23
Edward VI, King, 24–25
Edward VIII, King, 222–23
Eliot, George, 182–83
Elizabeth the First, Queen, 24–
    25, 204–5
Ellis, Havelock, 240–41
End of Faith, The (Harris), 188–89
"ensoulment," 257–58
equality, gender, and Aristotle, 112–
    13, 204
Equality Act 2010, 246–47
equity in warfare (Grotius), 129–30
ethics, "substantive" versus "norma-
    tive," 208
ethnocentrism, 164
eugenics, 104–5, 108

European Union, 224–28
Euthyphro problem, 129–30
evolution, through natural
    selection, 4–5
experience, 61–62

Farage, Nigel, 225–26
Faulkner, William, 80–81
Ferguson, Brian, 34–35
"final causes" (Aristotle), 5–6
"Final Solution," 108, 203–4
Fisher, Admiral "Jacky," 163
Fiske, Alan Page, 56–57, 132–33
Floyd, George, 238
Ford, John C., 148–50
Franz Ferdinand, Archduke, 133–
    34, 163
Franz Joseph, Emperor, 25–
    26, 133–34
Freud, Sigmund, 113–14, 240–42
Fry, Douglas P., 34, 37–38, 64–65
Fussell, Paul, 158–59

Gallipoli, 220
Gellately, Robert, 252–53
genes and genetics, 9–11
George V, King, 163
Germany and the Next War (von
    Bernhardi), 19–20
Gidron, Noam, 168–69
Gilbert, William S., 89
God Delusion (Dawkins), 188–89
Goddard, Henry, 104–5
Godwinson, Harold, 22–23
Goebbels, Dr. Joseph, 108–9,
    201, 203–4

Goldhagen, Daniel, 250–51
Good Samaritan, Parable of, 212
Goodall, Jane, 44
Gordon, Lord George, 186–87
"Gordon Riots," 186–87
Grayling, A. C., 47, 57–58, 149–50
Great Depression, 139–40
Greene, Joshua, 28–29
Grey, Lady Jane, 24–25
Grey, Sir Edmund, 163
Grotius, Hugo, 128–29, 214

Hadza of Tanzania, 40
Haidt, Jonathan, 61–62
Halifax, Lord (Edward Lindley
    Wood), 220–21
Hall, Peter A., 168–69
happiness, 209–12
Harald III, King, 22–23
Harris, Sam, 188–89
Harris, Sir Arthur ("Bomber/Butcher
    Harris"), 152–53
Hastings, Battle of, 22–23, 28–29
hatred, 17–19
Hayden, Brian, 73–74
Headquarters Nights (Kellogg), 141–
    42, 163
Heidegger, Martin, 200
Hemmings, Sally, 85
Henry the Eighth, King, 24–25
Henry V (historical person), 164
Henry V (Shakespeare), 163–64
Henry VII, King, 192
Henson, Bishop Hensley, 136–37
heredity, 9–11, 70–72
hermaphroditism, 183

Hexam, Lizzie, 245–46
Hillis, Newell Dwight, 137
Himmler, Heinrich, 210–11
Hiroshima, 27, 28–29, 158–59
Hitler, Adolf, 106–8, 123–24, 139–41, 142, 200, 202–4, 218–20
Hitler's Willing Executioners: Ordinary Germans and the Holocaust (Goldhagen), 250–51
Hobbes, Thomas, 54–57
Hogarth, William, 102–4
Holmes, Justice Oliver Wendell, 104–5
hominin, 1–3, 29–30, 34–35, 94–95
Homo sapiens, 3–4, 13–14, 35, 51–52, 234–35
    subspecies of, 81–82
homologies, 13–14
homosexuality, 70–72
    agriculture and, 89–90
    Christianity and, 90–92
    Freud and, 240–41
    prosecution for, 242–43
Hook, Captain, 194
Hötzendorf, Count Franz Conrad von, 163
How Far Can You Go ? (Lodge), 206–7
Howard, Michael, 223
Hughes, Thomas, 72–73
Hume, David, 20–21, 95, 176–78, 212
hunter-gatherer, 3–4, 21, 38, 40, 43, 46–47, 48, 61–62. *See also* agriculture
    evidence of, 75–76

gender divisions and, 204–5
legacy, 224, 249–50, 253
origins of religion and, 95–97
plausibly egalitarian society of the, 256–57
reproduction, 38, 115
Hussein, Saddam, 154, 156
Huxley, Thomas Henry, 14–15, 19–20, 208

Ignatius Loyola, St., 113
"Immaculate Conception," dogma of, 257–58
immigration, 66–68, 78, 93, 165, 225–30
    Asian, to America, 166
    benefits of, 228–30, 255
    demographics of American, 166
    economics of, 168–69
    European, to America, 166
    to Germany, 255
    Hispanic, to America, 167–68
    lynchings, 181–82
    nativist clubs and, 166
Importance of Being Earnest, The (Wilde), 86–88, 182–83
"Incarnational" theory (Irenaeus of Lyon), 58–59, 131–32
inclusion, 168–69
inequality, female, 39–40, 73–74. *See also* prejudice: gender
ingroup, 61–115, 161. *See also* prejudice
    "contingent altruism" and, 63
    defined (Brewer), 63
    holistic, 202

obligations, 213–14
versus outgroup, 60–61, 120,
    178–79, 251–52 (*see also*
    discrimination)
war and, 220–21
inhibitions, 31–32
intention, right/rightful (St.
    Augustine), 127–28, 156
interdependence, 64–65
obligatory, 161
internment, Japanese, 166–67
Irenaeus of Lyon, 58–59, 131–32

James I, King, 24–25
James II, King, 24–25, 51–52
Jefferson, Thomas, 85
Jehovah's Witnesses, 244
Johnson, President Lyndon, 236–38
Jud Süss, 108–9
jus ad bellum, 121, 123–24, 126–
    27, 213
jus in bello, 121, 123–24, 126–27,
    214
"Just War Theory," 121, 159–60
Aquinas on, 154, 155, 156, 159–60
Christianized, 125–26
from Cicero to Aquinas, 121–28
conditions/demands, 127–
    28, 154–57
from Grotius to the pres-
    ent, 128–33
presupposition of, 176–78
justice, comparative, 155

Kalash people (northern
    Pakistan), 235–36

*Kallikak Family, The: A Study in the
    Heredity of Feeble Mindedness*
    (Goddard), 104–5
Kameradschaft and *Volksgemeinschaft*
    (comradeship and
    community), 252
Kant, Immanuel, 129–30, 163, 209
Keegan, John, 223
Kellogg, Vernon, 141–42
Kelly, Raymond, 37–38
Kierkegaard, Søren, 173
killer
    -ape hypothesis, 28–33, 34, 52–
        53, 54, 57–58, 163 (*see also*
        Hitler, Adolf)
    distance and, 53–54
    innate, 52–54
killing, intergroup, by
    chimpanzees, 44
Kim, Nam C., 47, 50–51
Kipling, Rudyard, 116
Kissel, Marc, 47, 50–51
Knox, Robert, 183
Kodiak Island, 39–40
Kristallnacht, 106–7, 146–47
Kutuzov, Mikhail, 23–24

labor, "physiological" versus "
    ecological" division of, 12–13
Lady Chatterley's Lover
    (Lawrence), 198–99
law
    God's eternal, 127–28, 210
    natural (Aquinas), 126–27, 130
Lawrence, D. H., 198–99
LeDrew, Stephen, 188–89

Leege, David, 259
LeMay, General Curtis, 158–59
Lennox, Mary, 196–97
Lieberman, Daniel, 45–46
Little Dorrit (Dickens), 65–72
Lodge, David, 206–7
Lorenz, Konrad, 31–32, 54, 58–59
Lowe, Robert, 232
Lucy (*Australopithecus afarensis*), 3–4
Lueger, Karl, 219–20
Luther, Martin, 108–9, 130–31, 250–51

Malthus, Thomas Robert, 4–5
Marcus, Gary, 61–62
marginalization, 168–69
Marlowe, Frank, 37–38, 47
Marshall, Brigadier General S.L.A., 52–53
Mary, Queen, 24–25
McNamara, Robert, 158–59
means, reasonable, 155
Mein Kampf (Hitler), 143–44, 218–19
Mellors, Oliver, 198–99
Merchant of Venice (Shakespeare), 106
"metaethics," 210
Metaphysics (Aristotle), 5–6
Metzl, Jonathan M., 60–61
Milam, Erika, 58–59
Milgram, Stanley, 253
Mill, John Stuart, 209, 210–12
Mivert, St. George, 185–86
mobility, upward, 181–82
moderation, in revenge and punishment (Grotius), 128–29, 138–39

Montgomery, Field Marshall Bernard, 220
Montgomery, Lucy Maud, 135
Moral Man and Immoral Society (Niebuhr), 141–42
morality, 14–16, 119–20. *See also* conduct, moral
natural law theology and, 90–92
personal versus public (Niebuhr), 141–42
purpose of, 211–12
of war, 212–14
Munich
Agreement, 140–41
Putsch, 218–19

Nagasaki, 27, 28–29, 158–59
National Socialist (Nazi) party, 139–40
nationality, racism as basis for, 165
nature, human, 33–34, 208–12
Neanderthals (*H. s. neandertalis*), 3–4, 81–85
New Atheists, 188–91
Nicholas Nickleby (Dickens), 195–96
Nicholas of Russia, Tsar, 163
Nicomachean Ethics (Aristotle), 209
Niebuhr, Reinhold, 141–42, 147–48
Nieman, Susan, 254–55
Nietzsche, Friedrich, 173
Nuremberg Laws, 106–7
Nussbaum, Martha, 248–49

Obama, Barack, 239
obedience, evolutionary potential for (Milgram), 253

O'Brien, William V., 154–57

Oliver Twist (Dickens), 163

On Aggression (Lorenz), 31–32

Operation "Barbarossa," 142

*Ordinary Men: Reserve Police
    Battalion 101 and the
    Final Solution in Poland*
    (Browning), 250–52

organs, nonfunctioning human, 183

Origen, 124–25

Origin of Species, On the
    (Darwin), 4–5

Our Mutual Friend
    (Dickens), 245–46

outgroup, 161–62, 188

outsourcing, 173–74, 224

Owen, Wilfred, 198–200

paiderastia, 185

Pan, Peter, 194

Papists Act of 1778, 186–87

Parliamentarians, 25–26

Patience (Gilbert and Sullivan), 89

Patton, General George, 220

Paul, St., 113, 204–5

Paul VI, Pope, 210

Pearl Harbor, 27, 120–21, 203–4,
    219, 220–21

Philoctetes, 199–200

pigmentation, skin, 84–85

Pinker, Stephen, 32–33

Pius IX, Pope, 257–58

Plato, 94, 112–13

Pleistocene (ancestors), 38–39, 47–48,
    59, 106–7, 221–22

poliomyelitis (infantile paralysis), 99

Politics (Aristotle), 178–79

Popery Act of 1698, 186–87

Popper, Karl, 85, 160

population, 38. *See also* casualties;
        immigration; reproduction
    aging, 230, 232–33
    American female, 206
    American slave, 18–19
    density, 32–33
        holocene/pleistocene/meso-
            lithic, 38–40
        Relative, 35–37
    genetic clusters and, 235–36
    movement, 69–70
    natural (Darwin), 4–5, 9
    origins of human, 3–4
    rightsizing, 61–62

Powell, Enoch, 66–68, 77, 165–66,
        173–74, 220–21, 225

prejudice
    class, 72–78, 169–76, 230–34
    credentialism and, 170–72
    defined (Allport), 60–61
    disability, 99–105, 191–
            200, 245–50
        accessibility strategies and, 247–49
        Legislating Against, 246–49
    foreigner, 65–72, 162–69, 224–30
    gender, 109–15, 204–7, 256–59
    against Jewish people, 106–9, 143–
            44, 182–86, 203–4, 250–55
    racial, 78–86, 176–82, 234–39
    religious, 93–98, 186–91, 244–45
    sexual orientation, 86–93, 182–
            86, 240–44
    as a two-part process, 161

primates, 34, 44–46
"primordial hermaphroditism"
        (Knox), 183
Princip, Gavrilo, 133–34
prisoners, 149–51
proportion, 156, 158–59
Puritans, 24–25
purpose, 5–6
Pygmalion (Shaw), 77

Quakers (Religious Society of
        Friends), xi–xii, 34, 54–55,
        58–59, 93, 131–32, 197–98,
        199–200, 260–61
Queensberry, Marquess of, 86–89

race
    as a cultural phenomenon, 181–82
    genetic clusters/differentiation
        and, 234–36
"racialisation," 60–61, 170–72
racialism (Powell), 165–66
Rai, Tage Shakti, 56–57, 132–33
"Rake's Progress" (Hogarth), 102–4
Rassenhygiene ("racial hygiene"), 108
Rawls, John, 63–64
Reagan, Ronald, 168–69
reason, 122
    Divine/Eternal, 127–28, 130
    moral power and (Kant), 217–18
    natural law and, 210
    right, 122
    slaves and (Aristotle), 179–80
reciprocation, 54. *See also* altruism:
        reciprocal (Darwin)
Reform Act of 1867, 77

religion, 30–31, 46–47, 57–58, 93–
        98, 186–91, 244–45
    good and, 209
    outgroup hostility and, 92–93
    war and, 57–58, 127–28
Renfield, 194–95
reproduction, 4–5, 34
    in cultivators versus hunter-
        gatherers, 38
    gender equality and, 114–15
    geometric, 4–5
    Unokais and, 41
Republic, The (Plato), 112–13
resources, arithmetic multiplication
        of, 4–5
revenge, 144
Riah, Mr., 245–46
Richard, Duke of Gloucester (King
        Richard III), 191–92
Richard II (Shakespeare), 162
Richard III (Shakespeare), 191
Rights of War and Peace, The
        (Grotius), 128–29
Rilla of Ingleside (Montgomery),
        135, 214–15
Rommel, Edwin, 123–24
Roosevelt, Franklin Delano, 99–101,
        203–4, 219, 220–21
Roundheads, 24–26
Rousseau, Jean-Jacques, 54–57,
        180, 233–34
Royalists, 25–26
Rubenstein, Richard, 254–55

Sandel, Michael, 170–72, 190
"savage man" (Rousseau), 55–56

Schlieffen Plan, 133–34
Scholl, Sophie and Hans, 94–95
Schwarzkopf, General Norman, 154
Secret Garden, The (Burnett), 196–97
selection
    individual versus group, 9–11
    kin, 15–16, 63–64, 241–42
    natural (Darwin), 5, 6, 9, 208
        beneficiaries *of, 9–13*
        morality *and, 211–12*
    sexual, 13–14
"self-interest" (Smith), 11–12
"selfish genes" (Dawkins), 9–
        11, 19–20
Selous, Edmund, 186
Sermon on the Mount, xi, 124–25,
        131–32, 141–42
Servetus, Michel, 97
Shakespeare, William, 162–
        64, 191–94
shamanism, 95–97
Shaw, George Bernard, 77
sin, original, 57–59, 125–26, 131–
        32, 221–22
Singer, Peter, 212, 214
"1619 Project," 238
slavery, 209–10, 238. *See also* captive
        taking (slave raiding)
    Aristotle on, 178–82, 209, 210–11
    as a cultural phenomenon, 181–82
    "natural slaves," 178–79
    reason and, 179–80
Smike, 195–96, 197–98
Smith, Adam, 11–13
Smith, Howard K., 140, 201
Smolensk, Battle of, 23–24

sociability. *See* sociality, human
social beings. *See* sociality, human
"social community" (Darwin), 15
"social complexity" (Hayden), 73–75
Social Contract (Rousseau), 180
sociality, human, 13–14, 17–18, 208–
        12, 249–50, 256
societies, 34
    complex, 47
    contemporaneous, 40–44
Socrates, 199–200, 210–11
Southwestern Energy, 174–75
Spencer, Herbert, 15–16, 163
Squeers, Wackford, 195–96
Stalin, Joseph, 220
Stamford Bridge, Battle of, 28–29
state
    versus nation, 200
    National Socialist conception
        of, 201
Staunton, Sir G., 184–85
Steiner, Rudolf, 201
sterility, mule, 11
sterilization, 137
    eugenical, 104–5
    "racial hygiene" and, 108
Stoker, Bram, 194–95
"struggle for existence" (Malthus),
        4–5, 19–20
"Substitutionary Atonement," 57–58
Sullivan, Arthur S., 89
surpluses, 73–76
synthesis, 182

Taung Baby (*Australopithecus africa-
        nus*), 29–30

teleology. *See* final causes (Aristotle)
Thatcher, Margaret, 122–23, 127–28, 168–69
Theodore of Tarsus, Archbishop of Canterbury, 257–58
Third Reich, 139–40, 200–1
Till, Emmett, 78–80, 236
"Tiny Tim," 245–46
Tolstoy, Leo, 23–24
Tom Brown at Oxford (Hughes), 72–73
Tom Brown's Schooldays (Hughes), 72
Tooby, John, 32–33, 256
Tostig (brother of King Harald III), 22–23
Treaty
    of Paris, 26–27
    of Versailles, 139–40, 218–19, 222–23
"Tree of Life," 6
"tribes" (Spencer, Darwin), 15–16
Truman, President Harry S., 158–59, 236
Trump, Donald President, 109–13, 114, 166–68, 170–72, 176–78, 188–89, 224
Tuke, William, 197–98
Tuttle, Raymond, 58–59
2001 (movie), 29–30

Ukraine, xiii–xiv, 147, 223
United Nations, 222–23
United States of America, 26–28, 67–68, 80–81, 99, 112–13, 118–19, 139–40, 154–57, 176–79, 203–4, 219, 242–43, 247–48, 254–55, 257–58, 261
    demographics of, 178–79
"Unokais" (Yanomamö males who have killed), 41

Valentine, Alf, 229–30
variation, random, 9
Variation of Plants and Animals under Domestication, The (Darwin), 184–85
violence, "virtuous," 97, 119, 192–94
Virtuous Violence (Page and Rai), 56–57
von Bernhardi, General Friedrich, 19–20, 208

Wallace, Alfred Russel, and Darwin, 11
war. *See also* agriculture; archaeology; casualties; conflict; primates; societies
    aggressive, 213
    avoiding, 214–23
    as "a biological necessity" (von Bernhardi), 19–20
    certainty of, 56
    civil
        American, 26–27
        British, 24–25
    conditions for a just, 127–28, 144–45
    defensive, 122–23, 213
        World War II Allies, 144
    defining, 47–48

Desert Storm, 153–57, 222–23
as a distortion, 208
"emergent" (Kissel and Kim), 47
Falkland Islands, 122–23, 127–28
guerilla, 27
    Ugandan, 159–60
"Holy," versus "Just," 136–37, 138
Islam and, 120–21
Just, defined (St.
        Augustine), 127–28
Kenyan (1952–60), 28
kinds of, 22–28
morality of, 212–14
neutralized by trade (Spencer), 163
nuclear, 27
offensive, 22–23, 122–23
    crimean, 50, 122–23
prevalence of, 32–33
private, 28, 127–28
Prussian-Franco, 134–35
religion and, 57–58
revolutionary, 159–60
    American, 159–60
"Seven Years'," 26–27
"Thirty Years'," 51–52
without hate (Rommel), 123–24
World War I (the Great War),
        17–18, 38, 123–24, 133–39,
        182–83, 198, 213, 214–15
    as "Holy" war, 150
World War II, 52–53, 139–50, 151,
        158–59, 218–19

War and Peace (Tolstoy), 23–24
Ward, Mary, Cassey, and
        John, 243–44
Washington, George, 26–27, 238
Waterloo, Battle of, 23–24
Wedgwood, Josiah, 11–12
Weimar Republic, 139–40
Whewell, William, 6
Wigg, George, 68–69
Wilde, Oscar, 86–88, 182–83
Wilhelm II, Kaiser, 25–26, 134–
        35, 163
William the Conqueror (King
        William I), 22–23, 50–51,
        122–23, 127–28
Winnington-Ingram, Bishop
        Arthur, 136–37
"wog," 68–69, 164
women, 15, 113–15, 204–7, 256–59.
        See also inequality, female
    American
        achievements of, 205–6
        contraceptives and, 206–7
        mechanization and, 206–7
    birth rates and status of, 230
    Plato and, 112–13

xenophobia, 164, 167–68

Yanomamö of Venezuela and
        Brazil, 40–44
York, Archbishop of, 149–50